Benjamin Randals

The plumb-line laid to the wall

Benjamin Randals

The plumb-line laid to the wall

ISBN/EAN: 9783337101497

Printed in Europe, USA, Canada, Australia, Japan

Cover: Foto ©Andreas Hilbeck / pixelio.de

More available books at **www.hansebooks.com**

THE PLUMB-LINE

LAID TO THE WALL;

OR,

THE PHYSICAL LAWS REVEALED IN THE SACRED SCRIPTURES.

———

BY BEN RANDALS.

———

NASHVILLE, TENN.:
PUBLISHING HOUSE OF THE M. E. CHURCH, SOUTH.
BARBEE & SMITH, AGENTS.
1897.

(ii)

DEDICATION.

PREFACE.

This work. with its many imperfections, is submitted to the public. The story of why we selected these topics for a life-work would make our Preface too long, and be largely composed of the story of the author's self. We submit the work, asking no charity to hide its faults. We give a few broken passages, and, though the connection is in no way related to our topics, yet if you grant to the words in these passages meanings that are acceptable to-day, and without which these words would be meaningless, you will discern even in these the tintings of inspiration. The Bible is the most wonderfully illustrative book ever given to the world. We will furnish you with sentences of but a few words, that, were we to illustrate their interpretations and simply draw the illustrations suggested by the individual words and the whole combined, you would see that no circus was ever more abundantly or more profusely advertised or illustrated. We never refer you to the Bible or to the sciences. We give you the book, chapter, and the text, and, when necessary to refer to the text, we repeat it. We then comment. Then we give the teachings of our scientists. Each reader may be judge, for the testimony of both is before him. Do not understand that we hold rigidly to the above order, but strictly to the above truths. Sometimes we make the scientific statement first; then come with our Bible text and comment afterward. We vary this arrangement to suit the trend of the thought and to prevent monotony. Where a passage supports, unmistakably, a particular theory, and, at the same time, thoughts on some closely related topic, or even a foreign one, we deal with that first which is more closely connected with the topic under consideration. Then we investigate those other features. This very often will give the work the appearance of a lack of unity. What we may apparently lose in unity will be compensated by fruit from adjoining or even distant vineyards. In referring to Job we sometimes mean the book

(v)

for the man, or even some one else, from the fact that it is a statement found in the book of Job. We believe that all science, all human learning, is couched in the Bible. The effort is to classify Bible science and Bible learning from Bible authors, as developed from their statements, and then to orderly arrange these statements, adopting as titles of subjects the names given by the scientific world. The plumb-line we conceive to be science. The wall is the massive masonry of God's works as seen in the things which he has created, formed, and made, from the atom to the world, to our systems, to all the systems, to the motions and forces, and the laws that govern them, from the organ to its functions, to the invisible forces transmitted by these organs to the inner receptacle where dwell immortal forces, a living combination of faculties having the image of God himself. God stands on this wall and holds out the plumb-line. The object of this work is to lay this line (science) to this wall (inspiration's statements), and ask you to see how gently it touches from top to bottom, from end to end, wherever applied. In many places I can see the wall rise high and grand, but to me the line is lost. May God in his infinite mercy and wisdom raise up one who can and will show the line, and will swing it to every angle, to every face, and to every height, and prove him! We very often give the dates when these thoughts were sent forth by inspiration, and when first promulgated by the world. Not one time has the promulgation made by the world antedated that made by inspiration. Not one time can the simplest or most learned skeptic claim for science a precedent.

THE AUTHOR.

Sipe Springs, Tex., February 5, 1897.

TO THE READER.

Was the Bible given by inspiration? You answer that it was. Then each sentence also was the gift of inspiration; if that be true, then so was each clause, phrase, and word. Words make sentences; individual words contain all the thought. Then to study this book of inspirations we have but to study each word. Inspiration never generalizes one single time. Its office is to particularize, individualize. Understand what the word means, then apply it rightly; it will always give a true Bible conclusion, and one that will conflict with no scientific truth, nor with itself. I know some good men who make—and deservedly, too—some pretensions to scholarship that when questions pertaining to science and the Bible are brought up turn off with an "O, well," and put on a look as if to say that it is not safe for the Bible to be looking after that.

Afraid to investigate a book acknowledged by all Christian people to be the work of inspiration, from one that says He is perfect in knowledge! God says that he made the earth and all things therein, and I'm afraid to investigate the matter for fear that it may not measure up to that standard. O the power of unbelief! I satisfy myself with a general old-rut use of terms, keeping up an outward appearance, with a heart full of misgivings on this matter. I asked a good man: "What is meant by *ends* of the earth." He answered: "All the face of the earth." "Then," said I, "what is meant by *end?*" "O, well," said he, "any one place on the earth." "Well, what is meant by breadth of the earth?" "Well, it is similar to ends; it, too, means all the earth." This is what I call "old rutisms;" an insult to inspiration, a dishonor to a Christian world. A strange inspiration that would use terms so recklessly, with meanings so flexible. The strongest proof of inspiration is the exactness of the words used. No ordinary writer of this day can afford to send out an article as meaningless as our friend's Bible definitions. End means end, not side, nor face, but the extremity of the longer side of a thing. Find that point, and, if talking about the earth, drive a stake till the lower end of it reaches the internal fires of the earth. When end is mentioned again, go back to your stake, and you will be right, not only

(vii)

once, but every time. When it says breadth, go to the extremity of the earth's shorter diameter and let your stake down again, with every assurance that you are right; you will never miss it. How little we value inspiration when we fail to give to each word precisely what it means! Words are often sermons, very often. Give this work a word interpretation. *Let your Bible study be a word work.* Solomon says: "Bow down thine ear, and hear the *words* of the wise, and apply thine heart unto my knowledge. For it is a pleasant thing if thou keep them within thee; they shall withal be fitted in thy lips. That thy trust may be in the Lord, I have made known to thee this day, even to thee. Have not I written to thee excellent things in counsels and knowledge, that I might make thee know the *certainty of the words of truth;* that thou mightest answer the *words* of truth to them that send unto thee?" The very *Word* was made flesh, and dwelt among us. Every thought is but the kernel, of which the word is the shell. Break these shells gently, but surely, and the richness of a precious kernel is yours.

Suppose that we could find in the Bible a country named and described, the description of which was precisely that of this country, as given by our geographers; that it lay between the same parallels and the same meridians as does this country; that the general shape of the land was as the shape of this continent; that it lay between two oceans, the one on the east and the other on the west, with a great gulf on the south; that it had a great mountain chain along its eastern and a greater chain along its western border; that it had a river system to the northeast, one in the south, another in the southwest, and still another to the northwest; that this description entered into detail far enough to give the sources of these rivers, their courses, and their mouths; that it gave the positions of thousands of cities similarly situated as are many of our cities, with surroundings in every respect the same; that this account describes the people, their language, laws, and religions. If I should ask you how this came about, to explain how it came to be written so many years ago, who could know such things? There could possibly be left to you but one solution. Inspiration alone could have done this—so we think. We have tried to make our proof of inspiration along this line, or by a similar process. All the subjects discussed in this book are discussed from Bible texts. These texts every time antedate, very often thousands of years, any mention made of them by the world. Like the description of our country as above, who could say that the earth was round a thousand years before man knew it—any man? Who could say that the earth turned on its axis four thousand years before any man dreamed of such a thing? God alone, directly, or through his inspired instruments.

Let us first compare some of the statements made against the Bible to some strange facts found in our school-books. I am told that the Bible contradicts itself, that it does not stand to reason. Some years ago I saw in a paper a notice proposing to send twelve contradictions, found in the Bible, for twenty-five cents. I repeated: "Only twelve contradictions in my Bible." I was not a reader of the Bible, consequently had no extra supply of piety, and really thought that there were not only hundreds, but that the whole was a bundle of contradictions. Have you never noticed that when a man changes his Church fellowship he stills the public mind by: "I got to reading for myself." That's the plan. I repeated again: "Only twelve contradictions!" That shocked my infidelity, and gave me faith to read for myself. I reasoned that if all the remainder were free from contradictions, I could find enough to boat over to the land of no contradictions. I thought again that perhaps the finder of these errors had sought for errors only; that the life of his business, twenty-five cents a dozen, was in a measure the great feature to him. Then maybe there are only eleven. The finder being soulless, it could make no difference to him if all were errors. A living soul, floundering in one, has something to do with bias in truth and morals. I thought that the perversion of truth through moneyed interest might prompt to the adding of one. This reduced the number to ten. Then could not this searcher, like other men, make a mistake to the reduction of one? This reduced the number to nine. I felt that the Bible in places, in its childish simplicity, had so far undershot this mentor that he could not reduce himself even to the loss of one. Now, then, there are in reality only eight. I thought that perhaps one of these might be reconciled by going back to the original tongue. That, you see, reduces this number fairly to seven. This, you know, is a sacred number, and I felt all right. I thought then of a friend's story, told when I was a boy. This friend told that on one occasion his father promised to take him and his brothers fishing when a certain piece of fodder was stripped. The boys speculated on this wise, that they could strip faster by each stripping one row at a time. They made one through; then they thought that in nearly the same time each might have stripped two rows. So the next through each stripped two rows. This was an improvement. So the next through each took three rows. This was also a success. After fanning for a moment the father said: "Boys, there are only seven rows for each; let's breast it." So they did. Now we have our contradictions and errors reduced to seven. Breast it; we'll have time to go fishing then. Only seven errors in a book of a thousand double-column pages, written by thirty or more different authors, covering hundreds of thousands of topics; a book of sixty-six books (we omit the Apocrypha), twelve hundred chapters, thirty thousand verses, seven hundred thousand words, covering a period of five thousand years, written under every vicissitude of fortune; when favor and fear were weighed in doubtful balance; when writing was young; an age clouded by moral and scientific superstition; before the arts were born; before science had ever looked up or around; a book translated from tongue to tongue; sold as a curious story; stolen, a prey in war, buried, burned; its adherents and promulgators staked, stoned, and burned. Let us review the track that reason has left. We will review its simpler things and see how they harmonize. Let us go back to the history of our own country. Select from any number of authors on the history of the United States, going back to its discovery; or bring in all. Now this period will not exceed the time that Israel remained in Egypt. Is there a man so silly who will say that hundreds of contradictions can not be found? Now in the close of the nineteenth century as we look back to the days of witchcraft in our country, tell me what account given in the Bible is less inviting, and one that it did not condemn having such a nature. Do you see the pillory, the stocks, and ducking-board? Do you find the code of honor whose merchandise is death and its subscriber a wretch? An eye for an eye beats that. The wretch who had time to become skilled in taking human life stood ready to provoke that he might ply

his skill, and an approving country clapped hands when new
victims fell. Any such contradictions as that in the Bible?
I have before me two histories written by different authors.
One says: "All of Manhattan Island, where New York now
stands, was purchased for trinkets worth twenty-four dollars."
The other says that it was bought for twenty-five dollars. Let
us interpret the first quotation above; let us see what the people four thousand years to come will make of it. "That Manhattan Island was purchased for trinkets. That when made
into trinkets these will only be worth twenty-four dollars. The
magnitude of such trinkets will revive the story of giants, and
we be classed among the giants. How am I to know whether
Manhattan Island was purchased with trinkets or twenty-five
dollars? This is a contradiction. There is no Manhattan, nor
was it ever purchased." (Reason.)

How much philosophy can you squeeze from all these histories before us? You can not find in all one-half that is found
in several chapters of the Bible. Draw now the sciences of that
period around the histories of that period, and all combined
will not furnish the learning and philosophy offered by the
thirty-eighth chapter of the book of Job; and this book was
written three thousand years before Columbus was born. The
writers of the Bible were the scribes of inspiration; the writers
of history are very often the scribes of interest, of sectional
preferment; very often scribes for money. Either of the last
would incline a pen, if it did not seriously bend it. Let us present you with a case in point, one that will not take other histories to prove. Take the moneyed provision of the Blair Bill.
That was a good thing. Why did the South not accept it?
Why should the North present such a bill? Why should the
North ask a monopoly in telling to the rising generations the
tale of our late war? Was it the only true story? Why should
the South object? Was the story not fairly told? Do we have
two different stories of one and the same period in which each
had his part in every scene and act? In a few thousand years
how can the world reconcile these varying reports from one
and the same household? Every struggle has its adverse
parties, and furnishes its adverse stories. Inspiration had none
of this. To-day will hand down its contradictions. We sus-
pect and are suspected; we condemn and are condemned. We

are a people of varying versions. Could we rid ourselves of these characteristics, then we would face a new heaven and a new earth, and the glories of a higher and a better life would stream down upon us as freely as the never-failing sunshine by day, and the lurings from the declarations of God's glory, as they ceaselessly fall upon us from the stars by night, become inspirations more surely, and with less variations point out the line of life than the best-devised compass can direct a ship's course through the trackless ocean.

Let us examine our geographies. They say: "The rivers of Pennsylvania, contrary to the ordinary geographical laws, cleave through the mountains." I reject this because it does not stand to reason—my reason, of course. Therefore, there is no Pennsylvania. Geography also teaches that the Ohio and its northern tributaries are lower than the mouth of the Cumberland. Then the Ohio and its tributaries run up-hill to the mouth of the Cumberland; and these streams are wilful, physical law-breakers. Is this a contradiction? Say, does this stand to reason—your reason, not mine? This does away with the authenticity of the Ohio River or geographical laws. I am told that recent calculations vary the sun's distance from the old figures. Is it possible that this error has been kept in our oldest sciences, in our most learned books, and that for three or four hundred years? How can this be if science is inflexible and reason infallible? Let us carry this thought to the primary department, to the kindergarten; let us turn to Webster's "Speller." We find the words "center" or "centre," "niter" or "nitre," "meter" or "metre." Is Mr. Webster able to teach with certainty either mode of spelling the above words? Can you tell the true orthography of either of these words? What would you say to the little one in the A, B, C book? This is purely an admission on the part of our best lexicographer that here is a contradiction that confronts us, even in the very beginning of a learned life. I am told that Webster and Worcester differ materially in the spelling of certain words. Does this allow the assertion that Webster and Worcester are impostors on the learned world? Can we reject their valuable dictionaries on this fact. Let us take the spelling of "phthisic." Nowhere in the Bible are we more heavily taxed to believe its statements than are the little beginners in a literary life to accept the above. If our faith had depended on the above spelling, a much larger per cent of the human family would be sacrificing to other gods than are at the present time.

A paradox is something that seems unreasonable, yet is true. Our physical sciences are full of paradoxes. This is only a fault of myself. My comprehension only makes a thing paradoxical to me, whether it be a scientific or Biblical question. A correct comprehension removes every paradox. The shades and colors from a picture do not depend more upon the colors or the blendings made by the brush than the observer's position and whence falls the light. Put yourself in the very best position possible to see the Bible, where the light will have its highest effect; then for twelve contradictions you would not think it unsafe to offer a million dollars.

The Bible comes down through fifty centuries. It has its paradoxes that can be removed by a change of position. Science may go up through fifty more. To those improperly placed it will have its paradoxes. The center of gravity of the one is the center of gravity of the other, and will never change. Harmony will still be the law of stability in both.

One suggested that we should submit this work to critical scholars, that the original tongue be consulted, that in the revision perhaps the true meaning of the original was not kept up. The Bible is God's word, his gift to man for man's good and his glory. We have but to casually glance over the nations of the earth to determine the truth that the most enlightened nations are Bible-reading and Bible-publishing nations. Whatever of elevation the world enjoys to-day is due to this Book. This Book has not filled its mission yet. It was not given to one nation nor one age. It is as much a gift to this generation, and more so, as to the first, from the fact that a new and a more recent edition has been added. The fact that it is God's Book, his gift, is evidence to me that he is able and willing to take care of it, and that he will do it as he has in ages past. Would he put into the hearts of men what to write at first, for purposes that are not yet accomplished, and then not watch his purpose through its revision? I as much believe that he supervised its revision as I do that he gave the first copies. The thought that God would lose his Book or suffer its words perversely revised is pure blasphemy.

CONTENTS.

(xv)

xvi THE PLUMB-LINE.

THE PLUMB-LINE.

CHAPTER I.

SELECTIONS FROM THE BIBLE.

PSALMS: " I meditate on all thy works; I muse on
the work of thy hands." "Open thou mine eyes,
that I may behold wondrous things out of thy law."
"Make me to understand the way of thy precepts; so
shall I talk of thy wondrous works." " So shall I have
wherewith to answer him that reproacheth me: for I
trust in thy word." "I will speak of thy testimonies
also before kings, and will not be ashamed." "The
earth, O Lord, is full of thy mercy, teach me thy
statutes." " Many, O Lord my God, are thy wonderful works which thou hast done, and thy thoughts
which are to us ward." "They cannot be reckoned
up in order unto thee: if I would declare and speak
of them, they are more than can be numbered."

Ecclesiastes: " I gave my heart to seek and search
out by wisdom concerning all things that are done
under heaven: this sore travail hath God given to
the sons of men to be exercised therewith."

(1)

Romans : "For whatsoever things are written aforetime were written for our learning, that we through patience and comfort of the Scriptures might have hope."

Wisdom of Solomon: "Surely vain are all men by nature, who are ignorant of God, and could not out of the good things that are seen know him that is: neither by considering the works did they acknowledge the workmaster. But deemed either fire, or wind, or swift air, or the circle of the stars, or the violent water, or the lights of heaven, to be the gods which govern the world. With whose beauty if they being delighted took them to be gods; let them know how much better the Lord of them is: for the first author of beauty hath created them. But if they were astonished at their power and virtue, let them understand by them how much mightier he is that made them. For by the greatness and beauty of the creatures, proportionably the maker of them is seen."

———————

THE earth's creation and its shape, and the changes preparatory to fit it for life are told by astronomers thus: All the matter which now composes the sun and the various planets, with their moons, was in a gaseous and highly heated state. It filled all the space now occupied by the system, and extended far beyond the orbit of Neptune. In other words, the solar system was simply an immense nebula. The particles of matter, as the repellant force weakened, began to seek a center, following the law seen in the whirlpool, whirlwind, or water poured into a funnel; rotary motion was established in the mass. With the decrease of the repellant force the rotary motion increased till the centrifugal force overcame the centripetal force, and the exterior part was thrown off. Then a second, third, fourth, and on till one by one our planets take their places each in its orbit, revolving in the same plane and moving in the same direction. The earth passes from a formless mass to that of a sphere. Then comes the sea, then the mountains. Let us see how revelation will tell its story of these great creations and formations. Proverbs viii. 22-30: "The Lord possessed me in the beginning of his way, before his works of old. I was set up from everlasting, from the beginning, or ever the earth was. When there were no depths, I was brought forth; when there were no fountains abounding with water. Before the mountains were settled, before the hills was I brought forth: while as yet he had not made the earth, nor the fields, nor the highest part of the dust of the world. When he prepared the heavens, I was there: when he set a compass upon the face of the depth : when he established the clouds above : when he strengthened the fountains of the deep: when he gave to the sea his decree, that the waters should not pass his commandment: when he appointed the foundations of the earth. Then I was by him, as one brought up with him: and I was daily his delight, rejoicing always before him."

While this lesson recites the story of the earth from times prior to its being earth till it was earth, till the seas were poured out upon it, till the hills were settled and the highest mountains raised, the whole story as it advances from period to period is offered as proof of the wonderful age of Wisdom. Upon this fact in the 32d verse we are earnestly entreated to hearken to the lessons taught by Wisdom : "Now therefore hearken unto me, O ye children." "The Lord possessed me in the beginning of his way, before his works of old."

"The beginning of his way" is explained by the phrase "before his works of old." Not the beginning of God's existence, but the beginning of his work of old, his first work, a work done prior to that mentioned in the opening verse of the Bible, the astronomer's story of the creation of our system, a work begun when emptiness and silence held space, uncontested by a single atom, unlit by a single ray of light. Moses says that there was another work. His mode of calling our minds to this truth is suggestive. Genesis i. 16: "And God made two great lights; the greater light to rule the day, and the lesser light to rule the night: he made the stars also." While Moses is reciting the story of the creation of our system and the order of the earth's transformations we should know that he had another work that preceded this one: "He made the stars also."

"I was set up from everlasting, from the beginning, or ever the earth was." Two great periods are here named: everlasting and beginning, and in the order of their occurrence. In the first of these, perhaps, God did his work of old. The later period, you see, is subdivided, a part having gone before the earth appeared. This suggests to our minds the astronomer's theory, that our system was created as a whole and remained one undivided mass for a great period before it was earth. Here the Bible begins its wonderful statements: "In the beginning God created the heaven and the earth [solar system]. And the earth was without form."

"Or ever the earth was." From the time of the creation of the material of the system, while the earth mingled with the mass, was its formless period. This period was sufficiently long to be enumerated with other great periods, or a subdivision of one, and long enough to exemplify Wisdom's great age. If this covered only twenty-four of our hours, then Wisdom's boast of her age is a deception. After Moses recites the story of the creation of our system, he proceeds to cut it: "And the Spirit of God moved upon the face of the waters. And God said, Let there be light: and there was light."

Before the forces which do work in and with matter were named, all the changes wrought over matter were attributed directly to God himself. In some few instances we see certain influences ascribed to his ordinances, or laws. As a Christian people we attribute all things directly to God, through his laws, which the prophet Isaiah calls God's servants. "Spirit of God moved upon the face of the waters." "Spirit." The life, the strength of resemblance, moved, excited to action.

All the planets outside the earth, together with it, filled with, excited to action in the strength of resemblance to, God's Spirit, took their places each in its respective orbit, full of life and motion. The moment these fly loose, light springs up to the earth, which could not be the case prior to its separation. It is only light—no sun; 'tis but the blaze from the residue, parent of worlds.

"When there were no depths I was brought forth." This is, without question, the second great physical transformation. It was first the earth; then the sea followed. This was the second day's work, calling for the firmament, separating the waters, collecting the sea. Wisdom here takes cognizance of the time that drops between the formations, rather than to the time consumed in the formation itself. Now this was sufficiently long to add to Wisdom's age, and it furnishes proof of this fact.

"When there were no fountains abounding with water." This topic, you see, while it could only have reached from the time of the coming of the sea till fountains appear, adds to Wisdom's age. If the six days theory—days of twenty-four hours—be true, then this could not have exceeded a few hours. Could this in any way illustrate her long continuance with God, the Creator and Former of all things? Had all these intervening times consumed but six of our days, then Wisdom's boast, in a great measure, would cover only one hundred and forty-four hours. This period is covered by the period mentioned by astronomers. That when the first condensation fell upon the earth it was highly heated, sufficiently so to convert this ocean of water to vapor and send it up again. It thus rose and fell till the earth was sufficiently cooled to stop its vaporization. So we do not wonder at Wisdom's attention being called to it.

"Before the mountains were settled, before the hills was I brought forth." The next earth modification. The above statement makes plain the truth that the hills were made by the settling of the mountains, and, consequently, older. Geologists tell us that when the earth was young its crust was thin; that mountains thrown up by the force of expanding gases and vapors fell back to an unstable crust, one not able to support these elevations. Thus gradually they settled back; the process was repeated through centuries, the crust growing thicker all the while, till it reaches a thickness which is able to support these elevations, though slight at first, making the oldest mountains the lowest; while the younger and more recent ones tower above their elders. How could Solomon know that the settling of the mountains made our oldest elevations? Again this period was sufficiently long to receive the notice of Wisdom.

"While as yet he had not made the earth, nor the fields, nor the highest part of the dust of the world." The three great periods—before he made the earth, from the time of its creation, till from this nebular he made or formed the earth; before he made the fields (seas); before the sea in vapor had gone up from the earth to our present firmament; before he made the highest part of the dust of the world—highest mountains. Solomon reiterates the preceding order, condensed, maintaining the true geologic order.

"When he prepared the heavens, I was there." Heretofore Wisdom rather emphasizes the time that elapses between events. Now she refers directly to the time consumed in making transformations, and this too is offered as evidence of added age. The preparation of the heavens—aerial heavens—consisted in separating the waters that were under the firmament from the waters that were above the firmament. By this act the water and air were separated. The water drops upon the earth, and the air remains above it.

"When he set a compass upon the face of the depth." This was the next thing in order after the sea was made. We know that the surface of the sea is circular. As sure as this is a truth, so sure is it that there was a time when this rounding took place. Wisdom was present when this was done, and even named the instrument used. This period added to her age.

"When he established the clouds above." The sea is now ready for its purpose to help the world in its mission. Without the means for its dissemination it would be a useless appendage. The clouds are established for that purpose.

"When he strengthened the fountains of the deep." After the clouds are established to scatter the waters of the sea some restrictions must be thrown round the fountains of the deep to prevent a water catastrophe to this world by the breaking of the fountain, as the flood was produced.

"When he gave to the sea his decree, that the waters should not pass his commandment." This law is in some way closely connected with the foundations of the earth.

"When he appointed the foundations of the earth." It is a fact that the same force that holds the sea in its bounds was appointed the foundations of the earth: gravity. Wisdom, after having mentioned these periods as durations inconceivable to us, closes by "I was by him, as one brought up with him: and I was daily his delight." Were these periods daily visitations? If so, then they were not the six days such as we have. Wisdom was his daily delight from the time the work began down through all earth transformations, even before the earth was. Closely connected with the later topics is, how the sea was made.

By Bible statement we find the sea suspended above the earth; immediately after it becomes earth, occupying the space now filled by our aerial firmament. Genesis i. 6: "And God said, Let there be a firmament in the midst of the waters, and let it divide the waters from the waters." Geographers teach that at one time the sea was suspended in this same space. The time comes when the heat is no longer able to support these suspended vapors; vapors driven from the earth by its burnings, all the vapors that make the waters of the world, together with all the carbon and metals vaporized by the fierce heat mingled in this suspended ocean. Under the tremendous pressure of the dense atmosphere the steam was precipitated. These dropped upon a red-hot earth, were instantly converted into vapor and rose again; again fell, arose and fell, how long we cannot tell, we can only say till the earth was cooled sufficiently to stop this so great vaporization, or till a sea covered the earth. This period was noted by Wisdom: "When he prepared the heavens I was there." Scientists make this precipitation instantaneous and simultaneous. Job's Lord makes it no less so. Job xxxviii. 8–11: "Or who shut up the sea with doors, when it brake forth, as if it had issued out of the womb? When I made the cloud the garment thereof, and thick darkness a swaddling-band for it, and brake up for it my decreed place, and set bars

and doors, and said, Hitherto shalt thou come, but
no farther." Let us make a liberal interpretation of
this text and particularize after. When the cloud
was a garment for the sea, encircled it, and thick
darkness a swaddling-band for it—at that time it
broke forth from this cloudy garment and this swaddling-band, as, or like, an issue from the womb; at
that time it was shut up with doors, geographical
features controlled as doors by a physical force.
During all this time the sea bottom was being broken
up to decreed bounds, bars and doors were being
set. There were geographical features in one sense,
and physical forces in another.

"Who shut up the sea with doors, when it brake
forth, as if it had issued out of the womb?" Then
the sea was shut up with doors. A door is a
thing that opens or closes a passage, or is the passage. The force that opens or closes these doors
must be some physical force. See doors and bars in
another place.

"When it brake forth, as if it had issued out of the
womb." Do geographers make this precipitation
more sudden? Simultaneously this garment falls off,
this band breaks, and a sea drops upon the earth as
an issue from the womb. "Brake forth" illustrates
the mode of separating the two oceans, the vapor
from the air. No words can replace these. The
temperature is falling, the air particles contract till
the water breaks forth.

"Thick darkness a swaddling-band for it [sea]."
We said above that with the waters that make our
seas, lakes, rivers, etc., were mingled all the metals,
vaporized by fierce heat. To swaddle is to bind with

cloths, generally used of infants. At this day and time these cloths are stayed with metallic safety-pins. Do you suppose that the lesson was to teach Job that the thick darkness about the sea was made tighter by these diffused metals? Was our mode of fastening taken from this? Ours is an illustration. How simple the illustration! How the sea was formed seems a complex question. It is illustrated in terms that go to the comprehension of all the civilized world. Without question it indicates an infant sea; a young sea, a sea in the nursery, in sight, growing up for the duties of an active and an endless life.

"And brake up for it [sea] my decreed place." While the incidents mentioned above were transpiring fearful convulsions were going on in the earth. The sea bottom was being broken up; so it was told to Job. Geology, speaking of this very period, says: "Huge crevices were opened, and torrents of liquid lava, ejected from the cracks and seams, were poured in fiery floods over the scarcely solid crust, which was constantly being rent asunder by eruptions from the molten mass beneath." See this period in any geology. Job's Lord says, "brake up;" now it is really done by a brake and that upward. Now this would be an impossibility were the earth any other form than that of a sphere. No other solution would possibly do. We hold to a word interpretation. Please whisper and tell me why Job's Lord did not miss this delicate, intricate feature. Busy elements are preparing for a coming sea, one in sight. How fearful the means employed, how wonderful the result as blast after blast is fired from the trains laid by decree beneath!

"My decreed place." Irregularities in the earth's surface are the results of upheavals, and these upheavals we are taught occurred in obedience to a decree; therefore must have compassed bounds as definite as the purposes which these two agents, mountains and seas, were to fill and do fill in the world's economy. Though mountains appear on our maps as so many confused masses and rugged eminences, as though hurled out in blind and mad confusion, yet the reverse is true; precision was the law governing these great uplifts and these deep depressions.

The place was decreed, its bounds surveyed and marked; its execution affords the highest example of civil engineering. The equator, the poles, the line separating the darkened from the lightened hemisphere, the sun's place itself, were not more definitely fixed than were these mountains and seas. No other place could fill the great mission of the mountains and seas. They fit a universal plan. This we are conscious of, for they meet universal purposes.

Our geographers speak thus: "In the mountains similarity is found *everywhere*. There are certain features of relief which belong to all the continents in general. Each continent is bordered by mountains. Each continent is traversed in the direction of its greater length by a grand mountain system. For the most part a subordinate system occurs in each of the continents. The central portions of each continent are comparatively depressed." This uniformity points to a general plan and leads back to a decree. More, "these are important regulators of climate; they aid in the distribution of moisture and

are regulators of drainage." They are the reposi-
tories of mineral wealth. As much may be said of
the sea. Nearly three-fourths of the earth's surface
is covered by water. The northern hemisphere comprises three-fourths of all the land, while the southern hemisphere comprises three-fifths of all the
water surface. Does this show a purpose? Does
this show a preconceived plan? Plans are but spec-
ifications of a decree. "The offices of the sea are to
receive the drainage of the land, to wear away and
build up the land, to supply the atmosphere with
moisture, to regulate climate, to be the highway of
nations, that commerce, civilization, and Christianity
may be wafted on its bosom to the ends of the earth."
If scientists see a uniformity that can be no more
nor less than the result of a plan, as seen in the seas
and mountains of the globe, it requires no very
great strength of mind to see and know that these
great features of the earth's surface fill prepared
bounds, "my decreed place."

Let us introduce another witness touching the advent of the sea: its instantaneousness. Amos v. 8:
"Seek him that . . . calleth for the waters of
the sea, and poureth them out upon the face of the
earth." Read the entire verse, and see that this refers to the formation of the sea. Its connection
with other great works found in this verse makes it
no less than what we here represent it. In another
place we have given our opinion on the other constructions. The waters of the sea were called and
poured out. Not a part of the waters of the sea, but
the waters that make the sea; not sprinkled out, not
rained out, but poured out. If these waters came at

a call and were poured out, was the geologist's process more instantaneous?

Again, Job xii. 15: "He sendeth the waters out, and they overturn the earth." Turn it over. We offer this as a thought that perhaps at this time the center of gravity was changed and the inclination wrought. At this time bars and doors were set. We believe that these terms, "bars" and "doors," are in one sense forces—bars, the centripetal; doors, the centrifugal. These forces hold the sea in bounds. The one holds it bound to the center; the other draws it in part from the poles and holds it heaped at the equator. (For bars and doors as geographical features see "Frigid Zones.") The conflict between the fire and the water ends. A hot, muddy sea follows the moon round the earth—no obstruction, no impediments; all is water.

Psalm civ. 5-9 : "Who laid the foundations of the earth, that it should not be removed forever. Thou coveredst it with the deep as with a garment: the waters stood above the mountains. At thy rebuke they fled: at the voice of thy thunder they hasted away. They go up by the mountains: they go down by the valleys unto the place which thou hast founded for them. Thou hast set a bound that they may not pass over: that they turn not again to cover the earth."

"Who laid the foundations of the earth, that it should not be removed forever?" A beautiful question, that is answered. Were the foundations of the the earth laid? is not the question. The truth is, they were laid; now who did it? Him who is perfect in knowledge did this. Don't be uneasy, don't talk before the children about the world's coming to an end. These foundations cannot be removed forever. They are abiding.

"Thou coveredst it with the deep as with a garment." These foundations were hid beneath the deep, covered as with a garment, effectually hidden —"as with a garment." What simple illustrations the Bible offers! No other book ever written does this. O the grand simplicity of the Bible!

"The waters stood above the mountains." This is the period spoken of by geologists, the time when a hot, muddy sea covered the earth—"stood above the mountains." The time comes when they must be gathered unto one place, their decreed bounds.

"At thy rebuke they fled: at the voice of thy thunder they haste away. They go up by the mountains, they go down by the valleys unto the place which thou hast founded for them." This is the account: Being rebuked, they flee, they haste away, they go up by the mountains, sweep down by the valleys to their prepared bounds.

MARCH OF THE SEAS.

Now we look upon the scene that David speaks of. Psalm xc. 2: "Before the mountains were brought forth." (Read the entire verse, and see how truly David repeats in reverse order the geological periods mentioned in this chapter.) The bringing forth of these mountains was a period of sufficient note to attract the notice of the great singer. "Before the mountains were brought forth" is susceptible of two interpretations. Both, we think, are just and pertinent to the thought before us. It refers to the time when the mountains were brought forth from the fiery chambers of the earth, the ocean being a factor; and also to the time when they were brought forth from this investing sea. We incline to the latter.

Genesis i. 9: "And God said, Let the waters under the heaven be gathered together unto one place, and let the dry land appear: and it was so."

All is now water, no visible appearance of land anywhere. The deepest valleys slumber thousands and thousands of feet beneath the pressure of a mighty weight of waters. Far above the loftiest mountain peaks of the globe the waves, unobstructed, make their rounds with the moon, being led on by its attraction. This chase ends. Over the face of the waters, along all the parallels, up and down the meridians from pole to pole; from the deepest depths to the highest heights, even everywhere goes the command.

"Let the waters under the whole heavens be gathered together unto one place." "Let" was an order to that which had heretofore restrained. Instantly the moon loses its attraction for the wave, the ordinance of the sun and stars fail. The centrifugal force yields, gravity hears and obeys with open hand. Every force that would impede the progress of the waters was enjoined. Mighty worlds, powerless to check, could only watch these evolutions as seas, unrestrained, went home.

"At the voice of thy thunder they hasted away." The signal-gun proclaims the march, and tells the birth of a mountain. The thunder from the hundreds of guns that blazed from broadsides on Sebastopol compared to this were as a mere whisper. The movements of contending armies in action are said to form

the climax of sublimity, from human effort. Under
high discipline hundreds of thousands of feet are
simultaneously raised, as simultaneously they fall—
left, right, left, right—with a regularity which the
tickings of no clock can excel. As we look on our
minds seize the thought that all these feet are members of one and the same person, guided by the same
intelligence. "March;" from east, west, north, south,
a great army is gathered at Gettysburg. "March,"
and the armies of Europe center at Waterloo. Greater still than all these were the hosts that followed
Xerxes; these were greater than were ever assem-
bled in ancient times; or, perhaps, at any known
epoch of history. Xerxes ordered: "March." The
tramp of forty-six nations, over five millions of
soldiers bent their steps toward the little country of
Greece. But "Let the waters be gathered unto one
place;" instantly two hundred million square miles
of water, having a depth of ten miles at least, form
line above the terrible roar of forces, lifting mountains and excavating for a sea bottom. Amid these
thunders the sea sets out on its march to its decreed
bounds. "At the voice of thy thunder they hasted
away." Myriads of waves, extending from pole to
pole, move westward; while the center, impeded, loses
distance, the wings sweep forward, the columns break
right and left, directing their lines of march to the
poles; the right wing to the north and the left to
the south. Here they circle like mighty troopers
till at the north, a fearful sound, the columns break,
then round, round, down, down they spin from far
toward the south. The velocity slackens as their
funnel shape becomes less concave, higher, higher it

2

rises in the center till one last leap and a shout proclaims the Arctic Sea in its bounds. From here the
surplus moves toward the south, and joins in the
march there. Submarine convulsions, "the voice of
his thunder," have broken the columns; now they circle here, yonder, everywhere, as marked by vast
areas of circling foam. The face of the deep is in-
dented by valleys as the waves turn in or are pressed
up as elevations rise.

"Let the dry land appear." A miniature continent
rises up near the great lakes. Let us take position
upon this, and watch the waters withdraw, and the
mountains rise up, monsters, children of the sea.

Age on age goes by, little by little the water re-
cedes, inch by inch the continent grows, slowly the
land rises. "Dim outlines of mighty reefs, the Ap-
palachians on our east are slowly coming forth, while
the Rocky Mountains on our west are doing likewise.
The pale sun is struggling to penetrate the dense atmosphere of a yet heated earth. It sends a line of
light along these mighty ramparts, outposts, advance-
guards of an approaching continent." These are the
bounds and barriers that the waters can never pass
again. The mighty convulsions that threw them up
have subsided. Now these peering mountains begin
to furrow its surface like some playful fish at first,
deeper and deeper as the waters move and the mountains come forth, till the force of the shock is broken
against the base of tremendous mountains that defile
along our borders.

"Let the waters under the heavens be gathered together unto one place, and let the dry land appear:
and it was so." "They go up by the mountains;

they go down by the valleys unto the place which
thou hast founded for them." Fifty-three million
miles of land have been unmasked, and one hundred
and forty-four million miles of water have assem-
bled unto one place.

"Thou hast set a bound that they may not pass
over." This bound was decreed before the waters
were poured out upon the earth. It just fills these
bounds, not one single drop too much, nor one too
small. The excavation was precisely deep enough,
just long enough, exactly broad enough, to hold a
supply of water sufficient to last the earth, "which
endureth forever."

THE OCEAN.

Geography teaches that the ocean is the great reservoir to which all the rivers flow, from which all the
rivers come; that it is filled with fish and plants, fur-
rishing food for countless thousands; that in every
one thousand ounces of this water are held twenty-
seven ounces of common salt; that the coral and
pearl are here. Says Maury: "The coral groves of
the ocean floor are decorated like our gardens of the
land; the flower-like polyps answering to our pinks
and daisies, violets and lilies. Some are of the
brightest and softest tints, pinks, pearl-color, and
blue, green, purple, and yellow. They strew the bottom, which is of the whitest and purest sand, or hang
like leaves and flowers, or cling like mosses and
lichens to the branching coral, and lend rare enchant-
ment to the scene. Fishes of many colors with ex-
quisite grace of movement dart among the branches.
They are as multitudinous as bees over the flower
beds, and with their polished scales vie in brilliancy

with the feathered tribes of the land." We learn
also that the records of past ages, beyond the reach
of pen, beyond the dumb language of monumental
history, before Eden bloomed, were written, and bur-
ried here, leaf by leaf, the story of the earth's
growth. Psalm civ. 24, 25: "The earth is full of thy
riches. So is this great and wide sea, wherein are
things creeping innumerable, both small and great
beasts." Again says the Psalmist, xxxiii. 7: "He
gathereth the waters of the sea together as a heap:
he layeth up the depth in storehouses." The conformity of our Bible text to the statements above
need no words to tell that to David these were direct
inspirations. Too many good things have been said
about the ocean that attest the truth of the text 'for
us to say more. We will speak of it geologically,
giving the part it has played in the earth's formation
and in laying up these records of the events of the
world's history; and then show by Bible texts that
the study of these records is recommended, that the
hand of God was in the matter. There have been so
many things written on the subject of these records by
geologists that we will only notice it so far as it is connected directly with the burden of our work. The more
we know of geology, the more we know of him who
layeth up the depth in storehouses. For this reason
we have faith in the correctly read story of past ages
as found in the rocks. Geology does accord with
revelation; they are both direct gifts of inspiration.
If there is seemingly a discord, it is man's fault. To
say that it does not accord does geology an injustice
and insults revelation. These are brothers, and come ‐
to us as such. They were designed to identify each

other. It is said that geology makes the earth older than the Bible makes it. These things, they say, are taught by the rocks, the animal and vegetable remains found in them. The story is. this: "Amid all these revolutions, the changes in the earth have been attended with corresponding changes in animals; and their organic remains embedded in the rocks are the records of these transformations. The igneous and metamorphic rocks, destitute as they are of fossils, tell but little of the lapse of time in the construction of the earth; but the aqueous formation, filled with relics of life, unfold the successive chapters of the history before the creation of man." The rocks you see are leaflets of the earth's history. These dead bodies are the writings.

Let us now see how written. " Not only is the inanimate dust of the earth carried into the vast storehouse of the sea, but there lie millions of shells of every shape and hue. There into the soft oozy bottom settle the remains of countless fish, which have thronged the waters; thither float leaves and reeds and trees, torn up by the tempest, swept seaward from every shore; there sink skeletons of sea-fowls, exhausted land birds, borne to the sea by rapid rivers; drowned mariners lying in their quiet graves, unconscious of the fiercest storms that sweep above them. All the varied relics are slowly buried by the ever-settling sediment. The bottom of the ocean is a cemetery in which lie the dead from the three kingdoms of nature. Layer by layer are gathered the remains of each passing year; there leaf by leaf the history of every age is being deposited and built into the very foundations of the earth. Could we gain access to this sea bottom, we should find revealed with each layer turned up by our spade a fresh page of the history of the world. The ocean is now making up a continuation of this history. The geologist is reading the earlier volumes in the stratified rocks, the sea bottom of the olden times." These are the writings which the geologist interprets, and sometimes he makes them say what the Bible does not say—so they say. Job xxvi. 5: "Dead things are formed from under the waters, and the inhabitants thereof." Geology begins here. This is the first observation, this the very writing of which we have spoken. Dead things are formed—take form under the waters, at the bottom, from the inhabitants thereof. The millions of shells of every shape and hue leave their forms here. The remains of countless fishes take form with these. The skeletons of sea-fowls and exhausted land birds go down and take form with these also. Reeds and trees and the skeletons of animals swept in from every shore go down and take form with these too. One leaf on the sea bottom is written. The ever-settling sediment buries these, and then spreads the sheet for a new page. It is a language of dead things. Dead things take form, position, the very thing, the only thing that is intelligible, in estimating the ages. We know that one formation is older than another if it is buried deeper, or lies beneath. The younger formation is always above the older. We use the very term, "formation." Dead things are formed, make a formation, under the sea, aqueous. How truly does Job make the sea bottom a cemetery, where the dead take form! Job xii. 7-9: "But ask now the beasts, and they

shall teach thee; and the fowls of the air, and they
shall tell thee; or speak to the earth, and it shall
teach thee; and the fishes of the sea shall declare
unto thee. Who knoweth not in all these that the
hand of the Lord hath wrought this?" The ant is
accepted as the type of industry. "Go to the ant,
thou sluggard." By example this little insect was
to teach lessons of industry. In this case a special
lesson was to be learned, and that lesson was defined.
Now the beasts are to become teacher.

"Ask the beasts, and they shall teach thee." The
lesson to be taught, we think, is that the hand of the
Lord wrought this. The lesson to be learned is an
important, a valuable, lesson. What will they teach?
This great lesson above. They teach their own history as read in the rocks, the solid foundations of
the earth. In these we see the hand that did this.
They can not teach orally, for they can not talk. They
can not teach by signs, for these are found only along
the line of their particular needs. They can only
teach zoology and geology and that from their embedded forms in the rocks. We are directed to no
particular beast—but beasts. How else can this
multifarious assembly teach? To make the statement that they do teach and that through their dead
forms only makes this meaning certain. They teach
geology.

"The fowls of the air shall tell thee." What can
their story be? The silent dead forms of the fowls
of the air tell their story from their creation down
through all the ages. Their dead forms speak
louder and more intelligibly than their living bills.
We learn geology from these.

"Speak to the earth, and it shall teach thee." Will it not teach just as the beasts and fowls do? The dead, silent earth is teacher. "Speak to it," question it, investigate it, dig down into it. What does the earth teach? Were you going to buy a book that contained the lessons taught by the earth as teacher, what book would you call for? But you did not tell me for what work you would call. Geology. That is right, my man. That is what it teaches. Now do you suppose that the Bible would recommend you to go to school to the earth to learn geology, the only thing it can teach if the written and "formed" works did not agree? He says that the Bible is his word. He says that he layeth up the depths in storehouses. He claims to be the Author of both the Bible and the earth. Then he recommends geology. Go at the work determined to accept nothing as true if it is not in full and harmonious accord with the written Word. This you can understand, while you may fail to interpret dead forms. Would you recommend a work with which you are not conversant? Would you recommend a work that was not correct in its teachings? Would you recommend an incompetent, unworthy teacher? If you would not, I can not entertain for one second that he who made the record of the earth's history, and whose ways are as far from our ways as the east is from the west, would do so either. Now the east is about six hundred millions of miles from the west; if his ways, words, and works are that far above mine, or even yours, believe him.

"The fishes of the sea shall declare." The beasts shall teach, the fowls shall tell, the earth shall teach, the "fishes shall declare." We need not ask these a word; they tell at an immoderate tone. Declarations come more often by sight than from hearing. Their declarations are heard loudest as we see in that ocean cemetery where lie the three kingdoms of nature. Job's comment is wonderful: "Who knoweth not in all these that the hand of the Lord hath wrought this?" Some say it did; some say it did not. Psalm lxxxii. 5: "They know not, neither will they understand; they walk on in darkness: all the foundations of the earth are out of course." Such is the testimony of those that do not know and will not understand. The dead bodies of these that have grown into hardness tell us of their former habits, the kind of food upon which they subsisted. From others, by the shape of the eye we determine something concerning the conditions of the air. A single tooth betrays its master's diet. One bone, its size. Each form lies buried on the same plain with those that flourished alongside of it. Each form was a letter in the leaf, the whole leaf a combination of letters making a page in the history of the earth's growth.

Surface of the land under the sea. Deep-sea dredgings show the bottom of the ocean, like the land, to be made up of elevations and depressions, of mountains, hills, and valleys. Psalm civ. 6–8: "Thou coveredst it with the deep as with a garment: the waters stood above the mountains. At thy rebuke they fled; at the voice of thy thunder they hasted away. They go up by the mountains; they go down by the valleys unto the place which thou hast founded for them." Jonah ii. 6: "I went down to the bottoms of the mountains."

WAVES.

As long as the ocean and winds have existed so long have the waves swept over the sea. The ocean by the friction of the winds, modified by other circumstances, is often torn to great depths and waves heaped one upon another till their heights are estimated by the phrase "mountains high," or "to the clouds." Psalm cvii. 26: "They mount up to the heaven, they go down again to the depths."

WATERSPOUTS.

Of this phenomenon of the sea geographers say: "The whirlwind is frequently accompanied by a funnel-shaped cloud, having its point toward the earth. When it passes over a body of water this point frequently extends lower and lower, while the water beneath is violently whirled up in a column of spray. As the cloud descends it unites with this column, and a waterspout is formed." Here are the two oceans we have talked so much about; one of air descends in a cloud, while the other of water rises higher and higher ti'l they meet in mid-air, and form a waterspout. Psalm xlii. 7: "Deep calleth unto deep at the noise of thy waterspouts." Here we have the same terms, the same process, and the same result.

OCEAN TIDES AND THEIR CAUSES.

We are taught that the unequal attraction of the sun and moon upon different parts of the earth produce the tides. As the amount of water in the ocean is always the same, the effect of the moon's attraction is simply to change its spherical form to that of an ellipsoid, whose longer axis is directed toward the moon. The sea is thus raised under the moon to the extent of 55 deg. around the point nearest the moon, while it is depressed about the pole to the distance of 35 deg., leaving it heaped directly opposite the moon also. Were it not for the interference of the land, the waves would chase each other round the globe, led on by the attraction of the moon. Jeremiah xxxi. 35: "Thus saith the Lord, which giveth the sun for a light by day, and the ordinances of the moon and of the stars for a light by night, which divideth the sea when the waves thereof roar." Jeremiah attributes the cause of tides directly to these bodies. The sun and the moon produce tides independently of each other; but, as their relative positions are constantly changing during every month, their separate actions are alternately united and opposite to each other. Twice a month, at new and full moon, the sun and moon act together, and the tides are unusually high, since the solar and lunar tides are then heaped one upon another. As an assurance of the acceptance of the seed of Jacob and David, he pledges it, and makes it as permanent and as sure as are these ordinances. Jeremiah xxxiii. 25, 26: "Thus saith the Lord; If my covenant be not with day and night, and if I have not appointed the ordinances of heaven and earth; then will I cast away the seed of Jacob, and David my servant." He declares that he is the Author of all the laws of heaven and earth, that he appointed these, that they are immutable, permanent as his own inviolable promises to his own chosen seed.

Here the grand doctrine of attraction is taught

twenty-five hundred years before Newton was born. Mark the indestructibility of these ordinances.

OCEAN CURRENTS.

We have spoken of the ocean as a great store-house. Now let us look at the continents as different apartments of one great establishment, heated by invective currents or cooled by melting snow and ice, from this great storehouse of good things, which is sending out its streams of heat and cold, mollifying the rigors of frigid climes, or cooling others with their burdens of ice. It is strange to see the rivers of hot water seemingly with undeviating instinct move straight for the coldest seas; while cold, icy rivers take the straightest route for these hottest seas. Every ocean has its currents. Let us follow two of these ocean currents and notice their effect on contiguous lands. The Gulf Stream begins down in the Caribbean Sea, or we will begin with it there. It passes along our eastern coast, a mighty river of warm water, flowing through the Atlantic. From Cape Hatteras to the Grand Banks of Newfoundland the stream is warmer than the ocean by 20 deg. or 30 deg. Fahrenheit. After flowing three thousand miles to the north this stream still preserves even in winter a summer heat, and, inundating with its warm vapors the cold surface of the sea for thousands of miles, forms a constant reservoir of heat, which, borne by the prevailing southwesterly winds to Europe, softens the rigors of its climate. It has been estimated that the amount of heat arising from the Gulf Stream on a winter day is sufficient to raise the atmosphere over the British Isles from the freezing-point to a summer temperature. Hammerfest, the most northern seaport in the world, is never closed by ice; this warm current prevents it from freezing. On goes nature's process of heating by steam, affording perpetual pasture to shores far north of us, shores that would otherwise be locked by eternal snows and ice. This agent makes these countries rich, powerful, and happy. It also forms a great feeding way by the distribution of food picked up and dropped along the route. The inhabitants of the sea are induced hither in search of food, the weaker becoming a prey to the stronger of their kind. Who knows but that this is a part of a great plan? So potent is this that the mind of the prophet seized upon it to illustrate Pharaoh's growth in wealth and power. Ezekiel xxxi. 3, 4 : "Behold, the Assyrian was a cedar in Lebanon with fair branches, and with a shadowing shroud, and of a high stature; and his top was among the thick boughs. The waters made him great, the deep set him up on high with her rivers round about his plants, and sent out her little rivers unto all the trees of the field." Ezekiel xxxii. 2: "Thou art as a whale in the seas: and thou camest forth with thy rivers."

Let us follow a cold current, one that has its origin high up in frozen seas. We will begin about 43° north latitude. Here the cold current divides into two branches. One of these, flowing along the coast of the United States as far as Florida by the side of the Gulf Stream, forms the counter-current of the latter; while the other, running southward beneath the Gulf Stream as a submarine current as far as Florida, enters the Caribbean Sea. The

waters of this cold current below the surface are
found to be as cold as those off the shores of Spitzbergen at corresponding depths. Like our two air
currents that set the one from the equator and the
other from the pole, for a great distance the one
moves directly under the other in a course directly
opposite. This was told to Job thousands of years
before man had marked the course of the winds or
had looked upon the face of the great seas. Job
xxxviii. 25: "Who hath divided a watercourse for the
overflowing of waters?" Who can make one wind
blow due south and another due north, and directly
under it; or who can make one river flow north
and another south, and directly under it? That
these things are now known to be so is to my mind
the mystery. Who could know these truths? What
one could say such things before the days of Columbus?

These currents are great thoroughfares—ways leading and even driving on man's boat, forwarding
commerce. "By the aid of ocean currents mariners
are enabled to take advantage of favorable currents,
and to avoid those that are adverse, thus shortening
their voyage and facilitating the commerce of the
world. In the Indian Ocean a ship sailing from Java
homeward bound to Europe is borne westward by
equatorial currents at the rate of ten to twenty miles
a day. After passing Madagascar it is carried southwesterly at the rate, in some places, of one hundred
and twenty miles per day. The influence of the Gulf
Stream upon commerce and navigation is very remarkable." When we know this, and when we look
upon the great ocean, marked by her many paths, we

think of the coal that touched the lip of the prophet Isaiah (Isa. xliii. 16), "Thus saith the Lord, which maketh a way in the sea, and a path in the mighty waters," hundreds of years before a painted chart of the seas was ever made by man, and thousands of years before he had followed these paths in the mighty waters. Scientists say that the directions of these paths are influenced by the rotation of the earth on its axis. Revelation in the book of Job mentions it in connection with the same subject. The question that presents itself is: Where are the books inspired men studied so long before the story of these things is told by the world? Proverbs xxv. 2: "It is the glory of God to conceal a thing: but the honor of kings is to search out a matter." By kings is not meant he who sits upon a throne or is born heir to a kingdom. These are not of necessity the only real kings or princes of earth. Ecclesiastes: "I have seen servants upon horses, and princes walking as servants upon the earth." Thus we close this chapter with a breathing of social philosophy, compared to a like breathing from revelation.

CHAPTER II.

" LET there be light." It is not denominated sunlight. The sun is reserved till the fourth day. According to the detachment theory there could have been no light to the earth till it (the earth) was detached from this nebular mass, and light from the residue to it did spring up at the very moment of its detachment. Also, according to the same theory, the sun never appeared in his place till after the detachment of Venus, Mercury, and Vulcan, if there be a Vulcan. Let us suppose that on the second day He prepared the firmament and separated the waters and Venus was detached. The detachment of Venus, together with the sun's compression, could have so charged atmospheric temperature as to effect, in a measure, that universal precipitation that brought down the waters of the globe. On the third day the waters were collected in one place; grass and herbs and fruit-bearing trees put forth. This was signalized by the birth of Mercury. The sun, by contraction, is withdrawing from the earth, each time affording a milder temperature, suited to higher organisms. On the fourth day Vulcan was thrown off. This act, at one and the same time, made the two great lights—the one to rule the day, and the other to rule the night. Now the sun is in his place. The

(32)

moon receives her light from the sun, yet was not placed as a light till the sun was placed; that means put in place, for as lights "God set them in the firmament of heaven to give light upon the earth" at the same time. Is it not strange that Moses should show this dependence?

According to Laplace and Moses the material was created in bulk, and this bulk was divided and formed into worlds. The residue was left as the sun. Spectrum analysis shows kinship—that they are flesh of one flesh and bone of one bone. "Two great lights." We see in the work-days of God this comment: "The moon is called a great light from its being apparently equal, or nearly equal, in size to the sun; or, perhaps, from the fact that it seems much larger than the stars. But here, again, things are described as they would appear to a spectator, and not as they were in reality; for the moon is among the smallest of the heavenly bodies, and, as compared with the sun or fixed stars, is but as a grain of mustard-seed to a twenty-four inch globe." We have given this quotation to illustrate our idea of a word interpretation. Mr. Morris's apology for these revealed truths caused him to speak of these lights as they appeared to him. Had he dealt with them as they really are, and just what the text denominates them, and then advised his spectators to change their standpoints, that they might in reality see them as they are, would have sounded more like reason. The bulk of these two bodies enters no more into the thought than do the individual elements of which they are composed. They are great lights, not great bulks. Light has its laws, which are as fixed, as definite, as operative, as

3

those that govern earthly matter, even the constellations themselves. Is the sun not a great light? It goes out to light a dependent son nearly three billions of miles away. Think of a circle whose diameter is nearly six billion miles. Over all this great area is light enough going out from the sun to make every spot feel its influence, and look toward our sun as the source. It is said that it would take three hundred thousand full moons to make night as bright as day. Surely the sun is a great light, the greatest that our eyes can behold. Were the space over our heads and around us one unbroken Milky Way, yet this would not afford the light that one moon does, and that in its second quarter. We are told that along this Milky Way trillions of mighty suns blend their feeble rays. Then the moon is a great light— the next greatest that greets us from space.

If, as Mr. Morris suggests, we should speculate on these lights as they appear to every spectator, then the sun and moon would rise and set each by its own motion. The Psalmist sustains our idea. Psalm lxxiv. 16: "The day is thine, the night also is thine: thou hast prepared the light and the sun." They are distinct preparations. Light is one thing, and the sun quite another.

"Thou hast prepared the light." This preparation must have taken place in the laboratories of old, in the beginning of his way, before his works of old, before it gleamed from any object. The first order that fell on chaos was not to create, not to prepare, but "Let there be light." Prepare—to fit for a particular use or service. It is one of the most intricate preparations found in nature. It is a mixture of three rays. " These work everywhere the miracle of life and motion." In the white ray is hid all the colors of the rainbow. Light comes to us from the sun as a preparation for life, and finds its uses wherever a service is needed. It is a sure tonic, healthful and invigorating.

"Thou hast prepared the sun." The preparation of the sun was the preparation of a great globe. It was created with the heaven and the earth in the beginning; so after that it was only prepared, fitted for its particular use. The word indicates its development from materials already at hand. There is no theory more plausible than the detachment theory, There is not an expression, that we now remember, in the Old Testament stating that he ever made a sun, only in connection with all the matter that composes our system, and that is found in the first sentence in our Bible. " In the beginning God created the heaven and the earth." The first thing God created the solar system. From this he prepared the sun, shaped, compressed, removed, the sun to fit it for a sun's work as we see it. We have such expressions as: " To him that made the sun to rule the day;" "he maketh his sun to rise on the evil," etc. He always claims the authorship of the purpose of the sun, but never does he tell us that he made the sun. "He prepared the sun" is the only Bible statement touching the formation of the sun, so far as we remember.

THE SUN AND ITS FRUITS.

In the blessings given to Joseph, among the wonderful things given to him, is that most curiously wonderful gift, the fruits of the sun. Deuteronomy

xxxiii. 14: "And for the precious fruits brought forth
by the sun." This can not mean literal fruit dropping from the sun. It can not mean the growth and
production of fruit in any other sense than a philosophical one. It is stripped of every visible, tangible fruit-producing branch. "Fruits," as used in the
text, are "whatever is produced for the nourishment
of animals and man, or for clothing or profit. It
includes not only corn of all kinds, but grass, cotton,
flax, grapes, and the fruits of orchards, and spices and
sweet things gathered from the many lands and islands of all the world;" and all transformations produced by this agent, the sun.

"Fruits of the sun." This blessing to Joseph was
penned more than five thousand years ago. If all the
knowledge concerning the sun at that age were compiled, it would not extend beyond the truth that the
sun was the source of light and heat. What are the
fruits of the sun? As we are comparing revelations
to science we cannot do better than to quote from
these works.

Chemistry of the Sunbeam.—"In classical fable we
are told that Prometheus stole a spark of celestial
fire and warmed into life the earthly body he had
formed. The mythologic dream was parallel with the
truth of nature; the true Promethean spark is the
sunbeam, which, by its wonderful alchemy, transforms
dead matter into organized and living forms."

Extent of Solar Influence.—"Not only life, but all
the grand phenomena of force with which we are familiar upon this planet, have their origin in the sun.
His radiations govern the movements of terrestrial
atoms, and in these the movements of masses take

their rise. Should that body cease to give out ema-
nations, the earth would speedily lose its heat; life
would disappear, vapors condense, and liquids con-
geal. There would still be tidal influence, due to
the attraction of the dark masses of the sun and moon;
but, as the ocean would be solid, there could be
only a slight movement in the atmosphere. There
might also be volcanic force, due to the earth's central heat, although this too has been held as subject to astronomic agency."

Effects of Solar Heat Alone.—"Were the sun to
radiate heat alone, the earth would still remain dark,
but the oceans would melt, and tides begin to lash
the coasts. The atmosphere would be rarefied unequally as now; storms would arise, and there would
be the motive power of wind. Water would be converted into vapor and condensed into invisible clouds
and rain. Streams would channel their way to the
sea, and, falling in cataracts, would give rise to water-
power. The descending floods, bringing down the
sediment, would generally lower the continents and
fill up the oceans, while the tide would gnaw away
the shores. The distribution of land and water
would be changed, and there would be all the extensive effects of aqueous geologic agency. Further-
more, the electrical conditions of matter would be
disturbed; tropical tornadoes and the milder storms
of the temperate latitudes would be accompanied
with thunder and lightning; the unequal heating
of the earth in its daily rotation would give rise to
thermoelectric currents, and these would produce
magnetism. All these results would flow from solar radiations quickening the motions of earthly

atoms, so that ice would change to water, and water to vapor."

Effect of Increased Solar Action.—"If we again suppose the energy of solar radiation so exalted that light emitted with heat, the higher phenomena of organization becomes possible with the introduction of plant germs, the vegetable world would be called into being by the vitalizing chemistry of the sun. The animal world, dependent upon the vegetable, consuming its matter and its force, could then appear with all its multitudinous forms of power. The burning of wood and coal would also give steam power. Thus, in addition to all the forms of mechanical movement upon earth, its very energies and impulses of life originate in the sun."

The Organic Kingdom a Magazine of Force.—"The vegetable world, born of the atmosphere, consists of condensed gasses. The animal world, derived from the vegetable, is also but solidified air. So the food that we consume, the clothes that we wear, the houses in which we live, the fuel that warms us by the fireside, that transports us to distant places with lightning speed, and labors for us in a thousand ways, are all nothing but condensed air. *The sunbeam is the agent of condensation, and thus the organic world presents itself as a vast magazine of solar force.*" Precious fruits of the sun. But that is not all. The blessing to Joseph continues in the next verse, and in the same sentence. Deuteronomy xxxiii. 15, 16: "And for the chief things of the ancient mountains, and for the precious things of the lasting hills, and for the precious things of the earth and the fulness thereof." What are the chief things of the ancient mountains? What are the precious things of the lasting hills? These are without question gold, silver, lead, copper, iron, coal, and stone.

Continuing our quotations: "So the coal deposits —carbonized remains of vegetation which, flourishing long before man appeared upon the globe, were condensed from an atmosphere richer in carbonic acid, and perhaps by a more brilliant sun; and yet this coal, having slumbered in its ancient bed through uncounted eras of time, now comes forth to surrender its ethereal agents, light and heat, and return as carbonic acid to the air, from whence it came."

The Sunbeam the Antagonist of Oxygen. — "When treating of oxygen it was stated that this element enshrouds the globe, and tends to unite with and bring all things to rest, so that if the earth were left to the action of its own forces life would quickly disappear, and leave the world a desert. But the earth's vegetation is the beautiful instrumentality by which this action is arrested. The leaves extract poisonous carbonic acid from the air, deprive it of the elements it has seized, and return it again to the atmosphere, while the forces which impel these changes are the beams of the sun. These are the great antagonists of oxygen. Under its influence organized matter is rent into its elements and carried down to the mineral world; under the influence of the solar rays it is again raised to the organized condition. If oxygen dilapidates, they renovate; if that decomposes and breaks down, they construct and build up; if that is seen in the falling leaf of autumn, they are proclaimed in the exuberant foliage and blossoms of spring. If oxygen is the mainspring of destruction, wasting, burning, consuming all things, the solar rays constitute the mighty force of counteraction. They reunite the dissevered elements, and substitute development for decay, calling forth a glory from desolation, and life and beauty from the very bosom of death." O, "the precious fruits brought forth by the sun!" "And for the precious things of the earth and fulness thereof." These are enumerated among the precious fruits.

Continuing our quotation:

It Is the Motive Power of the World.—"Thus is the earth warmed, illumined, magnetized, and vivified by the sun. In the fall of the avalanche, the roar of the cataract, and the flow of rivers; in the crash of thunder, the glare of lightning, and the sweep of tornadoes, in the blaze of conflagration and the shock of battle; in the beauty of flower, of the rainbow, and the ever-shifting clouds; in the days and seasons, the silent growth of the plants, and the elastic spring of animals; in the sail of impelled or steam-driven ship, and the flying train; in the heavy respiration of the laboring steam-engine, and the rapid click of the telegraph—in all the myriad manifestations of earthly power, we behold the transmuted strength of the all-energizing sun." "The precious fruits brought forth by the sun." These were blessings to Joseph. But, says the same writer:

The Universe Culminates in Life.—"If astronomy has revealed to us a universe of unspeakable grandeur, chemistry has linked the mighty mechanism to the course of terrestrial life. She teaches not only that the leaves and flowers distilled from the crystal medium in which they dwell, but they are tissues

woven in the loom of the universe—their warp the
subtlest ethers of earth, their woof the swift radiations
of the stars; not only that the leaf is the crucible of
vitality, whose mysterious alchemy is interposed between ourselves and death, but that it is the wondrous
mechanism appointed to receive and gather the life
forces which God is perpetually pouring through
this universe." "And God saw the light, that it was
good."

THE MOON.

It is an accepted opinion that the moon has much
to do with the planting and growth of vegetation;
that it shapes to a very great extent our seasons.
Psalm civ. 19: "He appointed the moon for seasons." Genesis i. 14: "Let there be lights in the
firmament of the heaven to divide the day from the
night; and let them be for signs, and for seasons, and
for days, and years." Science teaches that the moon
has no light in itself; it only reflects the light of the
sun. The eclipse of the moon is a proof of this fact.
The earth, passing between the sun and the moon,
cuts off the light from that body, and it is dark.
We say the moon is in eclipse. Job xxv. 5: "Behold
even to the moon, and it shineth not." The moon is
not a luminous body, but opaque. It does not emit
light; it only reflects it. Hence, says Job: "The moon
shineth not." Job xxxi. 26: "If I beheld the sun
when it shined, or the moon walking in brightness."
How nicely and how philosophically is this distinction made! The sun is made luminous, while the
moon only walks in his brightness. This accounts
for the fact that the two great lights showed forth
at one and the same time. Thales taught this doc-

trine seven hundred years before Christ. Job saw
and understood it more than a thousand years before
Thales was born. Yet Thales was the boast of
Greece. The world gives him the title of one of the
seven wise men of Greece. He established the first
school of astronomy in Greece. Still he only springs
a question old to the Bible. With these side remarks
let us return and show a striking beauty, one in conformity to the theory of to-day: "Moon walking in
brightness." Her movements are all in the light.
Let us see if we can justify Job's expression, "walking in brightness." Astronomy teaches that the real
path of the moon is the result of its own proper motion and the onward motion of the earth. The two
combined produce a wave-like curve that crosses the
earth's path twice each month. Then the moon
moves along her path by alternate oblique movements, which is philosophically nothing more nor less
than walking. One step places her at her greatest
distance to the right of the earth's track as it moves
onward through space; the next brings her back to
its greatest distance to the left of the earth, at the
same time keeping pace with the earth in its forward
movement. Thus in about twenty-seven days the
moon has completed its sidereal journey around the
earth. In about twenty-five of these steps the moon
reaches the starting, or the same position with respect to the sun and earth, and the earth has completed its yearly journey.

Job tells us by no uncertain or vague illustrations that the earth and sun each have both a forward and a rotary motion; but he says that the
moon has a forward movement, and denominates that

motion by walking in brightness. This implies the office of the moon, that of a reflector. When we walk we move forward, with our face toward the thing approached, without turning; this is true of the moon. The side that faced the earth when the two lights were first placed is the same side that it has ever presented and now presents—none but moons do that. The moon with its face set in one direction has moved, is still moving, forward with eye on the sun and its face on the earth. The tabernacle moved through the wilderness with its eye on the Son and its face on Israel's hosts. We ask you to examine some work where this motion is pictured, that you may look upon a picture penciled by inspiration four thousand years ago. Take a common auger make the barrel into a hoop, have only one wing. Let the bit represent the positions of the earth, the wing the moon's orbit; now if we could move the earth (the bit) round the barrel and the moon at the same time should move along the wing, keeping pace with the earth or bit as it moves with the sun; as it slides off in the full blaze of the sun you can almost hear the left, right, left, right as it alternately moves this way or that as we look on. The earth returns to its starting-point. Its journey is measured by twenty-five moon steps. There is one question that the scientific world is not agreed upon: the comparative brilliancy of the moon and sun, or the number of full moons necessary to make night as bright as day. One says it would take six hundred thousand full moons to make night as light as day; again, that the brilliancy of the moon is only one three hundred thousandth that of the sun; that if the whole sky was filled with full moons they would scarcely make daylight. We have learned two things: that there is an existing relation between these two lights, and that astronomers or philosophers are not agreed. Revelation makes a comparison (Isa. xxx. 26): "Moreover the light of the moon shall be as the light of the sun, and the light of the sun shall be sevenfold, as the light of seven days." It is evident that the light of the moon is increased by an increase of sunlight. This is a figure, the same figure as manifested by the tabernacle and Jesus Christ. It is drawn from the two great lights. It manifests God's nearer approach to the Church. When the Church shall shine as bright as is the light of Christ, our capacities having grown by nearing him, his light will have become sevenfold brighter when we draw seven times nearer. Let us see if we can not illustrate this by the light that some of our planets receive. The amount of light any planet receives depends upon its distance from the sun. The same is true with reference to the Church. The nearest definitely known planet to the sun is Mercury. Mercury receives sevenfold this light that we receive, and the sun appears seven times as large as it appears to us.

Then our moon, with a diameter eight hundred miles shorter than that of Mercury, though brought two hundred and forty thousand miles nearer the sun, would then afford less light than Mercury, less than seven times the light that we receive, but somewhere near that amount. Is it not wonderful that the prophet should talk of these nice comparisons that require the most intricate of all calculations?

THE STARS.

We peep from every observatory, from every standpoint on the earth, and we see the stars. Every nation has them. The twinkling stars, like so many gems, fill the bow that spans every nation. These shower their declarations of glory upon every people. Deuteronomy iv. 19: "The sun, and the moon, and the stars, . . . which the Lord thy God hath divided unto all nations under the whole heaven." Some are so far removed that light, traveling at the rate of nearly two hundred thousand miles per second, would require over a hundred years to reach the earth; were we placed on these far-off stars, others would twinkle as far beyond; and should we move on from star to star, still the heavens would spread out beyond us as we see them here. Solomon says there are three things insearchable, among them the heavens for height. Jeremiah xxxi. 37: "Thus saith the Lord; if heaven above can be measured, . . . I will cast off all the seed of Israel." How impossible that feat! Nor can we even number them. Jeremiah xxxii. 22: "The host of heaven cannot be numbered, neither the sand of the sea measured." O the stars! the stars! the stars!

ARCTURUS.

Job xxxviii. 32: "Canst thou guide Arcturus with his sons?" This is the last of four questions propounded to Job concerning star clusters. "Canst thou bind the sweet influences of Pleiades, or loose the bands of Orion? Canst thou bring forth Mazzaroth in his season? or canst thou guide Arcturus with his sons?" It is apparent that either of these performances is too much for Job. To bind the sweet influences of Pleiades, or seven stars, would require a power as great as that exerted by the most conspicuous group in the heavens. To loose the bands of Orion would require a power equal to that that supports one of the most conspicuous constellations in the heavens. To bring forth Mazzaroth in his season requires the ability to bring our earth to the constellations, to each in due time. The performance of either of these feats would require very great strength.

"Canst thou guide Arcturus with his sons?" This, we think, is directed to Job's ability to lead or direct in a way, to conduct in a course or path. The direct inference is that Arcturus is in motion. Yes, Arcturus is in motion. It is a magnificent star of the first magnitude. We said that it was in motion, yet through all our lifetime we shall never be able to detect any change in its position. In three hundred years of constant travel over the starry vault the whole space passed would not more than equal the moon's apparent diameter. To me the moon's apparent diameter does not exceed in size a common water bucket; to others its apparent diameter is as large as a wash-tub. This is the space that Arcturus seems to pass over in three hundred years. There were no facilities in the days of Job for knowing such things, and none for thousands of years afterward. The world estimated things and based its philosophy on appearance. Until recently Arcturus, together with all the stars that had no perceptible motion, were called fixed stars. Now, if Arcturus was at that day considered a fixed star, or had been

in reality such, then the question propounded to Job
was a foolish one; but when we are told that Arcturus with his sons is flying through space many hundred times faster than the fastest cannon-ball ever
travels, we comprehend the challenge to Job, and feel
assured that the flight of this star was the thought
set forth; if not to Job, it is to me and you.   Isaiah
xlviii. 4–6: "Because I knew that thou art obstinate,
and thy neck is an iron sinew, and thy brow brass;
I have even from the beginning declared it to thee;
before it came to pass I shewed it thee; lest thou
shouldest say, Mine idol [our science] hath done
them; and my graven image, and my molten image,
hath commanded them. . . . I have shewed thee new
things from this time, even hidden things, and thou
didst not know them."   "Canst thou guide Arcturus
with his sons?" "With his sons." If it be true that
our system was at one time one boundless mass; that
all the planets, satellites, etc., were detached from
this mass, leaving the residue for our sun, we conclude that this same process evolved other systems.
As our earth and all the attendants of our system are
sons of the sun, so are the attendants of other suns.
Each, as a spark sent blazing from the central mass,
is a son of that mass. Job v. 7: "Yet man is born unto
trouble, as the sparks fly upward." We introduced
this for the marginal reading of the clause.   "The
sparks fly upward." The Hebrew rendering is: "The
sons of the burning coal lift up to fly." The particles
thrown off by heat are here made the sons of the body
from which they were thrown. "Lift up to fly."
These ejected bodies of our system were truly lifted
up to fly—sent on wings that need no rest, on journeys

that have no ends. So far as these thrown-off worlds resemble thrown-off sparks; so far they partake of the nature of sons of the residue.

So, then, the sons of Arcturus may be those bodies that were detached from him and that follow him in his incredible flight. Arcturus is a sun, then a parent—one who supplies those of his own house with the needs, comforts, and even the luxuries of life. His sons accompany him in his flight; they draw their supplies directly from him. They acknowledge his authority; they obey without murmurs, and are led on by an influence as sweet as that of Pleiades, as strong as the bands of Orion. "Canst thou guide Arcturus with his sons?" Think of Arcturus's apparent motion; think of what was known concerning this motion at the time of the penning of the text. Think of his great, real velocity. See the challenges, and you will be convinced that God alone knew and spoke to Job.

CHAPTER III.

Job xxviii. 5: "As for the earth, out of it cometh bread: and under it is turned up as it were fire."

"As for the earth, out of it cometh bread." Job has divided here the earth into two parts—that from which bread comes, and that which is beneath this part. "As for the earth"—that is, that part of it from which bread comes—Job's explanation makes it the crust of the earth, the outside part. "Bread." Eatable—that is, may be used by man for food. So it extends to the outside of the earth everywhere. The earth—the outside part—gives us, directly or indirectly, all our food.

"Under it is turned up as it were fire." Under it, this outside part, this crust, "is turned up as it were fire." Job teaches that beneath the bread-producing part of the earth is fire. We have many proofs that the central part of the earth is intensely heated. Hot springs, geysers, and volcanoes, found in many parts of the world, attest this truth. In deep mines, wherever sunk, in valley or on mountain, whether through rock or sand or clay, the same gradual in-

4 (49)

crease in temperature is found. So uniform is this that by knowing the depth we may readily determine the temperature.

Job says that this internal fire "is turned up." This statement of Job's cannot be true under any hypothesis than that the earth is round. For, was the earth not round, these internal fires would, in some points, turn out: in others, they would turn down or up.

The center of the earth is equidistant from every point on the surface. The center of the earth is its lowest point; every direction from this central point is up. Geographies teach that this fire is turned up, is arrested only by this non-conducting crust, the part from which cometh bread.

"As it were fire." Our own fires illustrate the upward tendency of heat. "As it were." This implies that it is not the fire with which Job's hearers were familiar, and that the combustibles that feed it are different. These statements from Job can have no other possible significance.

Proverbs viii. 27-30: "When he set a compass upon the face of the depth . . . I was by him." You observe that the marginal reading is: "When he set a circle upon the face of the deep." This statement from Solomon refers directly to a statement by Job xxvi. 10: "He hath compassed the waters with bounds, until the day and night come to an end." In the statement made by Solomon, all the verses show that this performance took place during the earth's transformation period. Wisdom testifies that she was present when this was done. A compass is an instrument for describing circles.

To set a compass implies its use. Then he shaped
the face of the depth with a compass. Is it not
singular that he did not use the spirit-level? Columbus taught that the depth was round in the latter
part of the fifteenth century, and received for it the
title of "idle dreamer." Let us examine the above
text from Job—viz., "He hath compassed the waters
with bounds, until the day and night came to an
end."

For brevity, beauty, and geographical accuracy
this quotation challenges the learning of the world.
No human mind has ever afforded as much in so few
words. At one sweep of the compass he rounded the
depth, marked the bounds of three oceans, and
traced the line where day and night come to an end.
This can be said of only two circles on the earth's
surface: the arctic and antarctic circles. Could
we place one arm of the compass on the geographical north pole, and move the point of the other
arm along the arctic circle, it would trace the limit
and the surface of the waters of arctic seas, not
even an arm south of this circle uncrossed by it. It
also traces the line that limits the Atlantic on the
north and separates it from the Arctic; and also
limits the Pacific on the north and separates it also
from the Arctic; and also it traces the line of illumination December 22. Could we place one point of
this same compass on the geographical south pole,
and trace with the point of the other arm, the antarctic circle, just touching the surface of the water,
it would trace the line that marks the southern
bounds of the Atlantic, Pacific, and the northern
limit of the antartic seas, and the line of illumina-

tion in the southern hemisphere June 21. "He hath compassed the waters with bounds, until the day and night come to an end." It is not possible to draw two circles through any other points on the earth's surface that will meet one of these conditions, much less all of them. Then without question these are the circles that Wisdom saw described and the ones spoken of by Job. We come now to the most wonderful part of this discussion.

"Until the day and night come to an end." Until is always the same part of speech, and has the same meaning. The only difference is that it is followed sometimes by a single word denoting time, and in other cases by a verb denoting an event, or a word denoting place or degree. The sense is in all cases "to." In this case it accurately and beautifully fills its double purpose of the time when, and the place where, the day and night come to an end. In the margin we find this rendering from the Hebrew: "Until the end of light with darkness." It is not sufficient to say that we learn from the text that day and night end together somewhere on the earth, but that this ending together is brought about by a come; not a go, not a catch. There are two places on the earth's surface, and two times during the year, where and when the light and the darkness neither advance nor recede. By examining the almanac you observe that the sun rises and sets from June 17th to the 26th, making only two minutes variation in time during these nine days and nights. During this period the six month's night traces the antarctic circle, while day and night north of this circle alternate with each revolution of the earth.

This period is called the summer solstice in the northern hemisphere from the fact at this time the sun seems to stand in the heavens. Again, from December 20th to the 24th the sun rises and sets, making not more than two minutes variation during these five days. During this period the six month's night traces the arctic circle, while day and night south of this circle alternate with each rotation of the earth. In the northern hemisphere we call this the winter solstice, for at this time again the sun seems to stand in the heavens. At no other times or places do such stops or standings of light and darkness take place.

"He hath compassed the waters with bounds, until the day and the night come to an end." These two points are the extremities of the major axis of the earth's orbit, the ends. The statement is positive. We said that day and night could not come to an end along the meridians. Then we must look for it along the parallels. About the 21st of March the days and nights are equal all over the globe; these alternate with each rotation. As the earth turns from west to east, the light sets westward and toward the darkness; all the while the darkness seems to recede, as these fly from meridian to meridian with a velocity greater than was ever attained by the fastest-flying cannon-ball; impossible, then, that day and night could come to an end along the meridians. Each day the sun rises farther north than on the preceding day. Each day he ascends higher at the north pole, and withdraws correspondingly from the south pole. Now the chase is along the meridians as well as along the parallels. As the light advances toward the north, the darkness keeps pace from the south, and continues until the sun's apparent motion northward stops. Then the chase ends. Had the sun left a line of light as the earth turned, this line would have wormed round the earth like the threads on a screw, and the darkness, true to its instincts, would have traced this as surely as the threads in the tap follow those along the screw. This chase was kept up till June 17th. Then, and precisely then, the northward advance of day ends; simultaneously the night ends also. Now the sun sends his rays twenty-three and a half degrees beyond the north pole, while the darkness has advanced twenty-three and a half degrees north of the south pole. Now we shall see how day and night *come* to an end; do not go to an end, do not even catch up, but *come* to an end. For nine days the sun pours its light toward the darkness without an apparent change, while the darkness, on the defensive, boldly faces the light. And for a time it traces the antarctic circle clear round the earth, making the bounds of three oceans. The critical time comes just when the sun turns and meets the darkness. Till now the earth has been moving south, while the darkness has been moving north. During this standstill of the day and night this earth motion has never ceased, has only changed its direction. The long day at the north pole ended precisely when the advance of the darkness at the south pole ended. Then they came to an end in this sense. These ended precisely along the compassed bounds given by Job.

The sun retraces his steps, the same chase as before begins, but in an opposite direction. It is kept

up till the light at the north pole and the darkness
at the south pole have exchanged positions. From
December 20th to the 24th the darkness traces the
arctic circle, that line that marks the bounds of three
oceans. The south pole at this time to the antarctic
circle is enjoying its summer of continuous day.
Again, as before, day and night come to an end, and
along these compassed bounds. The critical time is
again just as day turns and meets the night; then
they come to an end. These truths depend on three
things: The rotundity of the earth, the inclination of
its axis, and its motion about the sun. We can not
interpret this text, nor can it be understood without
a knowledge of the above truths. I could not claim
to be the author of such a text without this knowledge, nor could you, nor could even Job. Isaiah xl.
22: "It is he that sitteth upon the circle of the
earth." Is the earth circular? What do you say?
There is no place for a comment, nor could we offer
higher proof of a round earth and a circular sea.
How strange that an inspired prophet, fifty-eight
years before the great Grecian sage conceived this
theory, should seize the palm above the hand of
science and wreathe with it a crown for Inspiration.
This is no new deviation. Every great scientific discovery found a record in the Bible antedating hundreds and, in many instances, thousands of years
any scientific record or statement, or conception from
the world. In the discussion of many other questions
we gave passages that support the foregoing theory
as forcibly and as unmistakably as the above. We
made mention of the fact in these discussions, hence
omit them here.

Wisdom of Solomon, 11, 12: "For the whole world before thee is as a little grain of the balance. Yea, as a drop of the morning dew that falleth down upon the earth."

"For the whole world before thee is as a little grain of the balance." Astronomers use the above language when comparing this world to the mighty globes that so gently shine upon us in the far-off sky, that it is only a minute particle in a universe of worlds. To-day our best telescopes can not develop a visible disk of even the nearest star. Solomon lived twenty-five hundred years before the days of telescopes, in an age when astronomy was the merest foolery. Who told Solomon? We call your attention to "*is as*," as expressive of comparisons in size.

"Yea, as a drop of morning dew." *Yea* means "yes," and expresses affirmation. It enforces the sense of something preceding; not only so, but more. Thus he introduces another comparison, which is wonderful: "Yea, as a drop of morning dew." *As* means "like:" then the world before thee is like a drop of morning dew compared to balance. In many respects it is like it. Our geographers use this same illustration to tell us not only that the earth is round, but what rounded it. They say that at some time in the earth's history it was in a liquid state, that the same force that rounds the dewdrop rounded the earth. "Morning dew," does this differ from early evening dew, from dew deposited during the night? Very materially. Though it be the drop deposited at early evening, or during the night, it exemplifies by morning quite a change. It is less and rounder. At seventy-five degrees a cubic yard of air can hold over half an ounce of water. A reduction of twenty-seven degrees will cause half that quantity to be deposited. The less moisture the air contains the less moisture deposited, and lower the temperature when the deposit is made, consequently smaller the drops. At forty-eight degrees temperature the air has deposited half its moisture. When the dew-point is reached the air begins to give up its moisture; every drop taken from the air lessens the supply, and aids in lowering the temperature, which contracts more the air particles and presses out more dew, but of smaller drops. The comparison does not end here. Not altogether like a drop of *morning* dew, but as one " that falleth down upon the earth." So it matters not so much when the deposit was made, if it is only the drop that falleth down in the morning. The drop when first deposited extends more along the twig or leaf, is spread out, its adhesion to the limb being greater than its cohesion for itself. The temperature is falling from radiation, and the evaporation which lessens the drop increases its cohesion as the air grows less inviting, it rounds more, the surface to which it holds is lessened, its gravity proportionately increased, while its buoyant force is less. Just when nearest the freezing-point its adhesion is least. Then it falls; see it as it goes down; it is as the earth, like the earth, round.

Geographers tell us that the earth was rounded in the same way. The earth is as a falling drop of morning dew. The earth has a falling motion, a tendency to go to its center. Our deductions lead us to a more curious fact: that of specific gravity. Specific gravity, or relative weight, is the weight of a substance compared with that of the same bulk of any other substance; and distilled water at a temperature of 39.2 degrees Fahrenheit is taken as a standard to which we compare other bodies. The density of the other worlds as compared to the earth is based on the density of distilled water at a temperature of 39.2 degrees. Astronomers give the density of the sun and all the planets as compared to the density of water.

The specific gravity of a world is the weight of that world, compared to an equal bulk of distilled water at 39.2 degrees. The falling tendency expressed and seen in the drop is as this world. This is the thing to which the earth is likened; then it is as a falling drop. Its weight, as manifested by falling, is a measure of the force of gravity. Thus we discover the close connection and dependence of all things. The same force which controls the mighty systems of celestial orbs measures quantities of matter in the daily transactions of business life. " Even measures of weight were derived from the weight of a certain volume of water." Isaiah xl. 12: " Who hath measured the waters in the hollow of his hand, and meted out heaven with a span, and comprehended the dust of the earth in a measure, and weighed the mountains in scales, and the hills in a balance." How beautifully is shown the intimate relation of measure, weight, distance. Dew is distilled water. Let us see if we can not approximate its temperature. The dew-point is 48 degrees. This is within less than ten degrees of the standard temperature. When the temperature falls to 32 degrees it becomes not dew, but frost. We have it between two bounds—one that it can not pass and remain dew, the other less than ten degrees above, and a falling temperature. Experience teaches us that morning dew is not frost, and that its temperature is but a little above that, or about 39.2 degrees. Solomon makes two comparisons—this world as a grain, or as a drop of dew. The bulk, weight, and density of this world has a relation ("is as") to the balance, as is the relation in bulk, weight, and density of a grain to the bulk, weight, and density of a drop of morning dew.

Wonderful, wonderful, wonderful inspiration that comes to us in truths that prove its divine origin!

THE LANDS ARE ESTABLISHED—WHERE AND HOW.

WE come now to define the position of the lands. Psalm xxiv. 2: "For he hath founded it upon the seas, and established it upon the floods." We all know that every body of land ends where the water begins, and that the water ends where the land begins. There are certain peculiarities, however, attending the position of the lands, relative to the water, that are universal, common to all bodies of land of any significance. This peculiarity is well defined by the text, "For he hath founded it upon the seas;" the literal interpretation of which is, "The lands stand upon seas." A glance at the map of the world reveals the fact that the great continental masses tend to assume a peninsular form toward the south. North America, coming to a very narrow strip at Panama, stands on the Atlantic and Pacific. South America ends in the bold promontory of Cape Horn, likewise standing on the Atlantic and Pacific. Africa, with the Cape of Good Hope, crowned with the table mountains, stands on the Atlantic and Pacific, or Indian, which is but an arm of the same. Greenland, terminating toward the south in the same way, stands upon the Atlantic and Baffin Bay. Malacca, Arabia, Greece, Italy, and Spain exhibit in the same direction peninsular figures standing upon seas.

The earth in its course around the sun maintains at all points along its orbit the same position to the plane of its orbit. Had we a small globe with lands and seas properly drawn upon it, then insert a pin at the south pole, using this for a top, and spinning it upon the floor, we have a miniature earth, that will show us too plainly the truth that the earth is founded upon the seas; that the lands stand upon the waters. "He hath established it upon the floods." We have not failed to notice the nice discrepancy made by the Psalmist in the selection and use of these terms. He hath "founded" and "established." The literal meaning of established is "fixed firmly."

The matter is safe. The waters cannot return and again hold undisputed sway over the earth. The decreed place for the sea was broken up. When the sea came it found bars and doors, and heard the exclamation: "Hitherto shalt thou come, but no farther; here shall thy proud waves be stayed."

We have observed that the highest mountains in all the grand divisions of the globe face the largest oceans. In the Western Hemisphere the lofty chain of the Rocky Mountains and the Andes face the Pacific; while the lower ranges of the Alleghanies and Brazilian Mountains face the Atlantic, the lesser ocean. In Asia the Himalayas, the highest moun-

tains in the world, look down upon the largest expanse of ocean upon the globe. The lower Altai system skirts the great Siberian plain, washed by the
Arctic Ocean. In Africa the loftiest peaks are on
the side of the Indian Ocean, and in Australia they
are directed toward the Pacific, the larger of its bor-
dering oceans.

We have not passed over this without noticing a
design—a designer. Thus the earth is established, is
fixed firmly, fortified by the everlasting mountains,
whose turrets, towers, and ramparts will break, without harm, the might of the greatest wave that could
sweep over the bosom of any sea. But "it is established upon the floods." While it stands upon seas,
it is made strong against the floods. Tides are the
alternate rise and fall of the ocean twice in the course
of a lunar day (twenty-four hours and fifty-seven
minutes). The waters of the sea rise for the space
of about six hours, overflowing the shores and running into the channels of the rivers. This is called
the flood-tide. These waves, unresisted by the land,
would follow the moon as it passes around the earth.
So the direction of these tidal waves is against the
sides of the lands. Here the floods have been wasting their might twice every day for thousands of
years. These attest the truth that the earth is established upon the floods and founded upon the seas.
Tell me how the Psalmist knew the positions of the
lands beyond the globe from him—a land that had
not been heard of; one that no geographer had ever
described or had delineated its bounds on paper!
Tell me, will you?

It is a simple geographical truth that the breadth

of the land is perpendicular to the length of the
sea, while the length of the land is perpendicular
to the breadth of the sea. Job xi. 8, 9: "It is as
high as heaven; what canst thou do? deeper than
hell; what canst thou know? The measure thereof is
longer than the earth, and broader than the sea."
This is given to illustrate the unsearchableness of
God's wisdom. We will not refer to the purpose or
thought in the text, but the expressions themselves.
These show a familiarity with the geography of the
trend of the lands and seas of the world. The whole
expression is composed of two antitheses: "Higher
than heaven, . . . deeper than hell." Thus the
two opposites are brought together. "Longer than
the earth, . . . broader than the sea." How did
Job know that the length of the land was measured
in one direction, while the breadth of the sea was
measured in a direction perpendicular to that? In
the first we suppose the height of heaven greater
than the depth of hell, though each is immeasurable.
We do know that the length of the land is greater
than the breadth of the sea.

EARTHQUAKES AND VOLCANOES.

Earthquakes and volcanoes are closely connected,
since they arise from the same cause. The concussions of earthquakes are commotions of the solid
crust of the earth, more or less extended, which vary
in intensity from the slightest vibration to the most
violent and appalling convulsions. A volcano is a
mountain which emits from its summit or side fire
and smoke. Psalm civ. 32: "He looketh on the
earth, and it trembleth: he toucheth the hills, and

they smoke." The Psalmist has pursued the same course that our geographers have; he attributes the same cause, and mentions in the same connection these two dreadful phenomena. He attributes directly to God what the prophet and we attribute to laws. These are his servants; these obey him so directly, so implicitly. that it is he indeed; it is the touch of his hand that makes the hills smoke.

CENTRAL FIRES.

The central fires of the earth in all probability are the fires that blazed up in the beginning, and were driven inward by the condensation of the vapors as these fell on the earth. Progressive increase of temperature as experienced in sinking deep mines, together with the evidence afforded by volcanoes and hot springs all over the globe, attest the truth that the earth is highly heated in its central part. Job xxviii. 5: "As for the earth, out of it cometh bread: and under it is turned up as it were fire." "Out of it cometh bread." Bread is everything given to us by God for the growth and nourishment of the body. All our food directly or indirectly comes from the earth—bread in particular does; every one knows that. This comes from the earth, outside, while "under it is turned up as it were fire." Under the food-furnishing earth (sea included) is fire. This fire is turned up. This turning up of fire is a fact, and Job's statement can not be justified under any other possible hypothesis than that the earth is round. This fire is turned toward the crust—"up" from the center of the earth is every direction from that point. "As it were fire." Turns up as fire will turn up, as heat. The thought goes a little farther: "as it were fire." It does as fire, still (implied) the combustibles are not as you have; it does like fire does, "as it were fire."

The United States and Britain in Prophecy.

Jeremiah vi. 22, 23: "Thus saith the Lord, Behold, a people cometh from the north country, and a great nation shall be raised from the sides of the earth. They shall lay hold on bow and spear; they are cruel, and have no mercy; their voice roareth like the sea; and they ride upon horses, set in array as men for war against thee, O daughter of Zion."

"Behold, a people cometh from the north country." "People," in this sense, is not used in the plural, but it comprehends all classes of inhabitants, considered as a collective body, or any portion of the inhabitants of a country. Behold, see a people; not a nation, a people. "Cometh," by descent as son succeeds father. From this people a great nation is to be raised from the sides of the earth.

"From the north country." The bounds of this country are somewhat indefinite. It must be from a country north of the prophet. This indefiniteness adds some interest to this investigation. The neglect in giving the nationality of this people, while apparently indefinite, when joined to the thought of indefinite bounds, proves an advantage rather than a disadvantage. The Angles, Saxons, and Jutes, of the Teutonic race, lived about the mouth of the Elbe, far to the north of the prophet's position. These people completed the conquest of Britain A.D. 607. These people united into one stock, and from them the great English-speaking nations sprang.

"And a great nation shall be raised from the sides of the earth." On different sides of a great ocean, in two different hemispheres, we are one common people in parentage and tongue, holding to the same faith. "Great nation." "What nation is so great as they that have the Lord so nigh unto them?" In the arts, sciences, learning, civilization, and profound spiritualism, we have one common greatness.

"Sides of the earth." We said above that this nation extended, was situated in two hemispheres, sides. The line that separates these two sides of the earth is the line that separates the eastern from the western hemisphere, and the one given by geographers. One side faces the rising sun, the other the setting sun. It is a truth that this nation stands on different sides of the earth. The torrid zone marks the ends of the earth and is so denominated by the Bible, and is the geographical end, admitting of simple demonstration.

This great nation is not to be raised here from its ends, but from the sides of the earth. It is not here. The earth is flattened slightly at the poles, making its polar diameter twenty-six miles shorter than its equatorial diameter; this region is called by Job the breadth of the earth, and is its geographical breadth, admitting of simple demonstration. It is not said that this nation shall be raised from the breadth of the earth, but the "sides of the earth." The side of a thing is the space between the extremities of its longer and shorter diameters. Then this great nation must lie between the Arctic Circle and the trop-

5

ics. This great nation extends from one degree east of Greenwich to Behring Strait, one hundred and seventy-one degrees west of Greenwich, making the extent westward, one hundred and seventy-two degrees, nearly half around the globe. Two quadrants, two sides of the earth. These things could not be true had the earth any other shape than that of a sphere.

"They shall lay hold on bow and spear." This people, that the prophet saw coming from the north country, "shall lay hold on bow and spear," fell upon Celts, the inhabitants of Britain; a people that lived from the product of the chase, and whose weapons were the bow and the spear. This people is further described by the prophet.

"They are cruel, and have no mercy." History says that the Celts were extinguished, or driven to the mountains; that the few remaining words of their language are found in the names given to the rivers.

"Their voice roareth like the sea." Another clause expressive of the terribleness of this people. "Their voice," has no reference to the volume of individual voices of this people. Its significance is found in the means employed for the accomplishment of their purpose, which means added to their character cruelty. This people now have by the union of Angles and Saxons become Anglo-Saxons. From the first they were democratic. Passing on till the middle of the fourteenth century, with the battle of Crécy, 1346, Edward III. began the hundred years' war. This war and that with Scotland developed the spirit of English nationality. This was the beginning of that great nation to be raised from the sides

of the earth. At the battle of Crécy was used the first
gunpowder and the first artillery. This is the voice
that roareth. The voice of a people is the strength,
the might of a people put forth, like the motions cf
the waves on the sea, whose rending from fierce col-
lisions is scarcely less noisy than the roar of cannon
in the heat of battle. The voice of a nation is the
strength of a nation, as seen in its armies. These
talk and are heard in the rattle and roar of their guns.
The roar of this same voice moved westward and fell
upon the ears of the sons of Shem. "This people"
seized upon his bow, despoiled his tent; the same sad
fate that befell the Celts awaits the Indian of North
America. Nothing will tell his story save the pen
of fiction. His language, like that of the Celts, will
only be found in the names of our mountains and
rivers. From the landing of Columbus till now the
Indians have endured four hundred years of cruelty,
and have been the recipients of but little mercy.

"They ride upon horses set in array." This has
been the characteristic mode of all Indian warfare in
our country.

"As men for war against thee, O daughter of
Zion." They are like the men, and they will carry
on a similar mode of warfare as do they that "war
against thee, O daughter of Zion." Of this great
prophecy, this last topic is all that the people of
Jeremiah's day ever knew.

CHAPTER IV.

Descriptive Geography—Frigid Zone—Arctic Circle Traced—
The World's Explorations in Arctic Climes the Subject of
Prophecy—By Prophecy This Region Was Surveyed, Its
Bounds Were Given—Also Its Geographical Features, Its
Animal and Vegetable Life—Behring and Davis Straits Noted
and Located—Also Those Dangerous Ice-Bound Straits High
Up in Arctic Lands—The Source of the Winds and the Cold
Ocean Currents—Warm Currents—The Pole.

Job xxxviii. 16–26: "Hast thou entered into the
springs of the sea? or hast thou walked in the search
of the depth? Have the gates of death been opened
unto thee? or hast thou seen the doors of the shadow
of death? Hast thou perceived the breadth of the
earth? declare if thou knowest it all. Where is the
way where light dwelleth? and as for darkness, where
is the place thereof, that thou shouldest take it to
["at," marginal] the bound thereof, and that thou
shouldest know the paths to the house thereof?
Knowest thou it, because thou wast then born? or
because the number of thy days is great? Hast thou
entered into the treasures of the snow? or hast thou
seen the treasures of the hail, which I have reserved
against the time of trouble, against the day of battle
and war? By what way is the light parted, which
scattereth the east wind upon the earth? Who hath
divided a watercourse for the overflowing of waters,
or a way for the lightning of thunder?"

Let us give a simplified interpretation to direct
your attention along the line of thought to be pur-

(68)

sued. The thoughts here set forth follow closely the
rotation of the earth on its axis, and its motion about
the sun; these two motions influence the conditions
about the pole. Our present lesson is one in physical geography, pertaining to the north frigid zone.
There are eleven geographical questions direct;
twelve, if we regard two questions as being asked in
the twenty-fifth verse. The twentieth verse answers
directly the second question found in the nineteenth
verse. "Springs of the sea." Head waters of the sea
currents that originate on the lands of arctic regions.
To walk in search of the depth, sea, is a prophecy fulfilled by arctic explorers during the last four
hundred years. "Gates of death" are those ice-locked
straits in arctic regions. "Doors of the shadow
of death" are the straits that stand on the arctic
circle. "Breadth of earth" is the pole of the earth.
"Where is the way where light dwelleth?"—that is,
the road, route, or way to the lightened hemisphere.
Where is "the place of darkness?" Answer: "You,
Job, take it to be, understand it to be, the bound of the
breadth, the pole." "Ocean currents" are the paths
that lead to it. "Treasures of snow." Here snow and
ice accumulate by deposit. It is checked out as bills of
exchange—cold payable in warmth. From here it is
shipped to latitudes of burning suns and of droughts.
East winds, beginning here, are scattered over the
earth by an unequal division of heat. "Overflowing"
of a "watercourse" is applicable to both ocean and
aerial currents. These cause it to rain, and thus prepare a way for "the lightning of thunder."

We will notice these topics as they occur, noting
the individual significance of each, and the relation

that each sustains to the other, and to the train of thought.

"Hast thou entered into the springs of the sea?" "Entered into." To go in or come in; to pass into mentally; to penetrate; to enter into the principle of action. As the teacher was acquainted with Job's surroundings, it inclines us to the opinion, "Have you studied this lesson, Job?" is the thought; while the next question seems to indicate, have you waded, walked into these springs, Job? This entire lesson was to Job a prophecy that this generation is a witness to its fulfilment. Scientific men have spent a large portion of their lives making observations in this land, noting its light, darkness, and temperature, its atmosphere, magnetism, electrical conditions, the aurora, etc.; then they have measured, plotted on maps and globes the lands, waters, great and small, and these springs in their devious windings from their sources to the equator. These are carried into the schools as physical geographies, and there entered into, studied, by millions of the youths of our land, by ten millions of youths from every enlightened nation on the globe. "Springs of the sea." Streams which have their sources on the land (the next question evidences that) and flow through the sea as waters of springs flow through the land. There are two kinds of these currents: the warm and the cold. The warm current could not properly be called a spring. Its origin and progress will not admit of this designation. The causes that produce it are just the reverse. These are larger at or near their beginning than at any other points. They grow less as they advance, and very often separate, one part mov-

ing in one direction while another will take an opposite direction. David styles these as "ways in the
great waters." The sources of cold currents, so far as
we know, have their origin on the land, many of them
as springs. Arctic explorers call these head waters
that aid in making the ice-bearing currents by no
other name. Says Sargent: "In these inhospitable
tracts the snow, which annually falls on the islands
or continents, being again dissolved by the progress
of summer heat, pours forth in innumerable rills and
limpid streams which overflow their channels, break up
the ice, and start glaciers on the continent of Greenland that find their way into the ocean, and are borne
along by these currents." Says Dr. Kane: "Imagine
now the center of such a continent occupied through
nearly its whole extent by a deep, unbroken sea of
ice, that gathers perennial increase from the water-
sheds of snow-covered mountains and all the precipitations of the atmosphere upon its surface. Imagine this moving onward like a great glacial river,
seeking outlets at every fiord and valley, rolling
cataracts into the Atlantic and Greenland seas; and
having at last reached the northern limits of the land
that has borne it up, pouring out a mighty frozen
torrent into unknown arctic space. Every particle
of moisture had its origin within the polar circle,
and had been converted into ice. There were no vast
alluviums, no forests, or animal trace borne down by
these liquid torrents. Here was a plastic, moving,
semisolid mass, obliterating life, swallowing rocks
and islands, and plowing its way with irresistible
march through the crust of an investing sea."

We hope you will notice closely the above quotations, as they furnish, in a great measure, the characteristics of this fearful country, as seen by Sargent and Dr. Kane, and which are made no less fearful to Job.

"Or hast thou walked in the search of the depth?" In modern times "in the search of the depth," or northwest passage to the Pacific, had its origin during the periods of early discoveries in America, and that search has grown in interest till a seagoing world joins in the search; and now its present object, though modified only by a name, is still "in the search of the depth," now polar sea. "Hast thou walked," looking for this open polar sea? This has been a literal fulfilment attested by every explorer of arctic regions. Ask McClure, Belcher, Bellot, Kane, Hale, and all the others; each alike will answer in the affirmative. Some of these men walked thousands of miles, dragging sledges, sleeping at night in banks of snow, at times when the thermometer indicated ninety-nine degrees below the freezing-point. When their ships were ice-bound, they abandoned them and took up the real search on foot. This the rule.

"Have the gates of death been opened unto thee?" Let us take a look at these ice-bound ships, that we left when beginning the search of the depth on foot. Let us examine the geographical positions and the nature of the difficulties encountered. Gate signifies both the opening and that which closes the passage. Originally it was used to name the opening into a walled city. The name is well selected. These are openings that lead to a coveted city whose towers and turrets have resisted the wisdom, skill, and endurance of the world for nearly four hundred years. Explora-

tions in search of the depths have cost more in ships,
more in lives from exposure, more in intense suffering,
than did the discovery and settlement of America.
What the Hebrews called gate, in all probability, we
call strait. The strait that connects the Red Sea
with the Indian Ocean we call Bab-el-Mandeb. This
is a Hebrew word and means the "gate of tears."
These gates are the straits that have proven so dangerous to the lives and shipping of arctic explorers.
Let us follow these springs of the sea still northward
and toward their source. About latitude seventy we
find ourselves just west of Disco Island. This is
said to be the most northern abode of man. Now
look still farther north and considerably west of
where we now stand; see that continuous line of
straits extending in nearly every direction, reaching
over fifty degrees of longitude. You observe an ice-
bearing current worms its way through these, moving in a direction from the pole. These straits are
the gates of death; the past has proven it in one
sense, and we will show how otherwise they are the
gates of death.

"Have the gates of death been opened unto thee?"
This question as a prophecy is made wonderful. As
it became a leading feature in all arctic explorations,
it formed the highest wish in all the search for the
depth.

"O that these straits might be opened to me!"
was the universal prayer. In the straits or gates
were met the insurmountable difficulties that have
baffled every attempt to find this coveted spot. The
wording of the text shows barred gates. "Have
they been opened unto thee?" implies that they as a

rule stand closed. These gates are rarely if ever opened; they stand ice-closed, ice-choked, ice-bound, ice-locked. Should we ask each explorer what were the greatest fears entertained, the answer from each would be that these straits (gates) would be closed. Ask the cause of the speedy return of so many expeditions. Ask why so many were detained to pass winters in this inhospitable land. You will be told each time that the closing or the opening of the gates determined these questions. Ask where were the greatest dangers to life and ships; the answer every time will be: "In these straits." Every arctic explorer will say that these were never truly open. Reid and Bushman, who penetrated sixty miles westward along the southern coast of Cockburn Island, till they reached a pinnacle whence they saw, beyond all doubt, the polar ocean spreading its vast expanse before them; but tremendous barriers of ice filled the straits and precluded all approach toward that great and desired object. "Have the gates of death been opened unto you?" Let us stand within these straits. Cunnington describes one scene thus: "Icebergs of all dimensions came bearing down from polar seas like vast squadrons, and the roar of their rending came over the waters like the booming of the broadsides of contending navies. At times," he says, "they were carried through straits too narrow even for a ship to turn; were forced through by the great pressure from without, against which nothing could stand." Hartstien, on leaving with the Kane survivors, says that he left the arctic archipelago studded with abandoned ships. Melville's Bay, on account of its fearful character, is called the "Devil's

Nip." These are not extreme examples telling the fearful character of these gates of death. The story everywhere, every time, by every arctic explorer, is but a repetition of the above statements.

"Gates of death." Having shown them to be literally gates of death or destruction, let us look at the country around and see if they do not stand in a land of physical dearth, a land having scarcely a semblance of life. Capt. Perry, speaking of the coast along Barrow Strait, says: "The coast was the most dreary and desolate they had ever seen in the arctic world, scarcely presenting a semblance of animal or vegetable life." At Cape Kaler they entered another strait, Arctic Sound. They sent a party to explore a river, upon the banks of which they expected to find an Eskimo encampment. All, however, was silent and deserted. Even these hardy natives, bred amid the polar ice, had removed from so barren a spot. Again, when near the arctic circle, accustomed as he was to the scenes of polar desolation, he says that he was struck with the exceeding dreary aspect which these shores presented. The naked rocks, the snow still covering the villages, and the thick fog that hung over them rendered the scene indescribably gloomy.

Franklin, covering a distance of three hundred and seventy-four miles from the mouth of the McKenzie, in latitude seventy, he describes to be one of the most dreary, miserable, and uninteresting portions of seacoast that can be found in, perhaps, any other part of the world. Let us now pass to the eastern shores of Greenland. Mr. Claveland, after leaving Spitzbergen and landing on the eastern

shores of Greenland in, perhaps, the most favorable
season of the year, says that the scene appeared the
most desolate he had ever beheld. The mountains
rose to the height of several thousand feet, without a
vestige of vegetation or the appearance of any living
creature on the earth or in the air. Even the dreary
wastes of Spitzbergen appeared a paradise. Capt.
Perry, while making his sledge journey toward the
pole in latitude 81° 23', looking from the highest hummock on one occasion, says: "We beheld a
sight which nothing could exceed in dreariness."
In latitude 82° 45' he writes again: "Only one soli-
tary rotge was heard, and it might be presumed that
from thence to the pole all would be a uniform scene
of solitude and silence." Again we read from Dr.
Kane: "Darkness arrested all proceedings on No-
vember 20, and the sun remained one hundred and
twenty days below the horizon. The darkness was
so intense that it necessarily produced inaction.
The themometer fell to ninety-nine degrees below the
freezing-point. Human beings could only breathe
in such temperature guardedly and with compressed
lips. The influence of such severe cold and long
intense darkness was most depressing. Geese and
ducks leave in September. The deer and other animals as a rule leave these sterile wastes when the
long night approaches. The mercury runs down till
it freezes, and far below. Passing the magnetic pole,
the needle refuses to work without a stimulant." We
have given you these many quotations taken from
the various sections of this land of death. We refer
you to arctic explorations, where you will find the
story everywhere the same; each recital is but an

evidence that this is a land of death and darkness.
Man has braved every other danger, but he finds
nothing here, is not here himself.

A petulant kind of ambition leads numbers to walk
all over this land in search of the depth, for no other
consideration than the glory following this achievement. Its lurings beckoned Dr. Kane on to find a
grave, the outpost of this search amid fearful rigors.
No ship visits this land of solitude and silence with
its merchandize. It has no city with its hurry and
rush of business; no manufactures, no industries,
no thrift, no life. Below all is ice and snow, above
is heard the rush of mighty, cold currents of air
making their circuit to bless the habitable parts of
the earth. The sun sets; 'tis night. How awful the
stillness! No bells to ring, no steam-whistles, no
rattling cars, no beasts to disturb the stillness by the
roarings of its voice. A full moon rises upon the
scene. Its pale light walks noiselessly over the beds
of snow that have been falling here all the years,
and which the winds have piled here, yonder, and
everywhere, snow unpressed by any foot. The
lengthening and contracting of shadows as the moon
rises higher or sinks lower, or as a cloud sweeps over
its face, are the only visible motions; those formed
from the lofty, ragged, and distant ice-clad peaks
add loneliness to the scene and fill us with a feeling
that we are in a land where is no life. The white
peaks and mounds of snow remind us that we are
among the tombs that mark the burial-ground of the
years, in a land of darkness, silence, and death.
More recent explorations add their evidence to the
fact that it is a land of death or a land without life.

"On April 7, 1895, Dr. Fridtjof Nansen stood among the ice hummocks of the Arctic Ocean at a point about one hundred and ninety-five miles nearer the north pole than any man had ever been before. He could see nothing from the top of the highest ice-hill save these hummocks and ridges, stretching away to the horizon like frozen waves. The scene had the one condition needed to crown it as the most utterly desolate waste that can be conceived: it was wholly void of all forms of life. No polar explorer had ever before entered an area where the air, the ice, the land, or the sea depths support no living thing; but for the last one hundred and fifty miles of his journey north, by ship or sledges, Nansen had not found the slightest trace of life in the air, on the ice, or in the ocean depths. Somewhere near the eighty-fourth parallel he seems to have passed beyond the pale of life zones into an area around the pole where nature is wholly inorganic and inert." Surely Nansen stood in the very gates of death, in a land of no life.

"The doors of the shadow of death." We wish to show first that this is no graveyard question, but physical features of the earth. Job xii. 22: "He discovereth deep things out of darkness, and bringeth out to light the shadow of death." This cannot refer to the grave, nor does it express nearness to it. Has the shadow of death ever been brought to light? If it means near the grave or death, then we should say shadow of death brought to life. This the earth's own shadow brought by earth motions to the sun. The deep things discovered will be man's trophies when he shall have possessed himself of this

land of the shadow. "Seek him that maketh the
seven stars and Orion, and turneth the shadow of
death into the morning." This is the same thought
as above. There are a few passages that furnish us
the thought of death and the grave; the individual
expressions unmistakably will determine the nature,
whether physical or figurative. Every time it is one
or the other; when figurative, then it is a figure of
that physical shadow mentioned above. Job x. 20–22:
"Are not my days few? cease then, and let me alone,
that I may take comfort a little, before I go whence
I shall not return, even to the land of darkness and
the shadow of death; . . . without any order,
and where the light is as darkness." Here reference
is made to the grave. This is a figure expressive of
beautiful thought. I go down to the grave land of
darkness without order. This grave in its turn will
be turned to the light again, resurrection morning.
Jeremiah ii. 6: "Neither said they, Where is the
Lord that brought us up out of the land of Egypt,
that led us through the wilderness, through a land
of deserts and of pits, through a land of drought,
and of the shadow of death, through a land that no
man passed through, and where no man dwelt?"
Here it is distinguished as a country barren, without
animal or vegetable life, a land of deserts through
which no man passed, where no man dwells. Such
we consider "shadow of death" in our text. "Hast
thou seen the doors of the shadow?" We now talk
of a visible thing: door. A door is an opening or
passage into a house, or into any room or apart-
partment. These are the doors of the shadow;
the shadow that Job said was brought out to the

light, and the one that Amos said was turned
into the morning. If doors of the shadow, then
they must stand on the shadow line, and will be
found there. Shadow: marked with slight gradua-
tion of light.

Take your position with me at Behring Strait; let
us look around a moment to see just where we are
geographically. First we notice that we are on, or
very nearly so, the arctic circle; it is now the 21st
day of December; a faint line of golden light marks
our position; yes, we are on the line of the shadow.
See that cold current as it comes down from the
north? Watch it pass through the strait; this strait
is the narrowest passage that this current ever goes
through. This is one door of the shadow. Here this
current passes from one apartment of the sea into
another, from the region of night to one of day,
hence a door. Look coming up from toward the
south. See that warm current; it is directed toward this door; here it comes; see it pass through
this door. It, as did the cold current, passed from
one apartment of the sea to another, from a land of
sunshine to one of night. This line here separates
the Arctic Sea from the Pacific; this door connects
them. These two seas have been going in and out
here ever since the waters were gathered unto one
place. Say, aside from its office does this passage
not look a little like a door? This was a part of the
sea's decreed place, shaped before the sea was led
into its bounds. Let us now move east along this
shadow line. We need no compass, no one to guide;
we can follow this faint line of golden light; the
doors of the shadow stand on this; so we need no

further assistance, only protection from the cold. Here we are now at Davis Strait. Let us look around. We are between Greenland and Baffin-Land. See from the north how the land on either side contracts more and more; this is the narrowest part of the Strait. None so narrow south of us and none so narrow this side the gates of death.

See that ice-bearing current, fresh from the springs of the sea, as it approaches us from the north. It is now passing through the strait. Let us look about and see what changes are made here. We now stand on the shadow line as before. Davis Strait is another door of the shadow, or opening from one apartment of the sea to another. This current passes from the Arctic to the Atlantic, from a land of night to one of day, from a frozen to a sunny sea. See, here comes a current from the south; it is directing its course to this door; it is now passing through— from a land of light to one of night, from the Atlantic to the Arctic. This door connects these two apartments of the sea. Here these children of the sea have been passing in and out since the waters were gathered unto one place. Davis Strait was named door in the decree when the doors to the sea were set. Let us move on east. We need no further direction, only follow the line of the shadow. Now we find ourselves on the eastern shore of Greenland, as far as we can go on foot. Look to the north. Here comes the Greenland current; now it passes us, crosses the shadow line here, passes from a land of night to one of day, from the Arctic to the Atlantic. Now look straight across this current, along the shadow line. See that island; that's Iceland. See that promontory jutting

6

out to the west from Iceland. Reader, if you have
no map before you, get one. This promontory is in-
disputably the semblance of a hand with its palm to
the south, fingers extended, while the thumb from
the first joint to the end bends directly to the west
along the arctic circle, making this the narrowest
known point ever passed by this current. Here this
current makes the same changes that the others made.
That thumb is an index to a decree, a plan and a
planner. This is another door of the shadow. Between Iceland and Norway another current flows
steadily to the north, on the shadow line, the narrowest point separating these land masses. Here this
current passes from the Atlantic to the Arctic, from
sunshine to darkness. "Hast thou seen the doors of
the shadow?" This shadow line was traced by the
heavenly compass when the world was young. Its
bounds are definitely defined by Job; no author or
modern geography has more explicitly done so. Job
xxvi. 10: "He hath compassed the waters with
bounds, until the day and night come to an end." At
one sweep of the compass he traced the line of the
shadow, and modern geographers make this line separate the Arctic from the Atlantic and from the Pacific. I cannot look upon this circle and these doors
as I even see them on a map without a sense of awe.
I see the shadow of the mighty hand; I see the great
compasses, one point planted amid the depths, while
the other, sweeping around, marks the bounds of three
oceans and traces the line of the shadow which affords me the means to find its doors. If you are
skeptical, be glad that these curious things are revealed, that you may be made strong. These indicate

the majesty, wisdom, and the greatness and the goodness of the God of the Bible.

"Hast thou seen the doors of the shadow of death?" "Shadow of death." We often hear the expression "picture of death." This means far less than an average in health, bodily strength, and vigor; it does not mean actually dead. The "shadow of death." More signs of death than of life, a feeble condition of life. Standing in these doors, let us survey the country. It is a land of the shadow, of nights that last six months, of intense cold, never free from ice and snow, if at all for only short intervals, thus making its seasons of germination, growth, and fruitage extremely short. There are no forests; lichens and mosses spread over the rocks and frozen soil, their everlasting drapery of death. A sparse growth of little hardy plants of crimson hue grow amid the snow. Bread is raised in such scanty measure that the few inhabitants are compelled to subsist chiefly upon animal food. They depend for fuel upon the driftwood cast ashore by the currents of the oceans. The people is a nation few in number, and that few is a nation of dwarfs. The beasts and birds are dull and somber in color or of a snow-white. There are no homes save of ice and snow; no green pastures or lowing herds. How widely different are the lands south of this! These teem with life in all its forms. No delayed suns. No lingering snows. Bread everywhere. Cows are on every hill. Cities send up glittering spires from every hill, valley, and mountain. Happy homes, holy paradises, Eden returned, fill city, town, and country alike. A land of much life, physical, intellectual, and spiritual; one full of hope, that leads the highest energies of the highest type of life here, to expect still one higher in a land of endless life and light.

"Hast thou perceived the breadth of the earth? declare if thou knowest it all." Job's recitation in physical geography began with the springs of the sea. He followed these through those terrible straits on southward to the doors of the shadow, covering the frigid zone; now the startling question comes: "Hast thou perceived the breadth of the earth?" This declaration is made to him standing in the doors of the shadow, the very southern limit of the bound of the breadth. The question concedes an answer, thus: "I have shown you the breadth of the earth, Job; now, sir, tell me all about it if you know; or do you comprehend the breadth of the earth? Declare if thou knowest it all."

Reader, of the pole of the earth we know nothing. Reid and Bushman say they saw the polar sea, but barriers of ice in those terrible straits precluded all approach to that great and desired object. This is all we know of it. "Declare if thou knowest it all" indicates that much may be learned from this land of night and death. We can form no estimate of the priceless value of all the information that might be gained had we our laboratories and observatories here. This expression from Job makes it worth finding. Read the title-page of Cunnington's "Arctic Explorations," and be impressed with a part of the wonders of this land. The lesson continues on kindred subjects.

"Where is the way where light dwelleth?" Let us first see just where we are in the progress of this lesson

geographically. The preceding topic left us on the
shadow line, the southern limit of the bounds of the
earth's breadth. Standing here, we see on the one
side a shadow that deepens into night darker and
the cold growing more intense as we leave this line
and go north; while on the other hand we see a land
from which the sun never departs, where the light
stays or dwells. Viewing these opposite conditions
from a point between the two, is it at all singular the
question: "Where is the way where light dwelleth?"
" Where is the way " is susceptible of two interpretations; either is legitimate, and conforms to the idea
held in this lesson. You observe the question assumes that there is a place where light dwells; where
the way, route, or which of these currents, David's
"way in the great waters" leads to it? Or by what
process is the light made to dwell? Close on this follows: "And as for darkness, where is the place thereof?" This question is answered by the author in
terms that this age can not improve: "That thou
shouldst take it to the bound thereof"—the pole.
This intimates, by "take it," that Job knows that
the place of darkness is at the bound of the breadth
of the earth, the extremity of its shorter diameter.
"That thou shouldest know the paths to the house
thereof." Those warm currents that Job has been
watching and studying lead to it. Job, you know
it. Proof, next verse: "Knowest thou it, because
thou wast then born? or because the number of thy
days is great?" Demands how he learned it. Traveling along these paths, we find ourselves now in the
house of darkness. The lesson turns to the leading
features of this land. "Hast thou entered into the

treasures of the snow?" As is said of the springs
of the sea, "entered" has two significations: to literally go into, as did many of our explorers, who
slept in banks of it, who made houses of it and
passed winters there; or had you studied these things?
If you have studied this lesson, Job, have entered
into it, you see why it is called treasures. These
have been deposited here from year to year since the
world was made; from these banks—only banks of
deposit—the world is ever drawing its most valued
treasures. The winds start here as empty bottles,
are borne to the land of vapors, there filled and pass
all over the globe to bless life; returning, they are
bathed in these snows, renovated, and off again.
Psalm cxxxv. 7: "He bringeth the wind out of his
treasuries." Where does the wind come from? Determine that, and you can locate his treasures. Follow the wind; it will lead you there.

"Or hast thou seen the treasures of hail?" This is
so definitely modified by the next clause that we need
not be mistaken as to the expenditure of these treasures of hail, "which I have reserved against the time
of trouble, against the day of battle and war." This is
a reserved hail, hail kept back for a particular time,
against peculiar evils—a reserved fund for a special
purpose. It was not so specifically said of the
treasures of snow; still these would aid in giving the
winds their weight all over the globe, and be classed
among his treasures. Being reserved, hail would indicate that as hail they would remain for the time
and purpose for which they were reserved. Numerous icebergs, started by the springs of the sea, gathered in this clime of reserved hail, are borne south-

ward by the currents of the oceans to torrid climes; there they lighten the burdens of heat in a latitude of burning suns. These wield undoubtedly a very great influence over the temperature of this region, and perhaps answer other beneficent purposes in forwarding and blessing man. Five hundred of these icebergs were counted at one time by Capt. Scoresby— some many miles in extent. Psalm cxlvii. 17: "He casteth forth his ice like morsels." Every year these shipments are made; no year has failed to receive these precious cargoes. Jeremiah xviii. 14: "Will a man leave the snow of Lebanon which cometh from the rock of the field? or shall the cold flowing waters that come from another place be forsaken?" "Rock of the field." Plains of ice seas. Geographers call their product "field ice."

NOTE.—By reference to Exodus ix. 18, Job x. 19, Isaiah xxx. 30, Ezekiel xiii. 11, 13, Revelation xvi. 21, you will readily see there that the hail differs in every respect and purpose from the hail above. The above was deposited as ice, will be drawn as ice, not a tender by certificate.

"By what way is the light parted, which scattereth the east wind upon the earth?" We are still standing amid the treasures of the snow and the hail. "By what way" means: What process of operating on light causes the east wind to be scattered over the earth? The text does not ask if it is the parting of light that does this, but assumes that this is the thing that does, and the question is simply: How is the light parted to do this? Part means to divide. Geographers tell us that winds are produced by an unequal distribution of heat; that light and heat are the same; light is only luminous heat,

This talk is made to Job from the treasury department, the birthplace of the wind, those winds that blow from the east all over the globe. Speculating on the winds, the recitation proceeds.

"Who hath divided a watercourse for the overflowing of waters?" This may have reference, as we think, both to aerial and ocean currents. The objects following indicate that reference is made to aerial currents. The winds start from the pole south; as they move forward in their advance every point reached is traveling faster than they are, so the winds fall back till they appear to blow steadily from northeast to east. The return current must either flow above or beneath these east winds, which were told to Job as a fact.

"Or a way for the lightning of thunder." These winds are the bearers of moisture and the clouds, and thus become the great thoroughfare for the lightning of thunder.

"To cause it to rain on the earth." This is one of the great offices of the winds.

We said that gates of death and doors of the shadow of death were in some instances figurative; when so, were figures drawn from those earth motions about the sun which allow the darkness to remain for a period of months in certain quarters. We have the earth, its motions, and the sun, the source of light, which is fixed with reference to the earth, but which leads the earth in a great journey, a journey so great that the wisest cannot tell its period, whence it comes nor whither it goes. To make the figure we have man and his motions and Jesus Christ, the Sun and Center of the spiritual system. That part of the earth next to the sun has light; that part opposite to the sun has darkness. The same is true in a spiritual sense. "I am the light of the world." David represents the coming of his Lordship as the sun making his visitation to a land of death and darkness. Psalm xxiv. 7: "Lift up your heads, O ye gates; and be ye lifted up, ye everlasting doors; and the King of glory shall come in." We told you that the shadow of death stands just where day merges into night, while the gates of death stand in a land of darkness and of physical death. David observed the same order as do all the others. He came for the same purpose as a sun: to give light and to lead. Luke i. 79: "To give light to them that sit in darkness and in the shadow of death, to guide our feet into the way of peace." Lift up the doors of the shadow; let pass the mutual currents of love. If you send him cold currents, he will ever send you warm ones, fresh from his light-giving and heat-imparting bosom. Christ was born December 25. The shadow of death is marked by the arctic circle at this time. In March, about Easter Sunday, he was crucified. His life and death are sending his light over all the world. In March the earth has light from pole to pole as each revolution turns it to the sun. The onward motion of the earth and its turning to the light lift these gates and these doors to the sun. As we journey with Him the uplift will be higher, till the gates rise and the doors fly open and the King of glory will come to us and we will be trees planted by the rivers of water, fruitful, abounding in good works, living in hope of the promise made to them that follow the mighty One.

Note that the two great physical lights are the sun and the moon. The two great spiritual lights are Jesus Christ, the sun; and the Church, the moon. Directly the sun gives light to the earth by day, and the moon by night reflects the light of the sun to the earth; so that the earth at no time is wholly without the light either directly or by reflection. The earth turns to the sun daily and goes around it yearly. The moon goes around the earth, and accompanies it on its yearly movement around the sun. Jesus Christ, our spiritual Sun, to whom we turn, gives us his light directly, and we journey with him in life's circuit. The Church, our spiritual moon, is to accompany us, and its office is to reflect the light of the spiritual Sun as we and it are carried around him. When the world passes between the sun and moon the moon is said to be in eclipse. When the moon passes between the earth and the sun then the sun is said to be in eclipse. When the world gets between a man and the Church that man is in eclipse. When the Church gets between the man and the spiritual Sun then the spiritual Sun is eclipsed. That can only occur to those who expect the Church to save, and not Christ. The moon is said to be full when it faces on the same plane the sun. That man or Church only is full that stands in the full blaze of his spiritual Sun.

CHAPTER V.

Winds, Where and How Produced—The Air Has Weight, How Determined—The Buoyant Force of the Air—The Constant, Variable, and Periodical Winds—Vapors, Rain, How Produced—Lightning—Rainbow—Ice—Storms.

THE CONSTANT WINDS.

Job xxviii. 24-27: "For he looketh to the ends of the earth, and seeth under the whole heaven; to make the weight for the winds; and he weigheth the waters by measure. When he made a decree for the rain, and a way for the lightning of the thunder; then did he see it, and declare it; he prepared it, yea, and searched it out."

"For he looketh to the ends of the earth."

"And seeth under the whole heaven; to make the weight for the winds."

"And he weigheth the waters by measure."

TIME.

"When he made a decree for the rain, and a way for the lightning of the thunder; then did he see it, and declare it; he prepared it." We will notice these questions in the order above.

"For he looketh to the ends of the earth." The ends of the earth, as we have defined, are equatorial regions. In these geographical bounds the winds get their weight. "For he looketh." He expects these regions to make the weight for the winds under the whole heaven. This locates the workshop where the winds are made, and defines fully

(91)

the scope of their motions. "Under the whole heaven." Our text is so exactly in accord with the teachings of our geographers that we cannot refrain from quoting lengthily from one of these. Mr. Maury, speaking of the general circulation of the atmosphere, says: "Within the tropics [ends of earth] there is perpetual summer. The vertical rays of the sun are incessantly heating the torrid zone and its atmosphere, and filling the air with vapor; while the air on either side of that zone is comparatively dry and cold. What must be the effect of this unequal distribution of heat and vapor? It creates a general circulation of the atmosphere." "Under the whole heaven." Continuing, Maury says: "In the first place, as in the case of the fire upon the hearth, the heated, moist air of the tropics is pressed upon by the heavier air on either side. It is forced upward, and there is an indraft both from the north and the south to supply its place. Now, if the earth were at rest, and if its surface were covered with water, the flowing currents would go straight from the polar to the equatorial regions. There would then be a simple circulation of light air from the equator to the poles, and heavy air from the poles to the equator. The winds would be steady and unvarying. Winds are classed, according to the regularity with which they blow, as *constant, variable*, and *periodical*. The constant winds blow without interruption in the same direction and at nearly the same rate. So constant are they that vessels often sail in them for days and days without, as the sailors say, changing a stitch of canvas. It was the steady blowing of these winds which so

alarmed the crew of Columbus on his first voyage
to America and caused them to fear that they never
should get back to Europe. From their importance
to the navigator these winds have been called the
trade winds or trades. They are currents of air
which are ceaselessly winging their flight from the
polar and temperate regions toward the equator."
How truly do our geographers teach us to look to
the ends of the earth to give the winds their weight,
incessantly, all over the globe! Our first topic is
a cause; the object, "to make the weight for the
winds." The foregoing quotation from Maury shows
that the winds do get their weight at the ends of
the earth. Here the prop that supports the air is
taken away, and the air falls.

"He weigheth the waters by measure." There
can be no mistake but that the atmosphere in motion
and at rest constitutes the questions under consideration. Our text-books define the atmosphere as
the great invisible ocean of air that surrounds our
earth to the height of fifty miles or more. These
same books define wind as air in motion or a disturbance in this aerial sea. Genesis i. 6: "And God
said, Let there be a firmament in the midst of the
waters, and let it divide the waters from the
waters." Then the firmament was ordered to be
precisely in the bounds then filled by the waters that
make our oceans, seas, gulfs, lakes, rivers—all the
waters that are now in and on the earth, together
with the air that circumfuses our globe, that invisible ocean or aerial sea, as the air is defined by our
geographers. Then the lowest line of the firmament is the dividing line that separates these two

waters, one of which is evidently the air. Genesis
i. 7: "And God made the firmament, and divided the
waters which were under the firmament from the
waters which were above the firmament." One of
these waters is the air, the one weighed by measure.

"And he weigheth the waters [air] by measure."
Our text-books teach that the air has weight, and
that the weight of air is determined by measure.
"Take a flask that holds one hundred cubic inches,
exhaust the air, balance the flask accurately; now
turn the stop-cock, let in the air, and the flask will descend; it will take thirty-one grains to restore the
equipoise." "He weigheth the waters by measure."
It is not necessary that the flask hold just one hundred cubic inches; any size vessel will do. Its nature is such that of necessity it must be measured.
If one hundred cubic inches weigh thirty-one grains,
we can determine the weight of any number of
inches. There is no other method of determining the weight of air except by measure. So we
harmonize in language, in thought, and in process
for determining the weight of the air. The history
of this matter says that the idea of associating air
with material things was never thought of by the
ancients. Job dispensed this doctrine nearly four
thousand years before Galileo or Torricelli were
born. In talking on these great questions Job does
not claim the authorship: "I know that thou canst
do everything, and that no thought can be withholden from thee. Who is he that hideth counsel
without knowledge? therefore have I uttered that I
understood not; things too wonderful for me, which
I knew not." Here the Source of all wisdom is Him

to whom Job attributes all the deep things uttered by himself. The "him" cannot refer to men; this theory of which we speak, to man, is less than one hundred years old. If I were the least skeptical touching the science of the Bible, I would just plead infancy; then I would have manhood enough to return to my first childish simplicity, and come into manhood anew, full of strength and vigor, built up by the truth. Again, the very components, or atoms, of the air are weighed by measure. There are seventy-nine parts of nitrogen and twenty-one parts of oxygen in every one hundred parts of dry air, and with them is mingled a small quantity of carbonic acid. These, with their specific weights, are mingled in ratios by volume; are weighed measures of particles into weighed measures of one whole. Moreover, it is believed that these weights and measures have never varied since the creation of the first particle of air; at least, since the time of the separation of the waters in the midst of the firmament. Even to admit that the waters here referred to are the waters that make our oceans, rivers, etc., makes it none the less wonderful, but leaves the brightness of inspiration still hanging over it. It, too, is subjected to this same mode of mixture. It contains by weight — and this weight comes by measure—eight parts of oxygen to one part of hydrogen; and by measure, one volume of oxygen to two volumes of hydrogen. It matters not whether this water is obtained from natural sources or is formed by direct combinations of its elements, it always contains the above measures and weights.

"When he made a decree for the rain, and a way

for the lightning of the thunder; then did he see it,
and declare it; he prepared it, yea, and searched it
out." When did he make the weight for the winds?
When did he weigh the waters by measure? When
did he make a way for the lightning of the thunder?
Precisely when he made a decree for the rain. It
is curious that the Psalmist would unite these three
things, whose dependence was not known till the
middle of the eighteenth century. The three results
of the above decree are produced by the three factors, heat, air, and water: heat, to expand the air
and vaporize the water; air, to be expanded to receive the vapor; winds, to scatter the vapor over the
earth. "The waters are weighed by measure."
Precisely according to the expansion of the air, to a
measure, vapor insinuates itself; the buoyant force
every time is weigher. Among the known sources
of electricity none seems so probable as the evaporation and condensation of vapor. The friction of opposite currents of wind or a high wind against opposing objects generates more or less of the same
agent. While we have shown these to be factors
in its production, they truly become the way for the
lightning of the thunder: the vapor, its conductor;
the winds, the motive power; their appointed paths,
the way. Jeremiah x. 13: "He causeth the vapors
to ascend from the ends of the earth; he maketh
lightnings with rain, and bringeth forth the wind
out of his treasures." The torrid zone is the spring
of the great aerial currents, the belt of greatest heat,
the principal source of the vapors that make our
rains over the globe, and chief among the sources of
electricity. The ends of the earth become the line

of workshops from which so many earthly bless-ings are shipped to every land by trunk and branch lines of the four great systems of winds.

"He causeth the vapors to ascend from the ends of the earth." This means to mount up. Do they go up? How?

BUOYANT FORCE OF THE AIR.

We are taught that the principle of Archimedes holds good in gases as in liquids—that is, that par-ticles lighter than air will float in the air, as light substances, such as wood, reeds, etc., will float in water. Illustrations of this abound in many of the common things of every-day life. Smoke is an ever-occurring example; it floats in the air because it is lighter; the buoyant force of the air lifts it up. Isaiah ix. 18: "They shall mount up like the lifting up of smoke." We notice this from the fact that Isaiah uses the same term that we use. There could be no lifting without a lifter. As we see the smoke going up we see no more nor less than what the prophet saw. He could apply the lifting to nothing more nor less than to a force in the in-visible air. This force we call the buoyant force of the air, which means a lifting force. He could not have made it more intelligible to this generation had he used its own terms. These ascend like the lift-ing up of smoke. When these vapors have ascend-ed then they are turned over to the winds for ship-ment.

"He bringeth the wind out of his treasuries." His treasuries, we have shown, are the snow and ice gathered at the poles of the earth, in a land

7

of night and death, a land locked and barred. "He
bringeth." They come this way, toward the habitable parts of the earth. If it comes to the region of
the *greatest* rarefaction, then it must come from the
region of the *least* rarefaction. The region of the
greatest rarefaction is along the equator; the region
of the least is at the pole, from whence the winds
come. Thus we locate the world's treasury department and the treasures stored there. Job xxxviii.
22-24: "Hast thou entered into the treasures of the
snow? or hast thou seen the treasures of the hail,
which I have reserved against the time of trouble,
against the day of battle and war? By what way
is the light parted, which scattereth the east wind
upon the earth?" The last verse strikes the very
cause of the east wind, the wind that is scattered
over the earth. The east wind, to Job, is the trade
wind; this same wind sweeps over the earth, and
comes from the poles. The questions are: How
could any one tell this to Job? How could this same
one know that the east wind was due to the parting
of light? How could this same one know that light
could be parted? These things, to the world, are
younger ·than the eighteenth century, born since
then. The sunbeam is composed of three classes of
rays: heat, light, and chemical rays. Tyndall ob-
serves that "ninety-five per cent of the rays of a
candle are invisible or heat rays. These," said he,
"may be brought to a focus and bodies fired in the
darkness." Whether there be three classes of rays
emanating from the sun in reality, or these effects
be due to unequal distribution of ether waves made
by the prism, still we see the light, feel the warmth,

and perceive the changes going on around us —
changes wrought by the sun in the growth and decay of vegetation. While we think that it is a literal parting of the light ray, it refers as well to an
unequal distribution of heat on the earth, produced
by its relation to the sun and local causes that aid
in preserving or propagating a more than average
temperature.

The prime cause of the east wind is the parting
of light unequally in different parts of the earth.
The ends get the greater share, and these parts become the birth-place of the winds, of the rains, and
the way for the lightning of thunder by decree—he
declared it, he prepared it. The vertical rays of the
sun are incessantly heating the torrid zone and its
atmosphere and filling the air with vapor, while the
air on either side of that zone is comparatively dry
and cold. What must be the effect of this unequal
distribution of heat and vapor? It creates a general circulation of the atmosphere, thus scattering
the east wind over the earth. The earth is not at
rest. Its surface, instead of being one vast, level,
unbroken plain, is made up of great elevations and
deep depressions. The rotation of the earth on its
axis and these elevated land masses largely affect
the circulation of the air. The winds are classed as
constant, variable, and periodical. The east winds
are the constant winds, commonly known as trades;
but all winds are attributable to an unequal distribution of heat as the first great cause. If the
earth had no daily motion, these winds from the
north and the south would blow perpendicularly to
and from the equator. In consequence of this rota-

tion, the winds starting from the pole, where the rotation is nothing, are continually coming to parts having accelerated motion. When they arrive in the latitude of the equator the earth is moving eastward at the rate of one hundred and twenty miles faster per hour than in the region of latitude 30°. During its whole journey to the equator the wind has lagged behind, and the earth, which is revolving from west to east, is slipping from under it all the time. Thus north of the equator are east or northeast winds; while those that set out from the south pole pour in from the east or southeast for a like reason.

The atmosphere in the torrid zone, being intensely heated, is expanded and its density lessened; in this condition, being pressed upon by the colder and denser masses of air from the poles, the vast volume of hot air rises, flowing off in two opposite currents toward either pole, while two cold lower currents set in toward the equator from the north and the south. Ecclesiastes i. 6: "The wind goeth toward the south, and turneth about unto the north; it whirleth about continually, and the wind returneth again according to his circuits."

"The wind goeth toward the south." Had Solomon said that the wind goes due south, or simply south, I would be put to a very great loss what to say — only "toward." Or had the great preacher said that the wind goeth toward the north and turneth about unto the south, we could not have reconciled this passage. Let us see the difference. The heated air of the equator first goes up, then the current sets first from the pole—could not possibly go first toward the north. Reader, don't leave this thought till you have fully comprehended its meaning. We said in the beginning of this work that we would give the Bible a word interpretation. Now we say more: Press these interpretations with the vehemence of an enemy, and you will be wiser and the Bible vindicated; make no loose interpretations. Sparks fly from the flint that is smitten with steel. These sparks can burn up cities. Who would take lead and clay and expect these to give fire, warmth, or light? Then be steel, your Bible flint, and you will see the sparks.

"It whirleth about continually." This brings us to consider the variable winds. We stated that our text-books give three classes. The same cause produces each: the parting of light. We call close attention to the fact that the wind first goeth toward the south and turneth about unto the north before it ever whirleth about continually. Then this whirling about continually must take place somewhere between the north and the south, and cannot take place either at the north or the south. Let us take the two expressions and see if we cannot form from them an estimate as to where this whirling about continually takes place. First the wind goeth toward the south. Now we know that it is some distance from its starting-point; the statement says so. Secondly, it turneth about unto the north. Now the current is only fairly turned unto the north when this turning about continually takes place. This must be near the tropics, and then this turning about continues to the polar circle. Says geography: "North and south of the trades are the zones of the variable winds. They extend from the parallels of thirty degrees north and south to the polar circles. Within these limits the winds blow without regularity."

"And the wind returneth again according to his circuits." This brings us to consider the other class of winds: the periodical winds. These have their origin in the parting of light, as do the others. Periodical winds are those that blow for a certain time in one direction and then for an equal or nearly equal time in the opposite direction. "And the wind returneth again according to his circuits." These make the four winds of the Scriptures: the two currents that set from the poles to the equator and the two that set from the equator to the poles.

VAPORS.

Geography teaches that our springs, rivulets, creeks, and rivers flow into the ocean. There, under equatorial suns, they are carried up as vapor and returned to us in the form of rain. Ecclesiastes i. 7: "All the rivers run into the sea; yet the sea is not full: unto the place from whence the rivers come, thither they return again." How are these brought back? Philosophy says "by the conflict of great aerial currents which, differing in temperature, are constantly traversing the atmosphere in all directions, bringing rain to almost every part of the globe. When large bodies of air, differing in temperature and charged with humidity, are rapidly combined, as by the action of the winds, a sudden and powerful condensation occurs, and electricity is developed on a large scale. As the clouds form and the rain descends it plays in vivid lightnings amid the darkness of the storm." Let David tell it. Psalm cxxxv. 7: "He causeth the vapors to ascend from the ends of the earth; he maketh lightnings for the rain; he bringeth the wind out of his treasuries." There must be vapors, different temperatures, winds, lightnings, rain. This comparison is too striking to need any comment. We call your attention to an application in our opening statement from our text-books. In the beginning of this subject we stated that geographers taught that our streams flow into the ocean; there, under equatorial suns, their vapors are carried up. David says: "Causeth the vapors to ascend from the ends of the earth." We have proved by revelation that equatorial regions are the ends of the earth. (See "Rotation of Earth.") Now we are together in terms and geographically so. Science teaches that an increase of temperature by dilating the air increases its capacity for moisture, while a decrease lessens its capacity; that the rainfall depends upon the vapor absorbed. Job xxxvi. 27, 28: "For he maketh small the drops of water: they pour down rain according to the vapor thereof; which the clouds do drop and distil upon man abundantly." Our many authors are not ashamed to reach back forty centuries for this expression "distil." They say: "Water distils from the ocean and the land." Converting liquid to vapor and condensing it is termed distillation.

The Rainbow.

Genesis ix. 13-15: "I do set my bow in the cloud, and it shall be for a token of a covenant between me and the earth. And it shall come to pass, when I bring a cloud over the earth, that the bow shall be seen in the cloud: and I will remember my covenant, which is between me and you and every living creature of all flesh; and the waters shall no more become a flood to destroy all flesh."

If the rainbow is produced by the reflection and refraction of light through falling drops of water, did the bow exist prior to the time of the flood? If so, it is said that "it could not have been set at the time spoken of above." Such propositions are not designed to obtain information, but simply to disorganize, to bewilder, and confuse. The laws of refraction and reflection are universal; wherever light and falling drops exist, there the bow exists. Our observation is that the operations of universal laws are, as a rule (we remember no exceptions), expressed in the present tense, making them past, present, and continuous operations. "I do set my bow in the cloud."

It is God's bow, a fixture according to his own purpose and plan, for his own use or glory. He can set it where he pleases. Then he took his own bow. "I do set"—that has been my business, is still my business, will continue as long as flesh exists, as long as the earth endures; for with these he covenanted. The token is as permanent as the solid earth. The covenant had been made before; now it is witnessed by the bow. "It shall be for a token." It had not been for a token before this, but became a token after God's covenant with the earth. One man says, "I work in wood;" another, "I work in iron;" another, "I teach" or "I preach." Had the first man ever worked in wood before he made this statement? All the work he had ever done in wood was prior to this statement. The same is true with each of the others. There is no term used explaining what his bow was, indicating that it was no new thing. "In the cloud." The rainbow is an arch of colored light which spans the heavens during a storm. It is seen only when the sun is shining at the same time that the rain is falling.

"And it shall come to pass, when I bring a cloud over the earth, that the bow shall be seen in the cloud." A cloud is simply a mass of mist or fog floating high in the air instead of near the ground. It consists of either minute vesicles—that is, tiny hollow globes of water—or fine ice crystals. So far as we know, they are falling constantly; but the lower part of the cloud, as it comes into warmer air, is dissolved again to vapor and disappears, while a new portion may at the same time be formed above. So, while the vapor in the cloud is constantly being condensed and falling, the falling particles are evaporated and rise again. So the cloud is held between the vapor and the condensation temperature. The beautifully painted clouds are but sifted rays of light as they are reflected and refracted by these falling particles. Moonlight often shows the delicate tintings of the bow in the cloud. "It is set in the cloud." Rings around the sun and moon are but rainbows, which are due to the refracting power of ice crystals composing cirrus clouds. How truly is the bow set in the cloud!

Isaiah xlv. 7: "I form the light, and create darkness: I make peace, and create evil: I the Lord do all these things." Was not light formed before the days of this prophet? Was darkness not created till then? Was there no peace till then? no evil till then? The conclusion of the whole matter is: "I name an object, which is set in the cloud, as a reminder of the covenant between me and the earth: the rainbow."

The American Congress set the 4th of July as a national holiday, to be spent in rejoicing and in celebrating the event that made the nation free and independent. On the return of this day, since 1776, the story of former grievances and wrongs has been told and this declaration read. This declaration is a covenant; this day is but a token, reminding us that all men are born free, having inherent rights to worship God according to the dictates of individual consciences. Was there no 4th of July prior to this date? Not in this sense. Would you have asked so simple a question? This is not more simple than "I do set my bow in the cloud, . . . for a token."

ICE.

Water, in passing from the liquid to the solid state, expands. In cooling it follows the general law of contraction until it reaches the temperature of 39.2° Fahrenheit. Below this, it disobeys the general law and expands as the temperature falls, till it reaches 32° Fahrenheit, its freezing-point. Then suddenly it hardens into ice, and attains its maximum expansion. The face of the ice is extended always beyond the surface of the water. Water, when freezing, exerts a force that is practically irresistible. It sunders the solid rocks from the foundations of the mountain and crumbles them into fragments.

Job xxxvii. 10: "By the breath of God frost is given: and the breadth of the waters is straitened." These two occurrences—frost and the straitening of the breadth of the waters—take place at one and the same temperature. "Straitened." To make tense or tight, to press by want of sufficient room.

STORMS.

These are atmospheric disturbances, produced as other winds. It is a difference or inequality of pressure or weight in different regions of the atmosphere. "The principle may be thus stated: Into an area of low barometer a wind must always blow from an area of high barometer." Job xxxvii. 9: "Out of the south cometh the whirlwind: and cold out of the north." These are two plain truths. We know that the whirlwind comes out of the south and that cold comes out of the north. It is a little strange that the very two agents that produce the whirlwind are named together in the same construction, and come together in the manner to produce this frightful phenomenon.

CHAPTER VI.

CONDUCTION, REFLECTION, ABSORPTION.

Mr. Steele, after discussing the above topics, propounds, among his practical questions, this one: "Why do furnace men wear flannel shirts in summer to keep cool and in winter to keep warm?" Mr. Steele has for twenty years furnished a very acceptable course in the sciences. We wish to compare this with a similar question propounded in the book of Job (xxxvii. 17): "Dost thou know how thy garments are warm, when he quieteth the earth by the south wind?" If this question from Mr. Steele comes within the province of philosophy, what will you say of this one taken from the book of Job? If the first involves reflection, radiation, absorption, and conduction, what will you say of the second? Is Mr. Steele's question really practical? He propounds his question to a pupil: "Why do certain men wear a certain article of clothing?" One might say, "Oddities in dress;" another says, "Economy, less washing, less wear;" another, "The sparks from the forge would be less likely to burn such shirts;" another, "They are brighter, faster colors." Mr. Steele presumes by this question why. He asks me why other men do so and so. The question goes straight to Job and Job's own garments under one condition:

(108)

"Dost thou know how [not why] thy [not furnace men's] garments are warm?" This is purely a practical question—one man, a simple "how," one surrounding, and one condition. Now, it is not *why?* —this would involve an opinion; but "Dost thou know *how* thy garments are warm?" etc. This springs a philosophical principle: *how* did your garments become warm? not the man warm, but his garments. The heat from the warm south wind was absorbed, the warmth from the body helped to warm them by conduction. This is the third of four questions propounded to Job in this recitation. This recitation opened with the fourteenth verse: "Stand still, and consider the wondrous works of God." This is one of the wondrous works of God.

Now you are saying that I answered Job's question; that he did not do so. That is very true. Mr. Steele did not answer his. We think that he might spend an opinion only, and might give a correct answer to Job's question. If we estimate ability to answer questions by ability to frame a consistent, intricate question, we would give the palm to the author of the question found in the book of Job. The question suggests investigation.

STEAM.

We have talked of ocean currents, a thing about which perchance the world may have known something. But now we come to man's greatest servant, his greatest natural factor, one that has had more to do perhaps in elevating him in a social, a literary, and a spiritual sense than any of the means given him; at the same time, one that had not been known,

had not been heard of, had not been imagined by
him even in his idlest dreamings till but a few years
ago.   Its achievements have been wonderful indeed.   Could the whole story be told it would seem
a mere fiction.   One unacquainted with its powers
and its adaptability to serve man would think it a
vision, a fairy tale taken from the "Arabian Nights."
These powers will embalm the name of Watts and
Fulton, and make them as lasting as fire and water.
Rivers are made great thoroughfares against the current as with it; oceans have become traversable; distance is counted as nothing; across great continents
move vast caravans like burning meteors; men and
women journey around the world for business or
pleasure.   To this agent hundreds of tons are no
burden.   It leads most splendid palaces both upon
the land and upon the sea.   It is the banner of an
advanced civilization, leading on the arts and
sciences, learning and literature, in our own country, and sending these, like light, to all the world.
This power, the factors that evolve it, the causes that
bring it about, passed the eye of the prophet.   Isaiah
lxiv. 2, 4, 5: "As when the melting fire burneth, the
fire causeth the waters to boil, to make thy name
known to thine adversaries, that the nations may
tremble at thy presence!"   "For since the beginning
of the world men have not heard, nor perceived by
the ear, neither hath the eye seen, O God, besides
thee, what he hath prepared for him that waiteth
for him.   Thou meetest him that rejoiceth and worketh righteousness, those that remember thee in thy
ways."   This is a prophecy from an eminent prophet; and all the world knows that this prophecy is at

least twenty-five hundred years older than man's discovery of the latent energies of water as developed in steam.

"As when the melting fire burneth." "As when" is equivalent to when, at the very time, the fire is imparting its heat to the water in a way to put work into it.

"The melting fire burneth." The heat that it takes to boil ice-cold water will raise iron to a glowing red. The temperature of water cannot be raised above the boiling-point unless the steam be confined; then the extra heat force is expended in expanding the water into steam, and is of the same temperature as the water from which it is made. Nearly one thousand degrees of heat become latent in this process. It really requires more heat to raise water to a high degree of specific heat than any other substance, save one or two unimportant exceptions. In the furnaces that are used for producing steam grates are melted, bars bent, doors burned—a melting fire is kept up.

"The fire causeth the waters to boil." The melting fire of the furnace is only to raise the temperature to the boiling-point — "to make thy name known." This is the steam-generating point. At this temperature, 212°, water boils, and, as we have said, it cannot be raised above that point unless the steam be confined. Thermometers are not two hundred years old. It is true that Isaiah knew water boiled, and it is not necessary that he should have known it boiled at 212° Fahrenheit; but it is curious that he should have named that temperature and that only that does work. How did he know but that a less temperature would do the work? Steam is but melted water. How did he know that any temperature would do this? How could he say that boiling water would make His name known?

"To make thy name known to thine adversaries." This is the object. Great means are employed for a great purpose. It begins with God's friends, that his adversaries may know and acknowledge him.

"That the nations may tremble at thy presence." What an extended influence is wielded by this boiling water! It is to make thy name known to thine adversaries. It is to make nations tremble. It is not for a personal influence. Nothing has had more to do than steam in making his name known. Go to our steam printing-presses; light and learning radiate in every direction. Bibles are printed by the millions and placed upon the shoulders of this agent and borne over the world. When they can not be sold they are given away. Tons of Sunday-school literature are scattered weekly. Every corner and nook learns of him. Go to Mohammedan countries; our Bibles and other publications were not admitted there till the day of steam printing-presses. Go to heathen lands where very debasing forms of idolatry are practised; these are his adversaries; they worship other gods. China, Africa, and the islands of the sea are accepting him. Watch the ship-loads of missionaries as they land to tell of his name. See the astonished, trembling populace as they look on with fear and misgiving. Think of the fearful superstitions that hang like clouds over their minds as they bend to the works of their own hands. Then you will know why the fire causeth the water to boil.

God's wonderful dealings have most frequently been
for a double purpose: to benefit the patient, faithful
believer and to carry fear to his enemies.

"For since the beginning of the world men have
not heard, nor perceived by the ear, neither hath the
eye seen, O God, besides thee, what he hath prepared
for him that waiteth for him." Nothing like it since
the world began. No one save God himself knows
what was prepared for him that waiteth for him.
Then he prepared a something for the man or nation
that waiteth for him, a something that eye nor ear
has ever reached. I do not say that he speaks of the
invisibleness of steam; will only say that it is invisible. It is "for him that waiteth for him." Who
discovered the hidden energies of steam? A people
"that waiteth for him." Who wrought appliances to
hold it in subjection? A Christian people. Who
grasped the unseen force of the electric spark and
gave it in bondage to man? A people "that waiteth
for him." The whole is answered by the fifth verse:
"Thou meetest him that rejoiceth and worketh righteousness, those that remember thee in thy ways."
Study God in his ways, and every time the result is
that you will find him and some good thing. He has
ever helped that people that acknowledged him and
have helped themselves.

"Thou meetest him." We have the assurance
that if we go toward him he will come toward us.
He will divide the distance with us in every undertaking when his name is to be made known and himself to be acknowledged. The history of great discoveries and great inventions shows that the first-
fruits of these were reaped by a nation that waited

8

for him, a nation called by his name. These high motive powers were prepared for and developed by that people of whom the prophet speaks. We should regard every great invention, especially one that does so much for man in working good, as a witness of him to make his name known among the less favored, as a living testimony against those who do not fear him.

Psalm xxxi. 19: "O how great is thy goodness, which thou hast laid up for them that fear thee; which thou hast wrought for them that trust in thee before the sons of men!"

STEAM-ENGINE.

Speaking of the leviathan, a striking analogy of the engine is drawn in Job xli., beginning with the fourteenth verse and including the remaining part of the chapter: "Who can open the doors of his face? his teeth are terrible round about. His scales are his pride, shut up together as with a close seal. One is so near to another, that no air can come between them. They are joined one to another, they stick together, that they can not be sundered." This is a very good comparison of the construction of a boiler. Its strength and the closeness of its parts are such as to prevent the admission of air, too strong to be sundered. "By his neesings a light doth shine, and his eyes are like the eyelids of the morning. Out of his mouth go burning lamps, and sparks of fire leap out. Out of his nostrils goeth smoke, as out of a seething pot or caldron." "By his neesings," or sneezing, which is the same. Sneezing is ejecting the air violently from the lungs through the nostrils.

"Out of his nostrils goeth smoke." By violent and irregular ejection of the air from the smoke-stack we have a spasmodic chug! chug! fizz! fizz! very similar to sneezing. "His eyes are like the eyelids of the morning." The open doors of the furnace at night, revealing the red-hot pipes, together with the bright, dazzling Drummond light from the head of the boiler, find a similarity in the eyelids of the morning. So "out of his mouth go burning lamps, and sparks of fire leap out." The expression "as out of a seething pot or caldron" means that these things are ejected as if or just like they are thrown out by the force of a steam-boiler. "His breath kindleth coals, and a flame goeth out of his mouth." The rarefied air in the pipe is pressed by a column beneath, which rushes in to fill the vacuum, and feeds the flame as on this moving monster goes. "In his neck remaineth strength, and sorrow is turned into joy before him." "In his neck"—the long, bent pipe that extends from the boiler and communicates with the engine—"remaineth strength." All the latent energies of this great seething pot are here held for use. The throttle-valve, or throat-valve, is situated at the end of the pipe that communicates with the boiler. This lets the steam into the steam-chest to feed the engine; then "in his neck remaineth strength."

"Sorrow is turned into joy before him." Wherever this great enterprise is directed, forests give way to coming towns and cities. Uninhabitable mountains become favored resorts, great plains are white with cottages, artesian wells are lowered till by irrigation parched countries are made green and fruitful by waters that are lifted hundreds of feet from beneath the surface. The dominion of the red man and buffalo gives way to railroads, telegraphs, colleges, and churches. Prospective sites often lay the foundation for the coming of the engine. Sorrow or desolation and waste, a lack of thrift and enterprise, are foes of railroads; but these "are turned into joy before him." Great railroad centers are the centers of wealth and prosperity.

"The flakes of his flesh are joined together: they are firm in themselves; they cannot be moved." Every particle of this tremendous body is bolted and bradded together, so that "they are firm in themselves." "His heart is as firm as a stone; yea, as hard as a piece of the nether millstone." His heart, like the heart of animals, is the vital organ, the one that forces the life-giving steam to all parts; it is the life situated within. This is the propelling force or steam. "As firm as a stone." As the steam generates within the boiler its pressure is distributed to all parts; higher rises the temperature, the pressure increases. When the steam-guage points to one hundred then we know that every inch sustains a pressure of one hundred pounds. This pressure is as great on every inch of water in the boiler likewise. We can demonstrate this by taking a flask filled about half full with boiling water and corked tightly. The boiling will be kept up for a while. The pressure of the confined steam will be sufficient to cause the boiling to cease. Pour cold water upon the flask, the steam will be condensed, the pressure relieved, and boiling commence energetically. We give this as a simple illustration of the pressure of confined steam. If it is sufficient to prevent the boiling in a

flask, what would be the pressure in a great boiler
containing many barrels of water and resting upon
a melting and continuous fire? It would be as com-
pact, as hard, as a stone. "As a nether millstone"—
the bottom stone. This might lead us to think that
the water underlying this tremendous pressure
would have its particles pressed very closely and
compactly together, sufficiently close that its hardness might be compared to the nether millstone.

"When he raiseth up himself, the mighty are
afraid: by reason of breakings they purify themselves." "When he raiseth up himself." He is
brought from the roundhouse all nice and clean,
spitting sparks and heated vapor, fizzing, frying, and
cracking, his sides trembling under the great pressure. We watch this ponderous machine as it is
switched on to the main line. Every eye is turned
to it. We feel an inexpressible something creep over
us as we trust life, safety, and all to its power, which
is in the hands of a man only. Hundreds of insur-
ance offices are opened all along the great railways,
that we may have our lives insured against the dangers of the trip. Hundreds of thousands of policies
are bought daily. "The mighty are afraid." The
bulk of the patronage comes from the mighty. The
commonality, without means or experience, look
upon it rather as a frolic than a matter of business;
they pass from coach to coach, stand upon the plat-
forms, are out before it stops, get on again as it
moves out. Free excursions are given, and the cars
are filled to overflowing by the fearless class. Idle
curiosity makes them unmindful of fear. There is
no choice of seats to them. The mighty, as they

enter, scrutinize closely the water-stand, the stove, or other fixtures. "We must not sit here or there. Should a wreck happen, these might tumble down upon us." "By reason of breakings they purify themselves." Steam is invisible. The steam-engine is a machine for using the elastic force of steam. The moment the steam comes in contact with the air its elasticity is broken and it is condensed into minute globules, floating in the air; thus steam renders the vapor apparently visible. This condensed steam gives us the purest water. "By reason of breakings they purify themselves."

The next four verses show him to be without fear, show him a powerful machine.

"Sharp stones are under him: he spreadeth sharp-pointed things upon the mire." This may have reference to his track. "He spreadeth sharp-pointed things upon the mire." In the swamps of Arkansas, Mississippi, and Louisiana—where long trestles are built by sharpening the ends of the trunks of long pine and cypress trees and forcing these by great pile-drivers into the mire, the clay, or rock, and the track then spread out upon these — we see what Job saw, "He spreadeth sharp-pointed things upon the mire," and our minds realize the striking analogy.

"He maketh the deep to boil like a pot: he maketh the sea like a pot of ointment." Here the field of its operation is transferred to the sea. The ponderous wheels drive the water in waves behind and leave it beaten into spray and foam along its track. "He maketh a path to shine after him; one would think the deep to be hoary. Upon earth there is not his like, who is made without fear. He beholdeth all high things: he is a king over all the children of pride." The last clause is: "He is a king over all the children of pride." Great material wealth is the chief support of pride. The devil thought to tempt the pride and vanity of the Saviour by offering him all the kingdoms of earth and the glory thereof if he would worship him. The tempting of spiritualism is poverty, while the tempting of pride and vanity is wealth. "Upon the earth there is not his like." "He raiseth himself up." To-day in New York; in seven days more he is in San Francisco, three thousand miles away. He drinks of the Gulf to-day; in three days more he quenches his thirst from the Great Lakes. Those who own and control him are transported from place to place in princely palaces. He is the pride, the boast, the sovereign of a nation. He equalizes the products, the manufactures, the minerals; he makes the places where they are not, as abundant as where they are. "He is a king over all the children of pride." His revenue is the revenue of pride.

Nahum ii. 4: "The chariots shall rage in the streets, they shall jostle one against another in the broad ways: they shall seem like torches, they shall run like the lightnings." This, we may say, was written by the prophet Nahum against Nineveh. We believe that Sodoms and Gomorrahs, Ninevehs and Babylons, are repeating themselves. The thing that would destroy Sodom then would to-day; the thing that would spare Nineveh then would to-day; the things that would be written against them would be written against this generation. The conflict has always been between his people and their opponents.

"They shall run like the lightnings." In speaking of lightning we call it a current. It is a force. So steam as force is transmitted from particle to particle by displacement. Steam transmits its force similarly; it has a conductor to guide it in its course. So have these chariots. Lightning moves in straight lines, with greater velocity than any other thing save light. These chariots move with greater velocity than any other contrivance framed by man. The comparison is well selected. In the days of the prophet no such chariots were known; none fill so well the comparison as do our lightning express trains of to-day. They receive this name from their swiftness. We have called them by just what the prophet said they run like. More, these are now driven, especially in our cities, by the very force that they "run like." These things are to take place in the day of his preparation.

TELEGRAPH.

We have noticed that lightning is distinguished in the Bible: First, those electric discharges that we see during a storm or an approaching storm. Such are denominated lightning of thunder, lightning for the rain. These expressions of attendant purpose show too plainly the truth that we are to consider these apart from any other class. Again, we find in our Bible a communicative, an enlightening, a message-bearing, a tongue-walking, a word-running, and a biddable lightning—one that can be sent and will return and talk to us. The Bible has made these two divisions not as two distinct kinds, for the divisions are founded only on the purposes for which they are used. Franklin proved that they were the same. This does away with every chance for a dispute as to what is meant by the term "lightning." We are further justified in making the statement that the Bible is not silent touching the process by which the test was made to prove the identity of lightning and electricity. We propose to notice man's first efforts to lay hands on the lightning, to make it serve him, after we have given revelation's process as a prophecy. Psalm lxxiii. 9, 10: "They set their mouth against the heavens, and their tongue walketh through the earth. Therefore his people return hither: and waters of a full cup are wrung out to them." Before commenting on these passages let us ask you to examine the preceding verses and the two verses that follow our text. In them are plainly set forth the characteristics of rich, prosperous, proud, and powerful corporations, such as have ever controlled this lightning-bearer. "Their eyes stand out with fatness: they have more than heart could wish." Is that not verified in every case? In the text under consideration we have two declarations and a conclusion:

"They set their mouth against the heavens."

"Their tongue walketh through the earth."
Conclusion: "Therefore his people return hither: and waters of a full cup are wrung out to them."

"They set their mouth against the heavens." The terms "they" and "their" show that more than one person had a hand in the matter. Mouth is in the singular, and the text makes it the property of they. the parties that set it. A mouth belonging to more than one person! No reflecting mind would consider this a mouth having a tongue and the other modulating organs of speech, and the property of more than one person. Then it must be something else. This was set against the heavens. *Against* means "opposition to." Heaven, we said, is the expanse of air above and around the earth. "Heavens," as used in the text, refers to the vapors in the air, the clouds. Now, with these explanations, suppose that I should say that Franklin and Richmond set their mouth against the heavens and that Franklin drew into this lightning, and that Samuel F. B. Morse sent their tongue walking from Washington to Baltimore May 27, 1844—is there a man of ordinary information in all this country that would be puzzled to understand this? Let us review the story. During a storm Franklin sent up a kite. To the lower end of the cord he suspended a key, which was inserted into the mouth of a bottle. This bottle-mouth was against the clouds, inasmuch as it was opposite to and connected with the clouds by a cord. Along this conducting cord lightning from the clouds descended and entered this bottle. Thus Franklin proved the identity of lightning and electricity. Prof. Richmond, of St. Petersburg, drew, in the same manner, from the clouds a ball of blue fire as large as a man's fist, which struck him lifeless. This same bottle-neck, and for the same purpose, is seen on every telegraph-pole in all the land. Millions are set. Of the one hundred thousand miles or more of telegraph-wire now in use, every one hundred yards, at farthest, has this mouth set, which is nothing more nor less than the roof and palate modulating the electric force into a living language and keeping it on its highway from station to station throughout the length and breadth of our great country.

"And their tongue walketh through the earth." How closely these performances follow each other! They set their mouth, their tongue goes to walking. If there had been any tongue walking through the earth prior to the time when their mouth was set against the heavens, we have no account of it. Franklin's experiment and its results were the forerunners of the electric telegraph. Franklin drew into their mouth the very same force that in less than one hundred years did begin its walk through the earth.

Tongue is most frequently used to denote a particular language. In speaking of different languages we often say a certain tongue. A language peculiar to a people is the tongue of that people. "Their tongue [the tongue of the clouds] walketh through the earth." The thing that Franklin caught is the thing that now walketh through the earth. It is a peculiar tongue. I have been brought up in a land of telegraphs. Not one word can I utter; not one can I interpret. I enter a telegraph office and hear the incessant rattle of the instruments, which is no more intelligible to me than the rattle of the car-wheels along the rails. The operator listens, looks steadily at nothing for a moment, touches a little knob, turns off, and says: "The train is now passing Big Spring, one hundred miles away." Their tongue is a language of abbreviations, while their voice is the vocalizing force caught from the clouds, is made articulate through the sound of smitten iron, and is

intelligible to the tutored ear, can only be repro-
duced by the tutored touch — these, the ones employed to operate these machines, for "they" who
set their mouth.

NOTE.—This experiment of Franklin's was made during the
stormy scenes of colonial times, just before our war for inde-
pendence. The verse that precedes the above text reads: "They
are corrupt, and speak wickedly concerning oppression: they
speak loftily." We do not say that this has a bearing on our
text, but it is similar to the expressions and very similar to the
breathings of that period, and to Franklin himself.

*"The armature lever is the living, speaking tongue of
the telegraph."* This is what electricians say of it.

"And their tongue walketh through the earth."
"Walketh through the earth." Walk, to move forward step by step. We can see a similarity in the
propagation of words through the air to that of the
process of walking. This is done by an alternation
of condensations and rarefactions of the air particles; the voice shoots out, moving step by step from
the one to the other, but not through the earth. This
can neither be literally nor figuratively true of any
tongue of man; is true, and only true, of this tongue
of the clouds, heavens. If we know how electricity is
transmitted through a wire, we can see not only a
beauty in the expression, but accuracy. Philosophy
teaches that "in galvanic, as in frictional, electricity,
when the current passes through a conducting substance, as a wire or rod, the force is transmitted not
on the surface, as is sometimes said, but through the
entire thickness of the body. Each molecule, becoming polarized and charged, discharges its force into
the next molecule, and so on. "The current thus
moves by a rapid succession of polarizations and dis-

charges of the molecules of the conductor." Thus
from molecule to molecule its tiny feet step—here,
yonder, everywhere—till their tongue is said to walk
through the earth and deliver our thoughts in the
language of *their mouth*. But their tongue walketh
through the earth. "Through the earth"—this is literally true. "If one pole of a battery be connected
with the earth and the wire from the other pole be
carried to any distance and also connected to the
earth, the current will flow as readily as though the
circuit had been completed by the use of a return
wire. The earth is practically one vast conductor.
Telegraph companies use the earth's conduction in
all cases for their numerous lines, whether long or
short. It saves the construction of return wires on
every circuit." If a tongue went out and the same
thing returned, and that through the earth, and if
this force is transmitted from molecule to molecule
through the earth, then how literally does their
tongue walk through the earth! The battles of Europe, the speeches of her great men, the state of the
market, are reported in the journals of New York
the next day. While the busy hand of the operator
in Liverpool is telling these things to New York,
back through the earth the story returns. The story
is told, the operator stops, the walk through the
earth is ended, this voice becomes silent in the
mouth of the open jar. This is the mouth that was
set, wherein is the vocalizing force of their tongue.
"Their tongue walketh through the earth." It is
not possible for any other interpretation to be correct.

"Therefore his people return hither: and waters of

a full cup are wrung out to them." "Therefore."
For this reason. We come now to the conclusion, to
notice the results and upon whom they descend. If
great and good results are measures of causes, then
we must estimate very highly the cause leading to
this conclusion and these results. It could not be a
thing less than the introduction of the telegraph and
the many uses for which this electric force is now
employed. If, then, we are to consider these as results emanating from that mouth-setting and tongue-
walking process, and these to descend upon "his
people," it will not be a hard matter for us to locate
geographically and nationally his people. "His
people." Those named after him, Christians. "Hither." It is a simple postulate. The more we know of
God in his works and ways, the nearer we approach
him. The converse is equally true: the nearer we approach him, the more we learn of him, his works and
ways. These are to return hither, come back to a
higher knowledge of him, find him out in his law, and
the forces he ordained for man's service and man's
elevation.

"Waters of a full cup are wrung out to them."
"Waters." Did you ever think about water? It is
one of the most wonderful gifts to man. It is a most
fitting type to represent our needs. It, as well as its
individual components, is a physical necessity not to
be dispensed with anywhere along the line of our
needs, though I will not speak of it with reference to
our individual needs and purposes in every-day life.
My theme addresses itself to a people. We will look
at it as a public benefactor. Water changes its
form with remarkable readiness. So we have water,

and may make ice or generate steam. Think of the
fruits gathered from this branch alone! It expands
when freezing. Were it not for this principle, our
Northern rivers and lakes would have been frozen
solid long ago. The descending cold would draw
toward the equator from both poles till but a narrow
belt along the equator would remain. In no physical act have we a more certain evidence of divine
care than in this provision. It has extraordinary
capacity for heat. God uses hot-water currents for
warming different apartments of the world as we use
steam for heating buildings. It has great solvent
power. This property is remodeling the world in a
measure. The beautifully colored fabrics that please
us so well are due to this property. The water supplies the air with moisture and this descends as rain,
without which all must die. It is one of the great
regulators of climate. Finally, the sea is the highway of nations. Commerce, civilization, and Christianity have been wafted on its bosom to the ends of
the earth. "Of a full cup." This admits of two
pleasing interpretations. I give both rather than
omit either. My cup, your cup, the cup of his people, is to be full. No stint; enough of this precious
type emblematical of all good things. "Cup." The
measure of all needs; this is to be full. Or we may
consider it as water wrung from a full cup for his
people. A full storehouse, held in reservation for
his people, to be wrung out continuously upon them.
It is to bring about a return of his people, a return
to duty. To none but the dutiful are waters of a full
cup wrung out—wrung out from this selfsame agent,
lightning; wrung out from steam; wrung out from

the ten thousand inventions that help man, that elevate him, that give him more comforts, that enlarge his views of the great world around him and its adaptation to his wants and wishes, give him more faith, open his eyes upward to Him who is perfect in knowledge and who fashioned all things for his people. The story of those individuals and nations who have the fullest cups is that they are the ones who are nearest duty. That life that is duty bound is heaven aimed. "For what nation is there so great, who hath God so nigh unto them, as the Lord our God is in all things that we call upon him for?" "His people." What nations have reaped the first-fruits of great discoveries? Christian nations. What people have made the greatest advancement in the arts and sciences? His people. What people enjoy the greatest liberty? His people. Earth, air, and ocean are pouring their diversified treasures into the lap of his people. "Light is sown for the righteous, and gladness for the upright in heart." This is the hither and these the waters of a full cup meant in the text.

Let us interview David at a later date. Psalm cxlvii. 15: "He sendeth forth his commandment upon earth: his word runneth very swiftly." Beginning with the twelfth verse and closing with the twentieth, the prophet exhorteth the Church to praise God for his blessings upon the kingdom, for his power, and for his ordinances in the Church. All these verses enumerate excellent gifts to man, except the last; it says that he has not dealt so with any nation. These are not running men nor running horses, but running words. We have shown you how the

electric force is transmitted through the wire. That
we explained as a walking process. Walking and
running are philosophically the same. Let us see
what philosophers say about words running very
swiftly. "With what inconceivable rapidity must
these successive changes [steps] take place in an
iron wire to transmit the electric force, as in a recent
experiment, from San Francisco to Boston and return in one minute!" How rapidly must these little
feet move to traverse five thousand miles in one minute and make two tracks on every little molecule in
an iron wire connecting San Francisco and Boston!
Surely "his word runneth very swiftly." Suppose
that I should say publicly that a word was sent five
thousand miles in a minute, then should note the
comments from the refined and unrefined, from the
learned and the unlearned—it would be denominated
by all as a swiftly moving word process, and the
mind of each would be turned alone to the telegraph
or telephone. Nothing is made to run but his word.
At first dispatches were received in certain characters made by a recording instrument on paper. Then
these characters, which represented letters, were
combined into words; but now they are received directly from the instrument; the sound of the instrument is interpreted into words. To the skilled operator these sounds are as intelligible as spoken
words. They are really, in this sense, running words.
They are not spelled, but abbreviated, words.

ELECTRICITY.

We come now to notice the results obtained by
this tongue-walking, this word-running wonder.

9

Psalm xcvii. 4: "His lightnings enlightened the world: the earth saw, and trembled." "His lightnings enlightened the world." Already we begin to see and feel its effects. Its lights are looming up till a new dawn is breaking upon us. The arts and sciences are elevating their eyes to a higher plain; they seek to breathe a purer air. Electrotyping is the process of depositing metals from their solution by electricity. It is used in copying medals, wood-cuts, type, etc. We need but an impression taken in wax and a common battery to do this work. Electroplating is the process of coating with silver or gold. Our baser metals become as bright as silver or gold; can be done by any hand, and with incredible speed. "While the plate is hanging in the solution there is no noise heard or bubbling seen. The most delicate sense fails to detect any movement. Yet the mysterious electric force is contiually drawing particles of ruddy, solid copper out of the blue liquid and noiselessly as the fall of snowflakes dropping them on the mold, producing a metal purer than any chemist can manufacture, spreading it with a uniformity no artist can attain, and copying every line with a fidelity that knows no mistake."

From ocean to ocean across the continent these lightnings flash, bearing our messages through wires three thousand miles long or more. It is not enough. The wire finds a footing and a resting-place on the bottom of the great ocean, till the Atlantic is measured by its length and we can converse face to face with the people of Europe. The electric telegraph, the telephone, microphone, and the use of electric lights for illumination are the latest applications of the electric force to the purposes of practical life. It can not stop here. Force is to be converted into electricity, secretly and silently stolen from deep chasms and lofty precipices and carried to more habitable places, and there unbound and converted into force again and great machines driven by it and populous cities lighted along the line of its egress. In ten thousand ways it will become man's servant for enlightening him. With all the wonders wrought by this enlightening element, it is now but in its infancy; yet it is a genuine symbol of an enlightened nation. No nation is classed among the enlightened that has no telegraph.

"The earth saw, and trembled." This is true from the very beginning of researches in this direction up to the present. Thales, six hundred years before Christ, knew that amber rubbed with silk would attract light bodies, such as straw, leaves, etc. This property was considered so marvelous that amber was supposed to possess a soul. Franklin was so overjoyed with his experiment that he was said to have burst into tears. Prof. Richmond was struck dead while performing a similar experiment. Such an occurrence must have electrified all St. Petersburg. Oersted, 1820, discovered his phenomenon: that electricity and magnetism are not distinct forces, but intimately connected. This was published everywhere, and excited the deepest interest of scientific men. In the mind of Ampère the experiment bore abundant fruit. Prof. Henry next exhibited the wonderful power of the electromagnet, and invented the electromagnetic engine. Says the history of this matter: "Scientific men in all parts of the world were now gathering the material necessary for the invention of the electric telegraph." "The earth saw, and trembled." Descriptive of the emotions produced by this discovery. Great achievements have always been followed by or attended with great emotions. Isaiah said of steam: "The fire causeth the waters to boil, to make thy name known to thine adversaries, that the nations may tremble." "The earth saw, and trembled." The world looked upon it with awe, with fear, with astonishment. Like a shock from its own batteries it swept till every circle, every condition in life, was electrified. "The earth saw, and trembled."

Now we come to the very language of the telegraph. Job xxxviii. 35: "Canst thou send lightnings, that they may go, and say unto thee, Here we are?" An electric battery consists of a piece of copper and a piece of zinc suspended in a jar filled with a solution of blue vitriol and sulfate of zinc. If a wire of any length have one of its ends fastened to the copper plate and the other to the zinc, the current will flow through its whole length and come back to the zinc just as surely as though the distance were but a few inches. They go and return; they are sent. The very lightnings that are sent are the very lightnings that return and say: "Here we are." This is a talking lightning, and in the very language of the telegraph. In the clause "here we are" I am pleased to observe that the verb "are" is not found in the original; that the answer brought back over Job's inspired wire was simply "here we." Let us see what it is to-day. The telegraph operator at Nashville calls the office of New York; back comes the answer, simply "I." Now the use of "we" for "I" in constructions of this kind has rendered the two synonymous, and "we" is most frequently used for "I." The language of the telegraph is surely a language of abbreviations. Job's wire brings the return, "Here we"—this the first dispatch ever sent, ever received; no, it is only a prophecy of the coming call and answer. Thirty-five centuries slip away before its fulfilment comes.

"He hath not dealt so with any nation." After having enumerated many good gifts in the preceding verses, and among them this word-running process, David closes the whole with the above. Now Morse's first message, or the first message ever sent over a wire, was: "See what God hath wrought!" Does it not look prophetic?

It is lightning that is controllable, biddable; that may be sent and will return; a lightning that can talk, and will do it. It comes to us a language of abbreviations. What are to be its achievements? Already the globe is nearly circumscribed by this wire netting. Our own country is traversed in every direction by them. These already span our eastern sea and tie us to Europe. When China and Japan lift their heads a little higher, San Francisco and our western coast will tie on to them, and, our lines stretching westward, the ends of the earth will become a unit. Job xxxvii. 3: "He directeth it [his voice] under the whole heaven, and his lightning unto the ends of the earth." "Ends of the earth." All the ends or extremities of the land masses of the earth. The sides of the earth reaped the first-fruit; now it is directing its course to the ends. "I was by him, . . . rejoicing always before him; rejoicing in the habitable part of his earth, and my delights were with the sons of men." Electricity furnishes the symbol of a high civilization. Wisdom delights to dwell here.

CHAPTER VII.

Indestructibility—Change of Earth's Surface—Vegetable Kingdom—Samson Burning the Wheat-Fields—Iron Chemically Considered.

INDESTRUCTIBILITY.

Philosophy teaches that indestructibility is a property that belongs to all matter that renders it incapable of being destroyed; that no particle of matter can be destroyed or annihilated, except by God, its Creator. It also teaches that no new matter has been created since the earth was made; that the world contains the same matter, with no new additions. Ecclesiastes i. 9: "The thing that hath been, it is that which shall be; . . . and there is no new thing under the sun." Ecclesiastes iii. 14: "I know that, whatsoever God doeth, it shall be forever: nothing can be put to it, nor anything taken from it."

"Whatsoever God doeth, it shall be forever." The indestructibility of matter and of force was never more definitely taught by any text-book. Matter and force are imperishable.

"Nothing can be put to it." The doctrine that the world contains no new accumulation of matter was never more definitely taught.

"Nor anything taken from it." No matter can be annihilated, except by God, its Creator. One of our great statesmen said: "We know of no way of judging the future but by the past." So thought Solomon. Ecclesiastes iii. 15: "That which hath been is

(135)

now; and that which is to be hath already been; and God requireth that which is past." Ecclesiasticus xviii. 6: "As for the wondrous works of the Lord, there may nothing be taken from them, neither may anything be put unto them, neither can the ground of them be found out." The doctrine of the indestructibility of matter is here taught in the very language of this day; and more, the impossibility of finding out the true basis of his wondrous works— not the atom, but a something beyond.

CHANGE OF EARTH'S SURFACE.

Geology teaches that powerful agencies are at work changing the face of the globe, tearing down and building up; that its surface has been remodeled time and again. Rocks, disintegrated by frost and heat, have been worn away by the waters and spread out into fertile valleys and plains, and rugged slopes of the mountains smoothed. Job xxviii. 9, 10: "He putteth forth his hand upon the rock; he overturneth the mountains by the roots. He cutteth out rivers among the rocks."

The three stages by which rivers bring about these changes are called (1) erosion — eating away the solid materials which form the channel of a river; (2) transportation—the carrying away of these materials; the lighter, finer particles are carried away mixed with the water; (3) deposits—when the river gives up its dissolved particles, and the heavier particles that can no longer be moved by the force of the stream stop, these make islands, deltas, and sometimes extend the seashore outward. "The erosive action of rivers is illustrated by the excavation of

rocky gorges. Those of Niagara and the cañons of
our Western rivers are the most striking examples
that can be offered. The falls of Niagara, it is evident, were at one period about seven miles lower
down the stream than they now are. The vast volume of water that passes over the falls erodes the
edge of the cliff over which it pours. Falling from
the height of about one hundred and sixty feet upon
the rocks below, it wears them away." "He cutteth
out rivers among the rocks."

Job xiv. 18, 19: "And surely the mountain falling
cometh to naught, and the rock is removed out of his
place. The waters wear the stones: thou washest
away the things which grow out of the dust of the
earth." Above we explained erosion; now we have
exemplified the second stage, transportation, carrying away these corroded stones and the things that
grow out of the earth in solution, and the rock
moved by the force of the current. "Within the recent period important geological changes have occurred and are still going on. The sea in some places
has encroached upon the land, and in others the land
has encroached upon the sea; so that the waves now
sweep over the sites of ancient cities, and bays and
arms of the sea have been transformed into solid
land. In 1399 Henry of Lancaster, afterward Henry IV., landed with his adherents at Raven Spur, on
the coast of Yorkshire. This was an ancient seaport which once rivaled Hull in commercial advan-
tages; yet nothing of it now remains but banks of
sand, which are covered by flood-tides. The Goodwin sands, so dangerous to mariners, constituted in
the eleventh century an extensive lordship, belong-

ing to the powerful Earl Goodwin. On the other hand, the place where Julius Cæsar landed when he invaded Britain is now far inland. Ostia, which in the time of the Romans was the port of the Tiber, is now three miles from the water. Great rivers are constantly carrying down to the coast immense quantities of earth, and cause the lands to gain upon the sea." Let us lay by this long quotation from geography a statement from David. Psalm cvii. 33-35: "He turneth rivers into a wilderness, and the water-springs into dry ground; a fruitful land into barrenness. . . . He turneth the wilderness into a standing water, and dry ground into water-springs." The expressions are so similar, one and the same truth being set forth by each, that these passages need no comment, no explanation.

THE VEGETABLE KINGDOM.

Psalm civ. 14: "He causeth the grass to grow for the cattle, and herb for the service of man." When we consider the great variety of herbs, the ten thousand ways in which they serve man, we must regard it as a very great, a very essential, blessing. They are so nicely adapted to gratify man's every physical want that the sentence "he causeth herb to grow for the service of man" expresses all. Says the botanist: "Vegetation extends all over the globe, existing under the most diversified conditions of heat and light and moisture." "The Greeks were acquainted with five hundred species of plants, but at the present day botanists enumerate one hundred and twentythousand, and the list is constantly increasing with the explorations of new regions of the earth." Like man and his wants, they are almost innumerable, and are found wherever man goes. Certainly they were created for the service of man. Says Michel: "It is frequently the case that where a particular form of disease prevails Providence has caused the specific to abound." Says Carpenter: "It would be wrong not to contemplate the important inferences which may be drawn from the vegetable kingdom in regard to the power, wisdom, and goodness of the Almighty Designer. His power is remarkably displayed in the immense variety of products elaborated out of three simple elements—viz., oxygen, hydrogen, and carbon. His wisdom is strikingly evinced in diffusing these products over the whole globe, and his goodness is peculiarly manifested in the adaptation of these products to the use of man." "Aside from furnishing food, clothing, and medicine, it ministers most bountifully to the gratification of man's more refined senses and to the wants of his higher nature. Balsams and resins yield their grateful fragrance, and flowers and blossoms in every habitable clime fill the air with delicious odors. The floras of the globe present to the eye countless and varied forms of grace and beauty, and glow with such rich and delicate combinations of tint and hue as no art can rival, and which it is among its highest attainments simply to imitate."

"And herb for the service of man." Ecclesiasticus xxxviii. 3-7: "The skill of the physician shall lift up his head: and in the sight of great men he shall be in admiration. The Lord hath created medicines out of the earth; and he that is wise will not abhor them. Was not the water made sweet with wood,

that the virtue thereof might be known? And he
hath given men skill, that he might be honored in
his marvelous works. With such doth he heal
[men,] and taketh away their pains."

SAMSON BURNING THE WHEAT-FIELDS.

The mother of Samson was directed to abstain
from wine, for she was to bear a son who would be
noted for greater strength than any other man. The
use of wine by her would impare the strength of the
coming son. Prohibitionists teach that it enfeebles
the strong who take it. Revelation teaches that it
begins its work even on unborn sons. What a terror
is this beast that preys upon us in three worlds!
When a boy I heard a man say, speaking of Samson
burning the wheat-field, that such a thing was impossible, that standing wheat would not burn. Several
thousand acres were burned near Modesto, Cal., July
12, 1884. It was with difficulty that the fire was extinguished. I am told that some wheat farms in Cal-
ifornia raise many thousand bushels of wheat each
year, some even a million bushels. In this section
we can form but little conception of the size of such
a heap. How is it thrashed? That is part of what
we started to tell. It was done, reader, by a machine
which Isaiah saw on private exhibition in the land
of Judah seven hundred and fifty-eight years before
Christ. Isaiah xli. 15, 16: "Behold, I will make thee
a new sharp thrashing instrument having teeth:
thou shalt thrash the mountains [great stacks], and
beat them small, and shalt make the hills [shocks or
small stacks] as chaff. Thou shalt fan them, and
the wind [steam power, the same that thrashed and

fanned] shall carry them away [from the fields], and the whirlwind [fast trains or ships] shall scatter them [send them to a bread-eating world]." Yes, that is a prophecy. Is it literal or figurative language? Figurative. A figure of what?

IRON CHEMICALLY CONSIDERED.

Job xxviii. 1, 2: "Surely there is a vein for the silver, and a place for gold where they fine it. Iron is taken out of the earth, and brass is molten out of the stone."

"Surely there is a vein for the silver." This needs no comment. It is thus that this metal is found in many localities in the Eastern continent. Those in Hungary and Sweden are among the richest. The western hemisphere far exceeds the eastern in its yield of silver. In South America, amid the heights of the Andes, this chiefly occurs. Copiapo, in Chili, is the richest. Silver was discovered in this region in 1832. Sixteen veins were found, and lumps of pure metal were gathered from the surface of the soil. A single mass was obtained which weighed five thousand pounds. "Surely there is a vein for the silver." This statement of Solomon's meets the conditions of the western hemisphere just the same.

"A place for gold where they fine it." Humboldt remarked many years ago that most of the gold of the globe is found in mountain ranges running in a direction from north to south. Since then this theory has been remarkably corroborated by the gold-fields of every country. "Where they fine it." Nature's forces, for it comes to us in the most part in a native or pure state.

"Iron is taken out of the earth." Let us see how this is done, that we may test the truth of Job's assertion. "It is thought by many chemists that all iron ores are of marsh origin. The growth of this so-called bog iron is as follows: Iron is contained in the soil in slight amounts as ferric oxid, or common iron-rust, which is insoluble in water. But if there is vegetable matter present in the water, it deoxidizes the iron, changing it to the soluble ferrous oxid. On exposure to the atmosphere the iron takes up the rejected oxygen again, and with it water, becoming ferric hydrate. This, being insoluble, is deposited at the bottom of the pond." Thus, by a chemical process, iron is actually taken out of the earth. This is the theory of the nineteenth century, and Job's theory was four thousand years before. "Knowest thou it, because thou wast then born? or because the number of thy days is great?" Silver is found in veins. Gold comes to us from a refinery. Brass is molten out of the stones. These have special places, and are found in these places the world over. But iron is taken out of the earth. How common are these localities where iron is found! Here is found indisputable evidence of design and a beneficent Designer. It is a fair standard by which we measure national advancement; it is the symbol of civilization. It "is taken out of the earth." Everywhere its abundance indicates how indispensable the Creator deemed it to the education and development of man. Its abundance, like its uses, is universal.

> " Iron vessels cross the ocean,
> Iron engines give them motion,
> Iron needles northward veering,

Iron tillers vessels steering,
Iron pipes our gas delivers,
Iron bridges span our rivers,
Iron pens are used for writing,
Iron stoves for cooking victuals,
Iron ovens, pots, and kettles,
Iron horses draw our loads,
Iron rails compose our roads,
Iron anchors hold in sands,
Iron bolts and rods and bands,
Iron houses, iron walls,
Iron cannon, iron balls,
Iron axes, knives, and chains,
Iron augers, saws, and planes,
Iron globules in our blood,
Iron particles in food,
Iron lightning-rods on spires,
Iron telegraphic wires,
Iron hammers, nails, and screws,
Iron everything we use."

CHAPTER VIII.

Psalm xix. 1-7: "The heavens declare the glory of God; and the firmament showeth his handiwork. Day unto day uttereth speech, and night unto night showeth knowledge. There is no speech nor language, where their voice is not heard. Their line is gone out through all the earth, and their words to the end of the world. In them hath he set a tabernacle for the sun, which is as a bridegroom coming out of his chamber, and rejoiceth as a strong man to run a race. His going forth is from the end of the heaven, and his circuit unto the ends of it: and there is nothing hid from the heat thereof. The law of the Lord is perfect, converting the soul: the testimony of the Lord is sure, making wise the simple."

While we design examining each topic separately, it will be well first to notice the text in general, making a short and concise interpretation. The Psalmist begins with the heavens. We hope that you will notice the plurality here as compared to the same term used in the singular below—that is, firmament. The heavens, all the visible, starry worlds, declare. Then he descends to the aerial heaven or firmament. Though this is invisible, still it shows something of God. Approaching apparently nearer, to at least within the range of the ear, he cites our minds to days that talk, then removes the field of knowledge

(144)

as far as the scope or range of the eye exceeds the
scope or range of the ear. The days lecture; the
nights afford object-lessons; then follow five signifi-
cant terms. - In order to get a true understanding of
these terms we must consider them to matter just
what they are to us: names of communicable forces.
As names of forces in nature we determine the province of each by analysis of its lettered parts, just as
we determine the properties of matter and its make-
up. *Word* is to matter just what it is to us. It goes
from one particle to another just as my word goes
from me to you; matter words go from particle to
particle till all the earth hears, then on to the end
of the world. Now it is motion. The sun's tabernacle stands in the things that before were names;
they lead it along a limited circuit. Then as a great
amen the Psalmist declares this text to be just what
we shall try to interpret it to be: "the law of the
Lord," the physical law. These are the testimonies
of the Lord; these make wise the simple. The whole
is the grandest picture ever painted on any canvas.
It is a gallery of word features orderly arranged,
which, when viewed through a glass, give us by synthesis the whole of one great picture, the law of
gravitation, while the individual features are lost in
the blending of colors.

"The heavens declare the glory of God." The ex-
actitude with which the terms "heaven" and "heavens" are used in the Scriptures, when properly considered, will excite to wonder and astonishment the
best-thinking minds of the world and stamp their
use as a direct inspiration.

"Heavens," as used in the plural, is susceptible of

10

two meanings. First, the firmament with vapors diffused—Genesis ii.1: "Thus the heavens and the earth were finished, and all the host of them." Host here refers to the things that live in the air, water, and on the land. Fourth verse of same chapter: "These are the generations of the heavens and of the earth when they were created, in the day that the Lord God made the earth and the heavens." The generations enumerated by Moses are the generations here spoken of—Deuteronomy xxxiii. 28: "Also his heavens shall drop down dew." Job xxxv. 5: "Look unto the heavens, and see; and behold the clouds which are higher than thou." Psalm lxxiii. 9: "They set their mouth against the heavens" — the cloud. Secondly, it refers to a plurality of suns or systems, or to all these creations—Job ix. 8: "Which alone spreadeth out the heavens, and treadeth upon the waves of the sea." The work of spreading out the heavens, all the starry worlds. Isaiah xiii. 13: "Therefore I will shake the heavens, and the earth shall remove out of her place." This is a figure illustrating the dissolution of worlds. Isaiah xxxiv. 4: "And all the host of heaven shall be dissolved, and the heavens shall be rolled together as a scroll." The members of our system shall be dissolved first, and the heavens, all the systems, shall roll up. Isaiah xlviii. 13: "Mine hand also hath laid the foundation of the earth, and my right hand hath spanned the heavens." The passages that refer to the starry worlds as heavens are very limited when we review the great number of passages where this word is used. "Heaven" used in the singular when speaking of worlds refers to our system. See opening verse

in the Bible, the Ten Commandments, and many other places.

"The glory of God" is made clear or plain by the
declaration of this immeasurable vault, filled as it
seems with worlds and set with suns, stationed with
a geometrical nicety, and moving in unbroken harmony in obedience to laws that are recognized and
obeyed by the smallest grain of sand, or that sway
the brightest suns, that break the high arms of revolving spheres and control mighty caravans of
worlds as though they were but single grains or the
smallest atoms. These make clear his glory; not
alone for his power to create the materials of which
they are composed, but more especially do they make
plain his glory through the beauty and perfection of
those laws that govern them, for these are the
thoughts of God himself. We can only understand
and interpret these declarations so far as we understand the laws that control them. It is thus that
these sublime declarations, emanating from the stars,
can reach our minds and give to us the glory of God.
These twinkling stars can do it no other way; they
would be but disordered torches scattered throughout the great abyss around and above us; for when
we consider that the distance to the nearest star is
too great for the most powerful telescope to develop
a visible disk, it becomes an idle, empty gaze from
which no declarations of glory can ever come. We
are taught in the text that "night unto night showeth knowledge." Knowledge is the vocalizing force
that interprets these declarations and makes them
full of meaning. "The heavens declare the glory of
God." As these things have organs of speech or

are able to communicate to others by words, then these communicate to us by words. What do they say to us? The millions of ether waves that dance upon our eyes from these far-off worlds say: "Glory! glory!"

'Tis the triumph of law that brought us hither
And holds those spheres in the far-off thither.

They say that "cheerful obedience to God's law is the greatest glory that his subjects can give him." These are great object-lessons of obedience and its results. David winds up with "the law of the Lord is perfect." What law? The law that holds stars in place.

"The firmament showeth his handiwork." This is the aerial heaven, the air. The subject of investigation is now brought nearer, for we are called to his handiwork, a tidy, delicate, intricate work which the air must show. David has varied the terms "heavens" and "firmament" so appropriately, so beautifully nice, that we feel that he must have comprehended these things in a philosophical sense, or he never could have made this nice distinction. Moses makes the same nice distinction—Genesis i. 8: "And God called the firmament Heaven;" not "heavens," as David calls that which declares his glory. Genesis i. 1: "In the beginning God created the heaven and the earth." This can not be the heaven spoken of in the eighth verse, nor can it be the firmament, for that was not created at all. This is the solar system. Genesis ii. 1: "Thus the heavens and the earth were finished, and all the host of them." We consider this the plural of our present topic, or more particularly the air, vapors, and clouds. The hosts are the things that fill the air, water, and land. Genesis ii. 4:

"These are the generations of the heavens and of
the earth." Then he names plants, herbs, etc., and
the fowls, birds, beasts, and the things of the sea
and land—these "the host of them." But the firmament or air showeth. The air is invisible, and it is
quite evident that David knew it. "Showeth" means
to teach, to instruct. How strange that the world
would let two thousand years or more slip by without giving one inquiring look to the air! Patient
study of the air for nearly three hundred years, the
new and frequent developments, fruits of this search,
attest the truth that "the firmament showeth his
handiwork." One jesting remark of Galileo about
the middle of the seventeenth century turned the
minds of Pascal and Torricelli to the study of the air.
Great good resulted from it. A handiwork is one
done by hand. Were the air even a chemical compound, this would detract from the thought. Says
the chemist: "The atmosphere is not a chemical mixture, but a mechanical mixture." It is the work of
a handy mechanic. David declares that it showeth
this. "He giveth the winds their weight, and he
weigheth the waters by measure." The waters here
mentioned are the waters of that invisible ocean
which stands upon the land and upon the waters
that were below the firmament, a work executed
when he said: "Let there be a firmament in the midst
of the waters." How delicate must have been the
balance, how evenly held the hand that adjusted the
weight, how nice the calculation that gave to these
waters their place in the firmament and apportioned
their parts and fitted each to each, if we take philosophy for it! It teaches that "the air contains in

ratio by volume about seventy-nine parts of nitrogen and twenty-one parts of oxygen in every one
hundred parts of dry air, and with them is mingled
a small quantity of carbonic acid gas."

He fits these invisible elements in proportions that
are nearly invariable. By investigation we are able
to test and see and comprehend the truth that it is a
handiwork. The very air becomes teacher, showeth,
instructs us by its movements, products, and combinations of its invisible elements. The splendor of
the worlds above us, their varying lights and shades
of colors, their regular motions, their great numbers,
and their wonderful distances fill us with awe and
astonishment. And we give him glory, a glory as
to one perfect in knowledge. The unphilosophic
eye, looking out upon the broad expanse on a bright,
clear night, might involuntarily make the declaration, "The heavens declare the glory of God!" but
"the firmament showeth his handiwork" involves too
much philosophy for the untutored mind, and would
show it nothing; it would be but a misty, mazy gaze,
returning empty-handed, feeling nothing of that
pleasing conception shown in his handiwork. Investigation alone can develop this. The beauty of
his handiwork is seen only as we trace law in its
certain windings among particles many times too
small to be seen by the most powerful glass, and as
we find it binding with a powerful grip those invisible atoms, making a compound differing from the
elements composing it. The atoms cling with great
force, while the molecules move among each other
with greater freedom than any liquid. "In order to
decompose carbonic acid in our laboratories we are

obliged to resort to the most powerful chemical agents and to conduct this process in vessels composed of the most resisting metals, under all the violent manifestations of light and heat, and we succeed in liberating the carbon only by shutting up the oxygen in a still stronger prison; but under the quiet influences of the sunbeam, and in that most delicate of all structures, a vegetable cell, the chains which unite together the two elements fall off, and, while the solid carbon is retained to build up the organic structure, the oxygen is allowed to return to its home in the atmosphere. There is not in the whole range of chemistry a process more wonderful than this. We return to it again and again with ever-increasing wonder and admiration, amazed at the apparent inefficiency of the means and the stupendous magnitude of the result. When standing before a grand conflagration, witnessing the display of mighty energies there in action, and seeing the elements rush into combination with a force which no human agency can withstand, does it seem as if any power could undo that work of destruction and rebuild those beams and rafters which are disappearing in the flames? Yet in a few years they will be rebuilt. This mighty force will overcome. Not, however, as we might expect, amidst the convulsions of nature or the clashing of elements, but silently, in a delicate leaf waving in the sunshine." (Cook.) The starry worlds preach his glory, obedience to law. The delicacy of his handiwork is seen as we trace this law through the unstable, invisible air, like strange, sweet visions that steal upon us in peaceful, half-sleeping dreams. The physical senses comprehend nothing in all the firmament, but perception sees law enthroned on each of its atoms. . "The law of the Lord is perfect." What law? The law of the air.

The knowledge to be gained in the following part of this discussion is, more strictly speaking, a word interpretation than all the other questions we have been pleased to investigate. The word is weighed from inarticulation to the boundless variety of languages; its growth from the inarticulate on through the various combinations of letters to make words, the combinations of these words to make sentences, the combinations of sentences to make a book. In the other balance we place the smallest particle of matter as built up by the atoms, from a combination of these particles to the various substances, from a combination of substances to a world. More, there is beyond this fitting comparison an interphilosophical meaning of motion, force, and weight, and a proportion as truly correct as is that given by Newton's great law. The words that have these peculiar meanings are voice, speech, words, language, and line. No intelligible interpretation of our text can be given if we neglect or fail to observe closely the dependent relation of each to each and the one (the vocal or written) to the other (the material). If these are properly weighed and considered, then no words in our language are more fruitful or present a higher proof of David's inspiration than the selection of these terms.

"Day unto day uttereth speech." In our first topic we heard with intellectual ears the declarations of glory as they fall from the ever-exhorting stars above us. In our second topic we saw with intellectual eyes the work of the very hand that wrought all these. Now we are brought into communion with talking things around us, things that talk without ceasing. Our ears and eyes are the open avenues that bring to us material from which we make all our deductions. "Day unto day"—without cessation; no place is without it; unlimited as to time or space. It is true that the earth has its habitable and its uninhabitable parts, yet everywhere alike these utterances go on. Its utterance is speech. If faith comes by hearing, and if by faith we know how the worlds were framed, put together, then these daily sermons, utterances of speech, will impart to us this faith, and we shall see how the worlds were framed, put together. It is the utterance of inanimate things to inanimate things that we hear; or, more truly, the utterances of material to material; for these are the things we see, that utter — the speech of matter. "Day unto day." Light develops it. It is not addressed to the ear, for this organ is as acute by night as by day. It is a speech to be seen by intellectual eyes, or we hear it with intellectual ears. We hear it as definitely when we see it so unmistakably as we would should it fall in thunder peals from every material object beneath, above, around us. Speech to these silent objects is just what it is to man. It makes man more distinguished than all other animals. It is the center of the social, the political, the financial, and the moral world. It is the enervating force that gives life to every enterprise, that draws us together in our every relation to each other. It binds us to one common center of thought; it gives permanence to every thought. It is the medium of direct communication. Speech is the same with every nation and tribe on the globe. There are said to be about eighty languages and over three thousand dialects; yet to all these alike speech is the one common needful thing, emanating from the same cause, produced in the same manner, to answer the same end: to make the world of man one as a grand whole, composed of families distinguished by language. So to matter it is the one common thing, from the smallest particle to the grandest system. It is that which makes the world of matter a unit, one grand whole composed of boundless materials, distinguished by matter's language. The story never ends; it goes forth in one universal symbol, "speech," that needs only to be converted into words and a language to individualize it, to readily interpret it. Speech is a representative term; from it every language springs. Speech is the representative force of matter, gravitation; from it every communicable force in matter springs. Gravitation is speech; its utterances never cease. It is matter's tongue, and is found where and only where matter is found. Matter in its composition, its molecular structure, may differ; but only, and precisely only, as one language differs from another. Their peculiar structure alone makes them differ, as the peculiar structure of speech makes languages differ. These structures, either in matter or language, are brought to a common level; the one by universal gravitation, the other by universal speech.

"Day unto day uttereth speech." There is never a day that we fail to hear this speech; it is gravity,

gravity, gravity. It invests everything. Walking
is the process of falling, and falling is the yielding to
the influence of gravity. Proverbs vi. 13: "He speak-
eth with his feet." Every time the foot falls its
speech is gravity. This force brings to the ground
all unsupported bodies. The falling leaves speak
it in terms too plain to be misunderstood. We hear
it in the drifting snow and the pattering rain. All
matter is influenced by it, is filled with it. We see it
everywhere, in everything. There is not one single
hour of any day of any year that we fail to hear this
speech. It is without question the speech that came
to Galileo sitting in the cathedral at Pisa watching the vibrations of a bronze chandelier which hung
from the ceiling. It was gravity as seen in falling
bodies and in the motions of the pendulum. A falling apple whispered "gravity" in the ear of Newton.
His soul caught the philosophic fire, which gave him
the sublime music of the spheres and enabled him to
write in its own tongue its own law. "Every particle of matter in the universe attracts every other particle of matter with a force directly proportional to
its quantity of matter and decreasing as the square
of the distance apart increases." The moving chandelier and the falling apple thus talking to the earth
were the parents of great laws. Day unto day the
schoolroom doors stand open, and these object-
lessons are continually being presented as inanimate
things speak to each other. It is the speech of the
dumb, truly one of signs. Through these signs we
acquaint ourselves with all matter, and thus we see
only beauty and harmony as told by the unconscious speaking of objects around us. These do the

same thing everywhere, every time, under the same surroundings. There is no variation. "The law of the Lord is perfect.''

"Night unto night showeth knowledge." "Showeth," as in a preceding topic, signifies investigation. Every night since the fourth day of creation has opened above the book of knowledge. The fact that the world by its night watchings did glean here its richest fund of human knowledge is strong proof of prophetic breathing on the Psalmist, and even lends credence to our feeble interpretation. The progressive steps in each are similar. Galileo saw the motions of the lamp—to him a speech. The next step was to get knowledge out of this. Newton saw the apple fall—to him a speech; now he wants knowledge. So each alike rushed to the same field, that field which night alone opens, presenting the high authority of satellites, planets, suns, and systems. Alike each sought an interpretation first from the moon; then alike each passed to the other heavenly bodies, calculating and testing their orbits night unto night. For seventeen years Kepler watched the planet Mars in its night marches till it showed him, astronomers say, the richest fund of human knowledge, and he is accredited the highest achievements of the human mind. David pointed out the great field where knowledge is kept on free public exhibition. Strange to say, not a man looked for three thousand years. Stranger still, when one did look, in his search he followed the order as laid down by David, and developed the same laws as the ones here spoken of. Still, every night, these object-lessons, this panoramic show, appear in the blue vault. As one picture files out another dances on the canvas, bidding us get knowledge, get knowledge. Great minds obeyed; with strong arms they swept away the mystery that had shrouded the stars. They heard the speech, the song which the stars have been singing since the first dawn, when the morning stars began this song (speech) and all the suns of God raised their shouts of joy: "Glory! glory! glory!" All matter is full of sublime music tuned to catch our ears, feeding our intellectual selves with the richest feasts of knowledge and pouring into our inward selves the glory of an infinite God who wrought all these things for the children of men. "The law of the Lord is perfect."

"There is no speech nor language where their voice is not heard." Now we are confronted with three of the terms mentioned above. There must be some common connection between the terms expressing our knowledge and the visible acts of all matter from which this knowledge is gained. Scientists say that we are to study ourselves by the same methods that we study other phenomena of nature. They have demonstrated that living beings are not aliens and exceptions in the universe, but parts of a wonderful plan. Gravitation makes the world a unit; it is matter's speech that enables particle to talk to particle within our physical organisms just as particles do in the world without. This brings a closer connection between us and the outer world and aids our comprehensions perhaps to understand their wonderful doings. The outside world, by an ingenious lense, which is composed of particles of matter, focuses all these visible objects on the retina, which,

too, is of the focusing material; here the living eye
reads. The living wall that holds this eye has just
what other matter has: light, heat, weight, motion,
etc.; all of which are governed by the same laws
that govern particles of matter outside of us. The
body is common property of the physical, the moral,
and intellectual forces. The relation of these forces
is very similar to that of husband and wife, as
they live in the same house. Every conception is
an heir of its mother, the physical force, fathered by
intellectuality. Man was made a *little* lower than
the angels. When we consider that the matter which
composes his *made* parts is endued with living and
immortal forces that meet his high, living, immortal,
and angelic forces in organized matter, we justly
comprehend the term "a *little* lower than the angels."
Could he not be brought in contact with these by and
through the body, then he would have been made a
vast deal lower than the angels. Through kinship
of my material self with all matter* and my kinship with angels I commune with the smallest invisible atom or with suns too remote to present a
discernible disk through the most powerful glass.
It is from the behavior of the objects we see that
we deduce the laws that govern them. These things
only, make all human learning. The behavior of
matter is its language. I understand just in proportion to my ability to interpret matter's doings. I see
a stone fall to the ground, and I ask: "What did
you say, Mr. Stone?" "Gravity," says the stone.
This is its speech. Every body that falls, and every
body that would fall were it not prevented, would

---

* See note at close of this chapter.

say precisely the same thing. Gravity! How strange
that this word was selected to denote that force
which produces this downward tendency seen in all
things! To-day our authors can not assign a reason
why so called. It is only a speech. Then accept it
from David as a prophecy for the name of that universal force called gravity. "There is no speech nor
language where their voice is not heard." There is
no gravity nor cohesion where there is no matter.
Then there is a speech and a language wherever matter does exist. Matter not only talks to matter,
but a world in our sight communicates to our powers
tidings from one beyond our vision; we have proof
of this divine telegraphy and its correct interpretation. Perturbations in the planet Uranus led to the
discovery of Neptune. Herschel made this an-
nouncement touching this matter: "Trembling motions have been felt along the far-reaching line of
our analysis, with a certainty not far inferior to oc-
ular demonstration." The problem that followed
was this: "Given the disturbance produced by the attraction of the unknown planet, to find its orbit and
its place in the orbit." Two young mathematicians
(Le Verrier, of Paris, and Adams, of Cambridge, England) undertook, each unknown to the other, to find
by figures the place of this new planet. The disturbances in Uranus were observed at a distance of one
billion, seven hundred and fifty-four million miles
from the earth; while the planet talking to Uranus
was a billion miles beyond. Le Verrier, having only
the characters of this communication as given to
Uranus, returned to Paris, figured out its place in its
orbit and the time of its coming. Astronomers, hav-

ing faith in his prophecy, were watching for the new planet when it came into sight. We are akin. Force —the living spirit of matter born of the spirit that moved upon the face of the waters and filled and sent six worlds full of life on their mission of life— was the same that breathed into man the breath of life and made him a living soul. Now, as the whole is based upon the relation that these terms bear to each other and the conformity of relations of the forces of matter to each other and of these terms to these forces, we will try to explain here. The terms voice, speech, words, language, line, in the spoken or written word are absolutely dependent upon the above order; that which follows depends every time on that which precedes; not more so to the make-up of a speech or a sermon than certain forces do to the make-up of a world or the boundless systems of worlds and suns. These forces are affinity, molecular attraction, adhesion, universal attraction. The written word and the visible world present a striking similarity in their formation. The relations of the separate parts of the written word are the relations that the parts of the visible world or worlds sustain to each other. The alphabet of the written word is only visible signs of invisible sounds, which alone, with a few exceptions, do not materialize. They only do so when united in conformity to a law of likes and unlikes, with reference only to their vocalization—that is, every syllable must have a vowel or vowels, and may have one or more consonants; then each syllable must have a vowel and a consonant, excluding the exceptions mentioned above. The story of Cadmus introducing letters is

the story of the chemist's atoms; these are matter's
alphabet. There are known sixty-six of these matter
letters. These atoms are invisible, and are only
manifest by the things that we see around us. So
the things that we see are signs of invisible atoms.
We said that our letters were signs of invisible
sounds that only materialize when united into a
word. The same is true of the matter alphabet;
we see the sign of their existence only when joined
together. Our written word is made up of vowels
and consonants, unlike in vocalization. In the chemical gradation of effects of affinity things most alike
are most feebly attracted, while the wider the difference the stronger the affinity. Vowels and consonants, being unlike, must be combined according to
the law of unlikes to make strong the word. So the
law that unites letters to make words is the divine
orthography of matter. This is affinity. The smallest particle of matter is framed of atoms as a word
of letters. In the former we have a molecule of
matter; in the latter, a molecule of a language. It
thus rises to a system or a great book. To illustrate,
I take the smallest particle of salt that can exist
alone. I am told that it is composed of two atoms
(letters), chlorin and sodium, mechanically joined as
are the two letters in the word *no*. The word *no*
does not look like *n* or *o*, nor is the pronunciation of
no the pronunciation *n* or *o*. When separated they
are only meaningless sounds. The very second they
are thus joined all the English-speaking world says
"no." This word has its place in the make-up of our
communications, and is as potent as a molecule of
matter in a substance. Let us join these two letters

11

otherwise and we have *on*. We have the same letters as before. The pronunciation of these letters
individually is the same; combined, the pronunciation is widely different and has a meaning quite as
foreign. The way letters are united to make words
helps to make in part the variety of words that form
our vocabulary. The same is true in combining
atoms to make matter words. For a long time if
two substances of different properties were found,
upon analysis, to have one composition, it was held
that the experimenter must have erred. But so constant and increasing were such results as at length
to establish the fact that bodies of the same composition may still have different properties. For this
reason such bodies are termed isomeric. For example, the fragrant oil of roses and the chief illumi-
nating constituent of common street gas are isomeric: a compound atom of each consists of four
atoms of carbon and four of hydrogen. To explain
this we are compelled to assume that the constituent
atoms of a compound may have different arrange-
ments. The same atoms which if grouped in one way
give rise to one substance, if grouped in another way
give rise to a different substance. Then the things
that we see are not composed of the things that do
appear. The apostle Paul was not unmindful of this
truth in a philosophical sense. Hebrews xi. 3:
"Through faith we understand that the worlds were
framed by the word of God, so that things which are
seen were not made of things which do appear."
Faith was the glass through which Paul saw and
understood that worlds are the framed work of God
to the *word*, authority, pattern, or model. Frame

means just what we are talking about: putting things in a regular structure. We thank the great apostle for his enlargement. Worlds, all, are put together this way; not chemically mixed, put together, framed. There can be no more a chemical mixture of atoms to form a substance than a chemical mixture of letters to form an English word. Now the thing that did this work of framing worlds we said was *word* and a model. As such atom joined atom, molecule joined molecule, bulk to bulk, world to world, system to system, heaven to heaven, by word, the direct product of voice, speech, words, language, symbolical of affinity, gravity, cohesion, and adhesion. Similarly the law of construction or synthesis that unites words into sentences is the divine grammar seen in the united molecules that make a substance. The law of arrangement of topics in a great discourse finds its parallel in the logical arrangement of the boundless substances that make the world a unit. The line upon which the least letter in a book stands is the same line upon which every word, every sentence, every topic that makes the book stands, and is similar to that upon which every particle of matter, every substance, the combination of substances, the world, all the worlds, stand.

All the chemists, all the philosophers, during all the ages will never move these corner-stones; they may learn more of these things and build higher, add decoration to decoration as they find God here, there, everywhere, as their eyes turn to his visible creations. The world will improve our feeble interpretation, but Paul's atomic theory never. He offered in this the provisions that will feed through an endless life. Manifestations of his inspiration in the very offer are seen in his ability to know how the worlds were framed. Without doubt the world is forced to accept the physical truths offered by him. How, then, can it reject the proffers of life? The former will abide till general ruin dissolves the framed elements; the latter will be no older when this event takes place. So we live in a world of deaf-mutes having voice, speech, language as communicable as the lettered sheets that hold to view our harvests of learning as gathered from these. They tell their stories in signs, they are perpetuated only in signs. This pantomime goes on wherever matter exists. Man tells in signs all their doings, then studies his signs that he may know the make-up of the bodies of the players.

Let us look to the spoken word. This is invisible, yet audible, and thus finds a comparison in nature's vocalizing forces, which are also invisible. Let us pair these as we design comparing them. Voice, affinity, speech, gravity, language, cohesion; languages, adhesion. The written word and visible world may in their separate make-up be paired thus: Letters, atoms; words composed of letters, molecules composed of atoms. Sentences are built up by letters being joined to make words and words to form sentences; a substance is built up by atoms uniting to form a molecule and these molecules united to form a substance. A language is a peculiar mode of communication belonging to the same tongue; a substance is a separate and a distinct kind of matter. All our languages combined make our speaking or writing world; all the substances combined make our matter world. Thus the book of nature was compiled and sent on its mission; thus "the heavens declare the glory of God." These show the wisdom of a great Logician and make plain his exegesis.

"There is no speech nor language, where their voice is not heard." There is no gravity nor cohesion where there is no affinity. There is no weight, no substance, where there are no atoms. Without voice there can be no speech; without speech there can be no language. The atom is the parent of all matter; without it none of the things we see could be.

As we said, it is their boundless combinations that fill space with both matter and motion, both of which spring into life when atoms come together. See here are two separate atoms, letters; they come together, producing the first element of matter or the first element of speech. Affinity is matter's voice. Language, cohesion, makes bulks of likes; this gives us the various substances that make the world. Those who speak the same tongue are said to have the same language. Languages differ as substances differ. Some substances are noted for strength; others, for weakness. The same is true with the languages. Draw the comparison where you will, and the same similarity is found. While looking at the material the philosopher sees the forces that make a substance. These are attractive forces from the first, and these forces are measured by the substance. We see, too, it is attractive forces that make special communities and hold them to one and the same language. A repellent force breaks up substances, and may even destroy the language. Repellent forces may break up a community and de-

stroy a language. The Celts and Babel offer high
examples. This is cohesion; we study it as we study
a language. Position, surroundings, and contact
make the different substances; so position, surrounding, and contact make the various languages. To
man speech is universal, based on voice; voice is the
material of which speech is made. To matter gravity is universal, based on affinity; language is local, cohesion is local. Where there is no voice there
is no speech nor language; where there is no affinity
there is no weight, no attraction. If there is a spot
in space where matter does not exist, then there is
no voice, no speech, no language. It teaches that
there is no reciprocity between a void and a world
or a void and even the smallest particle of matter.

"Their line is gone out through all the earth, and
their words to the end of the world." "Their line."
Whose line is this that has gone out through all the
earth? Speech and language. Gone out through
all the earth, every particle. To go out through
every particle—no possible hypothesis other than to
assume the earth a sphere will satisfy this statement. More, this influence must be conceived as beginning at the center. If it does not begin at the
center, or if the earth is not round, the influence
would in some parts go in before it could go out.
The center of the globe is the only possible starting-
point from which this line could go out through
every particle. It goes out as sound in spheres.

"Line." In the previous pages, when we talked
of the make-up of matter and written language, we
placed the written words on lines ruled on the paper.
If in print these words are placed in line just the

same, these lines are to direct the operation. So from the center outward these lines run till every particle stands upon a line. These go to the end of the world. This takes in the whole system of created globes, the universe. Let us compare with Newton as we advance: "Every particle of matter in the universe attracts every other particle of matter." If we consider these lines in connection with these forces, it becomes the measuring instrument, as size and distance apart vary the influence.

In speaking of the attractive force Mr. Steele says: "It may help us to conceive how the earth is supported if we imagine the sun letting down a huge cable (line) and every star in the heavens a tiny thread (line) to hold our globe in its place; while it in turn sends back a cable (line) to the sun and a thread (line) to every one of the stars. So we are bound to them (by lines) and they to us (by lines). Thus the worlds throughout space are linked together by these cords (lines), mutual attraction, which, interweaving in every direction, make the world a unit." Then their line, cable cord, thread, is gone out through all the earth and their words to the end of the world, and a mutual attraction established with all the stars. "Every particle of matter in the universe attracts every other particle." We defined "word" as signifying the smallest particle of matter that could exist alone.

"And their words to the end of the world." Whose words? Speech and language. We awarded to language the thought of substance as manifested by cohesion. If we extend it beyond the earth, it becomes general and symbolizes a system. The lesson teaches

that all matter in the universe is built up in the same
way and governed by the same laws. "Words go"
as sound travels. Speech influences by word-travel-
ing or influences as sound from a line or cord. The
pitch of the fundamental sound of a musical string
is found by experience to depend on three circumstances: the length of the line or string, its tension,
and the weight or quantity of matter in the string.
Three things influence gravity (speech). To illustrate, the diameter of Venus is a thousand miles
shorter than the diameter of the earth. The volume
of Venus is about four-fifths that of the earth, while
its density is about the same. A pound weight carried from the earth's equator to the equator of Venus
would weigh about five-sixths of a pound. This
shows that the force of gravity does not decrease exactly in proportion to the size of the planet any
more than it increases with the mass of the sun.
The reason of this is that the body is brought nearer
the mass of the small planet, and so feels its attraction more fully than when far out upon the extreme
circumference of a large body. The attraction increases as the square of the distance from the particles (words) decreases. Then the three things upon
which gravity depends are distance, mass, and
weight. Distance apart to the length of the cord;
density to the tension of the cord, and weight of
body to weight of cord; to the cord as its weight
varies with its density so the pitch of that cord varies. Let us suppose A and B two bodies in space.
Let us connect these bodies by two cords; that the
weight of one cord represent the weight of A, while
the density of that cord be the density of A, and the

other cord represent the weight of B and the density of this cord be the density of B. The one represents the force of gravity of A for B, and the other the force of gravity of B for A. If the force exercised between these two bodies is directly as the product of their masses, so the pitch of the two sounds produced by these two cords must be to each other as the product of their masses. These strings were of the same length, varying only in tension. If this be true, the pitch from these cords would vary as we move A and B toward or from each other. The intensity of sound decreases as the square of the distance increases. The force of gravity decreases as the square of the distance increases. So with the lengthening or shortening of the musical cord. "Every particle of matter in the universe attracts every other particle of matter with a force directly proportional to its quantity of matter and decreasing as the square of the distance increases." Newton made the attraction between particles. We said that "word" was made of atom letters, and was the smallest particle of language. These, in one sense, go to the end of the world — that is, all matter in the universe is built up in the same way. If you would know how, begin with our alphabet, and a few months of study will teach you. Worlds are framed just as books are written. "Words to the end of the world." Words, we have shown, are the particles, the smallest particles, of matter that can exist alone. The word is the first and smallest particle of a language. The attractive influence begins in the least particle; affinity drew even before it was a particle. So potent is the

term that it was made flesh, and dwelt among us.
It is now to the letter gently drawing the world,
guiding the thoughts and acts of five hundred millions of souls. As gravity guides and leads suns
and systems, so this Word is leading Heaven-directed
galleys to destinations sure and certain. God's love
in this way went out to us in periods too remote.
Affinity is love, cohesion is love, gravity is that tendency of matter to come together center to center,
heart to heart. This is love, illimitable love. These
make the world a unit. Now we see how God loves.
He has named the forces that do all things by terms
as sweet as any known to us in this world. Words
give potency and permanence to thought, this they
do for us socially; in a similar manner the matter
word does for matter. The influence of words written or spoken makes men and even nations what they
are; they hold each in place. These create navies,
call out armies, demolish thrones, set up republics.
These give to a nation's currency its value, build
railways, build jails and penitentiaries, lead to the
scaffold, and loose the drop under the gallows.
These were the swords of priests and prophets.
These lead to atheism and succor infidelity. How
potent are these things that go to the end of the
world! They have in them the link that holds
matter to matter, the link that holds man to
God, God to man. Let us see Psalm lxxviii. 69:
"And he built his sanctuary like high palaces, like
the earth which he hath established forever." Just
as the earth is built up, the same thing that makes it
abiding supports his sanctuary. The law of material
love as expressed by their names makes the earth

durable. The law of love is the support of his sanctuary.

"Their words to the end of the world." Earthly
matter talks to the matter of Mars, particle to particle, as the most enlightened English talk to each
other word by word. The widely severed particles,
having the same voice, the same speech, the same
language, hold close and sweet communion. These
two planets, we are told, had the same origin, are
composed of the same material, possess the same
motions, look to the same center for light and heat,
are shaped alike. The earth has one moon; Mars, to
compensate for its greater distance, has two. Their
years, seasons, days, and nights are alike, differing in
length and light and temperature. All things tell
us that the same forces that are doing work here are
busy there doing likewise. Then we conclude that
there was a time in the history of Mars when it was
said: "Let there be light; let there be a firmament;
let the waters be gathered together in one place;
let Mars bring forth grass; let there be lights;
let the waters bring forth abundantly; let Mars
bring forth the living creature;" and finally, "Let us
make man." Seven of these commands were directed to the forces that had hitherto stood in the way
and had prevented all these on the earth. "Let us
make man" implies a consultation with predeter-
mined purpose to do so. "Let us make man after
our likeness." Immediately after he is made, God
talks with him. He names all the animals. Speech
to him is as natural as is the speech of matter; language to him is as natural as is the language of matter. He was created by talking beings to be like

these same talking beings. Speech can be no more an acquisition than is the sense of sight. The blessing that fell so early on him would have been as unintelligible to him as to the trees in the garden had he not been a talking man from the moment circulation was established and it was announced that "man became a living soul."

What language was used? Certainly the same language that had said: "Let us make man." Matter had a first, a universal language. Matter was obedient, and maintained it; man was disobedient, and his was confused. Is it not imaginable that one universal language went to all the worlds that are inhabited by this high order of intelligences? God made all things alike in so many respects. The truth of a triune God on earth would make him so on Mars. He endowed matter with a silent speech; this enables earth to talk to Mars. It is believed that the inhabitants of Mars are trying to communicate with the inhabitants of the earth. Should the time ever come that these two worlds converse with each other, it will be through the medium of our primitive language. Let us return.

How nicely do these high moral influences that go out in words from one common center, Jesus Christ, the Word made flesh, illustrate those influences that go out from every center! These words, the make-up of matter, go out in words as force. We said that we were akin to the earth and akin to the stars, composed of like material, which is under the same law as that which controls the matter that makes the most distant star in space. So we have traced the kinship of the better forces of our higher nature with the forces that govern matter. These forces, physical and spiritual, hover over, around, and in us, crowning us with an immortality as endless as the law of light or motion, as endless as that given to matter and force by physicists.

"In them hath he set a tabernacle for the sun." In what is the sun's tabernacle set? In those lines, speech and language; the line of gravity and attraction. The sun's cable and the earth's line, mutual attraction. The sun's tabernacle stands on these; all the matter that makes the solar system, that makes all the systems, stands upon a line as the words of every book. This is no other than the line mentioned to Job, upon which the foundations of the earth were fastened, and the one that filled the enraptured vision of the inspired singer. Not the sun only, but his tabernacle is set in these lines and words. A tabernacle is a movable tent. Among the Jews a tabernacle was a movable building, so constructed as to be taken to pieces with ease and reconstructed, for the convenience of being carried during the wanderings of the Israelites in the wilderness. This is taken as a figure, an object-lesson, teaching the motions and the forces, and the manner of these motions and the distribution of these forces that carry our system as one building, a unit, or as individuals, comrades, on a great sidereal journey. The taking of it to pieces implies a separation of its parts. With ease shows an adaptability, a fitness of parts. To be reconstructed implies a bringing together of its parts. For convenience of being carried on the journey fits it to an economy of the carrying forces which move it. Taking it apart and reconstructing it most beautifully illustrates planetary aphelion and perihelion distances. In aphelion they are at their greatest distances from the central orb or sun, and may then be said to be taken apart. In perihelion they are nearest the sun, and may be said to be reconstructed. But it is taken apart for convenience of being carried. Now, if the force of gravity as given in our law decreases as the square of the distance increases, then less force is required or exerted to carry these aphelion planets along the journey than when closer together, in perihelion. "The law of the Lord is perfect."

"Which [sun] is as a bridegroom coming out of his chamber, and rejoiceth as a strong man to run a race." The idea of the text is readily developed by a true grammatical arrangement. "Which" refers to the sun. The sun as a bridegroom coming out of his chamber rejoiceth to run a race as a strong man rejoiceth to run a race. Here we have two comparisons. The sun is compared to a bridegroom coming out of his chamber, and his rejoicing to run a race is like the rejoicing of a strong man to run a race. These two comparisons illustrate two thoughts: those attractive forces of which we have been speaking and the motion of the sun along a course. "As a bridegroom coming out of his chamber." At first we are astonished at his magnificence, his grandeur, and the number of his train, which, if truly illustrated by the number of pieces that composed the tabernacle, must be great. The bridegroom must be the center of attraction for the train that attends him. The thought of harmony adds grandeur to the spectacle. See him as he rises, full of manhood, full

of vigor, full of life, full of motion. Bridegroom—
a man about to be married.

> As are those dulcet sounds in break of day
> That creep into the dreaming bridegroom's ear
> And summon him to marriage.

Like a bridegroom, filled and enthused with a sweet
influence that binds him to his affianced, he rejoiceth, is happy in the consciousness that he is the recipient of her first, her highest love. These sustain
and hold him on his course. "As a strong man." In
the figure his strength, the very thing of which we
are talking, was not overlooked — an attractive
strength. The sun is a great central globe, so vast
as to overcome the attraction of all the planets and
compel them to circle around him. How nicely is
the law of attraction illustrated by the law of love!
That is its name. He is the king of day; is to shed
light and warmth upon his bride; to support and
cherish her; to lead on, hand in hand or line to line,
word to word, through the course of a continuous
life.

"His going forth is from the end of the heaven,
and his circuit unto the ends of it." Heaven as used
in the Bible is susceptible of three interpretations
and only three: region of the air or firmament, home
of the blessed, the solar system or space occupied by
it and through which it moves. Genesis i. 1: "In
the beginning God created the heaven and the
earth." The solar system was one and the same creation. See the position of the two great lights. Genesis i. 17: "And God set them in the firmament of the
heaven to give light upon the earth." Now these
great lights were set in the bounds occupied by the

solar system. Deuteronomy xvii. 3: "And hath gone and served other gods, and worshiped them, either the sun, or moon, or any of the host of heaven." Here seems to be a double meaning: first, that the sun and moon are situated within the bounds of heaven, solar system, and the hosts that live in the aerial heaven. Deuteronomy iv. 19: "And lest thou lift up thine eyes unto heaven, and when thou seest the sun, and the moon, and the stars, even all the host of heaven, shouldest be driven to worship them, and serve them, which the Lord thy God hath divided unto all nations under the whole heaven." This gives light. The host here, as above, refers to all animals under the aerial heaven, the hosts that are "divided unto all nations." This is to cover all animal worship, whether of the frigid or torrid zone. Isaiah xiv. 12: "How art thou fallen from heaven, O Lucifer, son of the morning!" This is figurative. The planet Venus, on account of its brightness, was called Lucifer. Its position was in the heaven, the bound of the solar system, and it is one of the stars mentioned in Deuteronomy iv. 19. Amos ix. 6: "It is he that buildeth his stories in the heaven, and hath founded his troop in the earth; he that calleth for the waters of the sea, and poureth them out upon the face of the earth: The Lord is his name." The marginal reading for "stories" is "spheres." If our rendering of heaven be just, then we would say that he made the other spheres of our system. We have never seen one single passage that conflicts with this mode of determining the meaning of heaven. If we are wrong in our opinion that reference is here made to the solar system, still the clause "It is he that

buildeth his stories in the heaven" was surely meaningless to the world for two thousand years or more,
and was to Amos a sweet kiss from inspiration.

"His going forth is from the end of the heaven,
and his circuit to the ends of it." The sun, like all
the other stars, is in motion. David says that his
course is a circuit which extends from the end to the
ends of the space filled by the heaven, solar system.
Astronomers say that it is sweeping onward with its
retinue of worlds one hundred and fifty millions of
miles per year, toward a point in the constellation
Hercules. The Pleiades are thought to be the center around which this great movement is taking
place, but the orbit is so vast and the center so remote that nothing is yet definitely known. Other
suns are doing just what ours is. Isaiah xl. 26:
"Lift up your eyes on high, and behold who hath
created these things, that bringeth out their host by
number." When we lift up our eyes by night what
do we see? Only suns. What are these doing?
Leading out their host; yes, these mighty suns are
leading each its host. Astronomers only by analogy call these suns centers of systems, and by analogy say that each has its train of planets, satellites,
meteors, etc. Isaiah says that it is a fact. The only
means afforded the prophet was that of inspiration.

Job xxii. 14: "He walketh in the circuit of heav-
en." The heaven here spoken of is the solar system.
The sun is the center of this system. The planets revolve about the sun in circular orbits. He walketh
in this circuit. His walks on Neptune are what they
are on the earth. His way on Uranus is his way on
Mars. From planet to planet he walks. Are there

12

things on these distant planets that can induce him
to condescend to walk there? He was made flesh
and walked on earth. Did these disobey? Does he
walk from place to place on Saturn, going about doing good? Was there a cross on Jupiter? Why tell
us that he walketh in this great circuit if the term
used was not a term for locomotion there as here.
The great truths that the paths leading to these are
circular, for each alike, and that the whole combined
is moving in one great circuit is proof that the Author was conversant with enough to make us accept
all the balance. To hear him call this walk a circuit makes us know that his special attention in
some way is directed to these as to us.

"From the end of the heaven . . . to the ends
of it." He made it a circuit by statement. He gives
the starting and the ending, which, coming together
as ends would, by illustration, also make his orbit
circular. Science only ventures a thought that the
Pleiades is a center around which this movement is
directed. The Bible has held up this doctrine for
nearly three thousand years. Still the great philosopher says: "The astronomers of our day have discovered that the sun is not the dead center of motion." The astronomers of our day have discovered
this! O my day! What a rebuke to Bible-readers!
What a comment on the character of the wise men of
our day! Bible-readers had not discovered it. Those
in search of knowledge sought it in other fields. No
wonder this discovery cost so much; no wonder that
confusion hovered over and around it till "our day."
Objections are made to the Bible on the ground that
it does not accord with science. How can it when

many of her theories do not survive our generation? The great question of which we have been talking is a discovery of the nineteenth century. Let us get our science right, then lay it to the science of the Bible with all the vehemence of a foe, but fairly. Like Gibraltar, it will still overlook the sea with its terrible ramparts that no foe can storm. "The law of the Lord is perfect."

"There is nothing hid from the heat thereof." Along this sidereal journey the earth makes its revolution about the sun, day and night alternate till each part of its surface has had the same number of minutes and hours of light and darkness. Wherever light falls heat is ever present. This truth needs no further comment than the one found in "hid." Nothing is concealed, everything brought to the light. Then heat is there too. These are supposed to be the same. "In all regions outside of the tropics climatic contrasts are found. At the poles these contrasts are at their maximum. The summer of the polar regions, strange to say, is exceedingly hot." "There is nothing hid from the heat thereof." These periods of heat at the poles remain for so short a time that vegetation, particularly food plants, do not flourish, except in very limited amounts, and that of those less able to support life. The sun does not take hold here—nothing is hid from him.

"The law of the Lord is perfect, converting the soul: the testimony of the Lord is sure, making wise the simple." We have shown the perfection of a law. The heavens, aerial and ethereal, have borne testimony; by it the simple are to be made wise. This, we stated in the beginning, was purely scientific. It could not refer to the spiritual laws, for the Sermon on the Mount had not yet been preached. The physical law is perfect, and was so the very day the work of creation ended. Whether matter creates force or force creates matter, the result is the same; and, the work ended, the law is perfect in its operation, full and sufficient. The same laws, guiding the same forces that held watch over matter the first instant after its creation, have never, not one, been amended or repealed, nor a single new act passed. The only testimony offered is that of the stars, firmament, and the sun's tabernacle. How do these things make wise the simple? Could they do so by one idle, empty gaze, seeing nothing? Such a look would tend, in my opinion, to superstition. Such is the fact attested by the history of astronomy and sun-worship. One makes this statement: "Standing in the light of our present knowledge, the ideas of the ancients seem almost incredible, and we can hardly comprehend how they could have been seriously entertained." Anaximenes (530 B.C.) held that the stars are ornaments, and that these are nailed to the upper sphere as we use breastpins, etc., as ornaments. Would that make wise the simple or make the simple appear as fools? Anaxagoras (450 B.C.) considered that they are stones whirled up from the earth by the rapid ethereal motion around us; that the properties of which they are composed took fire and caused them to shine as stars. These were individual opinions, yet they came from the wisest. Grecian philosophers of many schools, Stoics and Epicureans, believed that they are celestial fires kept alive by matter that constantly streams up to them from the

center of the heavens. The stars at one time were
said to feed on air; at another, to be the breathing-
holes of the universe. These men lived and these
schools flourished in the days abounding in superstition. These helped to make them so, or from dis-
torted fancies these were created. Suppose that
these men could have seen the perfection of the laws
that control the stars, new skies would have appeared to them. These ornaments, burning stones,
celestial fires, these air-eating stars, would have
gone with their superstition; the people would have
become wiser; converted from these, they would
have lifted their minds and their hearts with every
upward gaze. Even now, with so much light and
knowledge, what strange beliefs do we simple hold
concerning the stars, the firmament, and the sun!
We believe that the stars are mere specks that shine
alone by night and are extinguished when day
comes; or that these, like the sun and moon, rise and
set in obedience to motions of their own. Instead of
comprehending a firmament, we look upon the space
from the earth to the stars as really empty, a great
valley in which there is nothing. Nowhere do we see
the slightest evidences of a handiwork. Our own
early experience when a child attests this truth.
When once we see these things as they are, and see
the perfection in the law as it really is, we are made
wise. When the perfection of the law and the law
itself is dispensed from inspired lips, that, too, antedating any other dispensation of it, how much more
do we feel and know that there is a God, one perfect in knowledge! The soul is converted and we
stand upon his testimonies, evidences as seen all

around us. "The law of the Lord is perfect." While
it is not our object to investigate questions purely
spiritual, we will say, touching the above, that the
final object is the conversion of the human family.
When a physical question develops truths asserting
the existence of a God, that far it is spiritual, and is
his agent or instrument for that end. There are
other questions purely spiritual, the sole object of
which is to lead men directly to God. This chapter
is a beautiful illustration of this fact. There are
fourteen verses in this chapter. We said that the
first seven were scientific, purely so; now we say that
the last seven are purely spiritual. Seven, you
know, is a sacred number. First, man is taught
God's glory through perfect laws, that he is the author of all these, that he gets knowledge and becomes in every respect the highest type for the acceptance of spiritual laws. No, you are mistaken;
we did not say that it was necessary for him to become a philosopher or an astronomer to make him
ready to accept gospel teachings. He has laid these
so closely together and has preceded the spiritual
with the philosophical, impressing us with the opinion above.

Let us now review the two laws side by side, and
then by these place a simplified interpretation of David's law. Where there is no voice (atom) there is
no speech (gravity) nor language (affinity). Their
line (speech and language) is gone out through all
the earth, and their words (influence) to the end of
the world. In them (words, influence of words) hath
he set a tabernacle for the sun.

Newton's law: Every particle of matter (word) in

the universe (to the end of the world) attracts every other particle of matter (goes throughout all the earth to the end of matter) with a force directly proportional to its quantity of matter (as the vibrating cords are to each other as the product of their masses), and decreasing as the square of the distance increases (the sound of a cord decreases as the square of the distance increases).

David's law simplified: Where there is no atom there is no gravity, no affinity. Wherever matter exists there these forces exist. Their influence goes throughout all, every particle of the earth, just as speech or sound produced from a vibrating cord, decreasing as the square of the distance increases; and the intensities of these sounds are to each other as the masses or weights of the cords. The sun, together with his attendants, is in these influences or these lines and cords. These go on decreasing as the distance increases and directly as the products of the masses of the vibrating cords, on and on to the end of the world, to the outpost of matter. In emptiness, darkness, and silence there is no speech (gravity) nor language (substance) where there is no voice (atom).

How often have we read this Psalm, and as often been lifted through all the firmament to the stars, feeling each time, after the shock, something strange creep over us, imparting a feeling of we know not how to explain, then flit away as a shadow, leaving us without landmarks or corners to make even an intelligible survey, nor could we count one single solid gain! We read it as we hear the pleasing strains from some skilled violinist, without knowing anything about the notes before him, the size, length, and weight of the cords, or the philosophy of sound at all. A sense of profound philosophy comes to us through these beautiful declarations that lifts mind and heart through hope to an existence as real as these constructions are beautiful and sublime. Thus the beauty of fiction becomes chaplets of truth. Why was this law given in these terms? David lived twenty-five hundred years in advance of the development of these principles. Then they could have no name, for in his time no such forces or influences were known, consequently no terms to designate them. He seized upon terms as imperishable as the forces they name, terms that spring from others bearing in themselves meanings which exercise over the human mind and heart an influence operating in a way very similar to these then mysterious forces. The one is as old as matter, the other as old as man and perhaps much older. The former will perish only with the extinction of matter; the latter, with an existence no less immortal perhaps, will never die. These terms, full and complete, have withstood the shock of three thousand years with its innovations and diversity of tongues. Their prominence and absolute necessity alone freed them from that general and promiscuous ruin that has followed the wheels of time.

David and Newton.

Newton, in testing the moon's orbit, finding that the result was likely to verify his conjecture, his hand faltered with excitement, and he was forced to ask a friend to complete the task. What then must

have been the emotions that filled the bosom of the
Psalmist when, without a precedent, he looks and
sees the solution to the greatest question ever presented to the human mind? Newton gave down
under the consciousness that he was about to develop a great truth; but he really rewrites a law twenty-
five hundred years old when he was born, and writes
it in the stern, rigid, prosy language of a geometrical demonstration. David sees his result, soars the
higher, filled with an electric shock from the eternal
batteries, gives his philosophy the measure of poet-
ry and the melody of song, the truth of Newton, and
more, a sublimity unequaled by the songs of Homer,
unsurpassed by any tongue or pen. Newton, satisfied with his achievement, retires from the heavens,
leaving the discovery of the sun's motion for the
dawn of the nineteenth century. David, holding out
the laws of gravitation and attraction, declares that
the sun's tabernacle is set in these, swings the whole
around one common center, reaching from the end
of the heaven to the ends of it, till nothing is hid
from the heat thereof; then winds up these most
wonderful declarations with, "The law of the Lord
is perfect," be that law physical or spiritual.

NOTE.—All matter is related. It had one common origin;
compounded from the same formula; had one common parent;
attended one and the same common school, so was under one
and the same instructor. To-day, all human learning is but the
lessons taught by matter. The plant teaches botany; the earth
teaches geology; the beasts teach zoology; the birds, ornithol-
ogy; the sun, moon, and stars, astronomy; the atoms teach chemistry, organic and inorganic. Our bodies, being matter, are related to all matter. It had its origin with the first origin of matter. It matriculated in the same school, learned the same lessons, studied the same books, is under the same law; and,
untenanted, will do every time, under the same circumstances
and the same surroundings, just what any or every other par-

ticle in space will do.   It has the ability to teach the above topics as truly as they.   It is to us not so much teacher as interpreter.
The nervous system is that part of our physical organism through
which the mind receives its intercourse with the external world.
The five senses are supported by five silver cords, telegraphic
wires, having the central office within; while each has its foreign office on the confines of the self world, and the nearest
borders of the world of not self.   The end of the optic nerve
from the borders of the world of not self receives a communication, and transmits it to the central office.   The operator an-
nounces: "A telegram from a tree."   The tree did not come to
the optic nerve, nor did the optic nerve go out to it.   But the
tree transmitted a force to this nerve sufficient to put it to vibrating or pulsating.   This is vision.   Now we have the matter
tree, the matter nerve, and the motions of matter.   These are
real and visible, but the force that moves these swinging nerves
is invisible and indestructible.   The existence of matter, from
what we see, is less certain, less real, than the existence of a
force as manifested by these motions of matter.   We believe
that were our eyes bandaged and we placed in a dungeon and
had the power to start up the same vibrations in the optic
nerve, then we would see this same tree, together with all its
surrounding objects.   The same is true of the auditory nerve,
and the phonograph is an example proving this truth.   The
scope of inorganic matter, per se, is rest, made so by a force
which, undisturbed, would ever hold it fast; and we know that
any visible motion in this is every time the product of another
force than that which would keep it in a state of rest.   Now we
know that there are two forces in nature.   Our bodies are matter, and called organic, for each organ is an instrument of action
by which some process is carried on.   The nerves are organs of
perception and sensation, the instruments of conveyance or
communication.   The object of organism is that it may receive
support, sought or unsought, from its kinsmen.   We said that it
was infused with the same forces.   Solomon says, "All things
are full of labor," the power of doing work.   Now the forces
that fill all matter exterior to us talk to their relatives, individuals that make our intellectual organism, as matter talks to
matter through their vocalizing mediums.   Thus force communicates only with force.   We said all intellectuality was drawn
from these, was, like our physical organism, thus fed and built
up.   I place my hand on a red-hot stove.   The hand only was
burned; the heat was not, nor could it be, transmitted one
inch beyond the place of contact; so the heat was not transmitted, but a force sufficient to produce a peculiar nerve
motion which force alone can interpret, is interpreted a burn.
The earth teaches geology.   In the study, the real earth is never
thought of, but the formations, their positions, and the forces
that made them.   If we study zoology, we look beyond the
dead bones to the actuations that once filled them.   If we study

astronomy, we look within, to the matter that makes the planets, or the invisible suns, to the forces that united them into bulks, that shaped them, that move them, that keep them in certain circuits. Beyond these, we know nothing of matter. It is said that matter can not operate on spirit or spirit on matter. This seems true. The living spirit of matter, the forces God gave to matter, the great physicist says are immortal. To these, and only these, do man's speculations extend. His perception can comprehend these, and nothing more. Newton saw the apple—saw it falling. He lost sight of the apple and its falling, and sought the only thing, the invisible immortal force that carried it straight down. A cow sees an apple, sees it fall; she rushes to the apple only and appropriates it to that alone which saw the apple fall, her physical nature.

Vegetables and animals devoid of those higher internal forces are unable to see the higher forces with which matter is moved. Man alone has these higher forces. He is akin to matter, and likewise is a kinsman of the angels. His higher powers are those of angels, the breath that God breathed into him. Genesis xxviii. 12: "And he dreamed, and behold a ladder set up on the earth, and the top of it reached to heaven: and behold the angels of God ascending and descending on it." This vision occurred to Jacob seventeen hundred and sixty years before Christ. John, on the divinity, humanity, and office of Jesus Christ, seventeen hundred and ninety years after Jacob's wonderful dream, says (John i. 51): "And he saith unto him, Verily, verily, I say unto you, Hereafter ye shall see heaven open, and the angels of God ascending and descending upon the Son of man." Now we have the ladder that Jacob saw—a three-round ladder that stands on the earth and reaches to heaven. This shows our connection with both worlds. The three rounds are: Earth-man, man-Christ, Christ-God. Christ was introduced to the world by his humanity. In the flesh our spiritual natures were through the flesh introduced to his spiritual nature, and through his spiritual nature we, our spiritual selves, are reconciled to God. So we get our accumulations of knowledge. Our material bodies, composed as they are of matter and force, bring us in close communion with the matter world, and through this union our intellectual selves are introduced to the hidden forces of matter. Thus, I have in my hand a pound weight. I feel the pressure just when the introduction is taking place. The pound weight and the hand being of the same creation, schoolmates, brothers, these are acquainted, no introduction is necessary. Then the pound weight says: "Let me introduce Gravity to your intellectuality, my brother Hand." The same mode of reasoning gives proof of man's fall. When God made man and had placed him in the garden he pronounced him not only good, but very good—that is, in substance he was truthful and obedient. This was man's first estate in his two natures, physical and intellectual, earthy and

angelic. Matter to him was the schoolroom, the open avenue
to God. This tenement was his observatory, from which he
could learn God through his works. These are the thoughts of
God, his way. Man disobeyed. He was very soon pronounced
desperately wicked and full of deceit. Then his material self
was debased.

Proof: Outside of man did you ever hear of one disobedient
particle of matter? Have you ever found anywhere in nature the faintest coloring of deceit? Mechanics, the laws of
machinery, gunnery, the movements of the heavenly bodies;
in fact, all our learning is based on the truth that matter won't
lie. Now count the locks, bolts, and bars that make fast the
doors to our houses; see the massive lock that threatens us
from every business house in the world. See the massive safes
and vaults that taxed the highest mechanical skill that they
might the more accuse us. See the jails, penitentiaries. See
the gallows. Count them, and you will find more than one for
every man, woman, and child on the globe. Thus man acknowl-
edges his debasement, and brings out his testimony to this ac-
knowledgment. Then if this be true, before man's creation
matter was not debased, and was good for all the purposes that
God had in design for it. He put his law in it, and it has kept
it inviolable all the ages.

CHAPTER IX.

Influence of Gravity—Result Should This Force Fail—General Ruin Will Follow the Dissolution of This Force—The Fall of Worlds Illustrated.

ATTRACTION OF GRAVITATION.

Isaac Newton, seeing an apple fall to the ground, said, "Some force drew it thither;" and he named that force gravity. From this observation he deduced the law found in the preceding chapter, and by it explained the falling tendency toward the sun seen in the planets, and in satellites toward their primaries, making it the cause of circular orbits in these planets and satellites. It is the constant force that holds these to their centers, while another force impels them forward.

Jonah, referring to the time that he was thrown overboard, says (Jonah ii. 6): "I went down to the bottoms of the mountains; the earth with her bars was about me." One side remark: Jonah and the whale have been the subject of comment perhaps since that occurrence. Skeptics and critics have discovered that the swallow of the whale is not large enough to take in a man; that for want of air he could not have lived three days, nor even one. We have before us Jonah's own statement. In this short statement are two truths coming from him that ought to put to shame these man-devised theories of little throats and want of air as being insurmountable obstacles in God's way for carrying out

(189)

his plan. "I went down to the bottoms of the mountains." These critics are confronted by a very seri-
ous dilemma. They must admit that it is no fiction;
that Jonah absolutely saw this mountain, or that it
is a gift of inspiration. Mountains are found at the
bottom of the sea—a thing I can not see how Jonah
knew. If we accept Jonah's statement, these criti-
cisms are foolish. To accept it as a gift of inspiration puts clear out of sight the size of a throat or
scarcity of air.

The other truth found in the text, and the one in
line with our present discussion, is that of gravity.
"I went down to the bottoms of the mountains; the
earth with her bars was about me."

Mr. Johnson defines bar thus, "Anything by which
a structure is held together;" and, curious to say, he
refers to our text from Jonah. Bar — anything by
which a structure is held together. Were we to define gravity in a philosophical sense, we could not improve on Johnson's definition of bar. This is now
the earth's bars, that thing which holds the earth together. You remember this is the same thing that
was set over the sea after it was drawn to its bounds.
He set bars and doors, and said: "Hitherto shalt
thou come, . . . and here shall thy proud waves be
stayed." We said in another place that this was a
physical force; now we have shown that it is the
force that holds the earth as one structure and
chains the sea in its place. It has been well suggested that the atoms drawn together by cohesion
resemble a weight pressed to the earth by gravity.
Going out from these atoms is truly that which holds
our earth together, holds it and all the other mem-

bers of our system in one structure; that holds all
the systems as one mighty structure, a moving cara-
van in limitless space.

Job xxviii. 11: "He bindeth the floods from overflowing." This is the force expressed by the bar that
was set over the proud waves of the sea, that holds
down the floods, the same that went down to the
bottom of the mountains with Jonah and is there defined as bars of the earth. Bindeth—Mr. Webster
defines: "To tie together; to confine with cords or
anything that is flexible." After defining this word
Mr. Webster then refers to the above text. Flood
is not tied to flood, but flood to land. With anything
flexible—how beautiful! how convenient! how necessary! If gravity were not a flexible force, we could
either not lift a body at all, or, when once lifted, this
cord, if inflexible, would break, and the body, when
loosed, would not fall to the ground. Can we even
think of anything being bound with a cord without
associating with the thought the idea that this cord
encircles the thing and is a center-drawing cord? If
a cord is used to tie a thing, we draw the cord and
force the bundle or the thing tied toward the center
till the cord fills fully its object—that is, holds the
particles together. From this we get the very common word "binding-twine." Binding-twine! I repeated the word, and your mind flew away to wheat-
fields, reapers, binders, and the various bundles received from the counters of every store in all the
land.

Can a thing be free if it be bound in order to prevent it doing the very thing that it would do were
it not bound? Can we imagine a thing as bound

without presupposing a binding force? "He bindeth"—an ever-present, active, continuous force; a
circling, twine-binding illustration. Philosophy calls
gravity a center-binding force, and presents it to our
imaginations as a thread, line, cord, or cable, which
experience teaches are flexible. Every weight lifted
will when loosed spring back to the ground, demonstrating the truth of its flexibility. This is the tie-
string that keeps watch over the rising floods that
they go not beyond their bounds. Every particle of
matter is bound in the same way, and by the same
binding force is held and kept from going too high.
The breaking of the least of these cords would fill all
matter with confusion and license the floods with un-
bounded sway. We are taught that the clouds are
raised by the buoyant force of the air, and that the
force of gravity resists this upward tendency till the
clouds reach a point of such diminished buoyancy
that they can no longer resist, and are stopped. If
the buoyant force of the air be greater than the force
of gravity, the clouds rise; if less, they fall under the
influence of gravity. When the ascending cloud
reaches the height where these two forces are exactly equal— that is, the uplift of the air and the
downpull of gravity — surely then the cloud is balanced, and it now measures the buoyant force of the
air and also the force of gravity, because the one is
equal to the other. Again, when a cloud has risen
to any height and stops, the air that once filled the
space now occupied by the cloud is precisely equal
in weight to the cloud — that is, the weight of the
cloud just balances the weight of the displaced air
when laid on the scales. Job xxxvii. 16: "Dost thou

know the balancings of the clouds, the wondrous
works of him which is perfect in knowledge?" Is it
not wonderful that Job should talk so? Three hundred years ago the world knew nothing of this property of the air. To Job it was weighed in a balance
with a cloud perhaps four thousand years ago. Had
the world felt that this text meant anything, and
had it experimented along the line of its statements,
thousands of years ago would have found the world
as wise as we of to-day. O what a fearful penalty
the world has endured for the neglect of studying
God's word! To be balanced implies two equal
forces or weights. The term "balancing," connected with the clause "the wondrous works of him
which is perfect in knowledge," will drive us into
no thought other than the one above. It is a wondrous work. That this is true, no scientist will dispute or deny for one moment. Nothing short of extensive knowledge can comprehend it fully. It is
"the wondrous works of him which is *perfect in knowledge.*" It was done by a Scholar, and will take such
to fully comprehend it. Why be so explicit, so
strong in terms, if it had no intricacies? It is one of
the most intricate questions found in the field of
science. Its invisibility puts it out of sight; its in-
tangibility, out of reach. The idea of associating
air with material things was never thought of by
the ancients. Seeing the air rush in to fill vacant
space, the followers of Aristotle explained it by
saying that nature abhorred a vacuum. This answered the purposes of philosophers and constituted
their fund of knowledge pertaining to atmospheric
pressure for two thousand years. Torricelli, the pu-

13

pil of Galileo, experimenting with the pump, found
that the water would not rise as high as the lower
pump valve if this valve were so much as thirty-four
feet above the surface of the water. He reasoned
that there is a force that holds up the water. He
verified the conclusion that the weight of the air is
the unknown force. Pascal carried his experiments
to various heights, and found that the pressure decreased with the height. This gave us our barometer, and was followed by the law of gravitation and
our present views concerning the atmosphere. This
thought was the forerunner of the coming law of
gravity. Jeremiah xxxi. 35: "Thus saith the Lord,
which giveth the sun for a light by day, and the ordinances of the moon and of the stars for a light by
night, which [ordinances] divideth the sea when the
waves thereof roar." Now we are brought together
in terms and meaning. The tides are gigantic, wave-
like movements. They differ from wind-waves in
their extent, in their regularity, in their cause. The
principal cause of tides is the influence of the moon.
The sun exerts a tide-producing influence; being four
hundred times farther, its influence is far less than
the moon's. The stars exert a control over the conditions of earthly matter, which aid in producing
tides. The sun was given for a light. It is not
given to the moon and stars, which are for light by
night, but to the ordinances of the moon and stars,
which were given for a light by night; these ordinances divide the sea when the waves thereof roar.
This ordinance, which is but a term for law, is the
very thing upon which the foundations of the earth
hang, and which philosophy defines as attraction—

a force awarded the moon sufficient to 'ift mighty waves above the surface of the sea.

Twice in every twenty-four hours the waters, drawn on by the moon's attraction, fall upon the shore with fearful crash, as they are checked in their pursuit of that body around the earth. This force is being expended on our earth to draw it from its track. It is a safe sailing-boat of ours. David says: "The world also is stablished, that it can not be moved." It may divide the seas, lift the waters, draw them from the poles, carry these around the globe at the rate of a thousand miles an hour, but here it must end; it can not overcome the force that establishes the earth. These ordinances came to the moon and stars by gift for a special purpose; beyond that purpose they are helpless. Philosophers and astronomers call this sea-dividing ordinance by no other name than that of attraction, the ordinance of gravitation.

Psalm lxv. 6, 7: "Which by his strength setteth fast the mountains; being girded with power: which stilleth the noise of the seas, the noise of their waves, and the tumult of the people." There are two forces mentioned in the text: one a physical force, operating on matter; and the other a mental or moral force, operating on the dispositions of the people. The force that holds the mountains fast and stilleth the noise of the sea is one and the same. The force that stilleth the tumult of the people is quite another. These forces are by the text attributable to the same source, and are very similar in tendency to do work. He—whereas we say law of gravitation— is made the center to whom all matter gravitated similarly as all minds of men do; or, just as matter has a center, a force pervading and controlling its particles, so has the mind one to which it gravitates. The two worlds, physical and spiritual, are precisely alike in this, that each has its center and each has a force that binds each to its own center. In physics we call it the attraction of gravitation; in morals we call it attraction. As a proof of this, take Psalm lxxviii. 69: "And he built his sanctuary like high palaces, like the earth which he hath established forever." The foundations and the continuance of his sanctuary depend wholly upon attractive influences. Attraction carries men to the sanctuary and holds them there. God's sanctuaries are as abiding as the centralizing forces that succor them. Attraction establishes the earth forever.

"Which by his strength setteth fast the mountains." What makes fast the mountains? Strength. How is this strength applied? "Girded with power." No philosopher ever said more, nor with greater simplicity. Let us see if much more is not implied. Were the earth motionless and flat, a girding strength would not be necessary to set fast the mountains. It is a thing of many motions; some force is necessary, and none can answer so well as a circling force. This force must act in opposition to motions, or the text is meaningless. "Girded with power" explains all this, and more: the earth is circled with power; this circling power compasses the mountains. This is a circular operating force that pushes all terrestrial bodies toward the earth's center. Job, in speaking of the floods, says: "He bindeth." This we defined as confining with cords or

anything flexible. Now, in speaking of the mountains, the Psalmist says "girded with power." Girded, Mr. Webster defines, to bind by surrounding with
any flexible substance, as a twig or cord. While it
is a binding force, the term girded with a girdle implies a center-drawing force. By it the mountains
are made fast. Though the earth moves along her
path with great rapidity, and at the same time revolves on its axis at the rate of a thousand miles per
hour, still the mountains are secure, being girded
with power. 'Tis a wave-checking and a mountain-
holding power. In both instances we have defined
these cords as flexible. Flexible: that which may
be bent, capable of being turned or forced from a
straight line without breaking. Gravitation is truly
a flexible line or force. A ball is ejected upward
with a velocity that carries it a thousand feet per
second. As it leaves the projectile force this cord
begins to bend; as it ascends the tension tightens, till
the ball is stopped. Now the projectile force has
passed into this bent cord, and has put into it all its
force, that will be developed as this flexible cord
springs back to resume its quiescent state. We can
not conceive a force sufficient to drive this same ball
fast enough or far enough to break this flexible cord.
It is the great enemy of motion, but the great stay
from confusion. "Which stilleth the noise of the
seas, the noise of their waves." The relative "which"
refers to the same force that makes the mountains
fast. Gravitation stilleth the noise of the waves.
Says philosophy: "Waves are produced by the friction of the winds against the surface of the water.
The wind raises the particles of the water, and grav-

ity draws them back again." It is this center-binding force that bids the frolicking waves be still. Tremendous waves may toss and leap like mountains set out from the clouds, but the flexibility of this cord accommodates them with a bend only to bring them back again, to still the noise of the seas, the noise of the waves. We, at this day, attribute it to God's means, his laws. The Psalmist and Job attribute it directly to God himself. So we neither differ as to the author of these forces nor in defining the forces themselves. Job xxvi. 7: "He stretcheth out the north over the empty place, and hangeth the earth upon nothing." "He stretcheth out the north over the empty place." Lieut. Maury, of the United States Navy, says that "Sir John Herschel has been sounding the heavens recently, and that he finds the empty place spoken of in the text precisely where Job told Bildad the Shuhite it was." Now, reader, before we comment, which of the two questions given in the text above would you regard the more difficult—to determine that the north stretched out over an empty place or to determine how the earth was suspended in space? It seems to me that Job has answered the more difficult of the two first. How can he venture an assertion on the other without knowing the first truth? or how could we question his statement touching the latter, when it surely seems the simpler of the two? My reason for saying this is that the law of gravitation was known to man two hundred years or more before Sir John Herschel made his observations. Our simpler truths were the first ones learned. "Hangeth the earth upon nothing." Then it is a hanging earth, a suspended earth, an earth that hangs on nothing. Let us see the difference that philosophy will make. Says Mr. Steele: "It may help us to conceive how the earth is supported if we imagine the sun letting down a huge cable and every star in the heavens a tiny thread to hold our globe in its place, while it in turn sends back a cord to every one; so we are bound to them, and they to us." Philosophers agree that the earth hangs upon an imaginary line, one that does not exist visibly, only an influence found in the very expression, "hangeth."

Job ix. 6: "Which shaketh the earth out of her place, and the pillars thereof tremble." Read the fourth to tenth verses inclusive of this same chapter. See supplement to rotation of earth on its axis and its motions about the sun. "The pillars thereof tremble." As the earth shakes, moves back and forth out of its place, the supports or pillars tremble. A pillar is that which upholds. These are placed beneath the thing to be upheld. Then the pillars of the earth must be beneath the earth. The earth is a great globe, the center of which is its lowest point; every other point throughout the earth is above this one. Stand at the center of the earth and point in every direction, and each is up. From this point there is no down; all is up. All bodies are drawn toward the center of the earth, not because of any peculiar property or power in the center, for all we know, but because the earth, being a great globe, the aggregate effect of the attraction exerted by all its particles upon any body exterior to it is such as to direct the body toward the center. The total amount of attraction exerted by the earth upon bodies exterior to it is the same as though that force were all concentrated at the center. Then the pillars that support the earth must be, if not at the center, so arranged that the total amount of support is the same as though these pillars were placed directly under the center. Stability in practical life we know depends much upon the direction of the pillars. Very great pains are taken to have them plumb. So with these earth-pillars; no plumb-line can excel them. These are the very patterns of which ours is but a poor representation. These pillars that support a thing have foundations that rest upon something far greater than the thing to be supported. Every particle of matter in the universe sends a pillar to the earth, and is placed where its support, together with the aggregate support of all its pillars, operate as though they stood directly under the center of the earth. But these pillars tremble. "Tremble" means to shake involuntarily; not left to the option of the pillars. This is an effect produced by a moving earth. Gravity acts as a tense spring. As the earth moves from the sun this spring bends, more and more retarding the earth's motion, till it reaches a point beyond which the spring will not allow it to pass; here it stops. As a ball thrown upward, it gently turns, when this spring brings it back again. As the earth moves rapidly back and forth (this is the meaning of "shake") let us watch this spring, the aggregate of all the springs or pillars, and we will be convinced that no expression can be more beautiful, more expressive, than "the pillars thereof tremble." Those imaginary lines that philosophers suggest, that we may conceive how the

earth is supported, are less real, less potent, and far
less representative. They make it imaginary, while
Job compares it to a thing about which all know.
Philosophers make these lines as so many guy-ropes,
allowing no motion to the thing tied nor expansion
nor contraction of the springs that tie. Everywhere
in the Bible they are flexible. In the above topic
they tremble or shake—that is, these pillars or lines
become longer or shorter; otherwise, they could not
move back and forth involuntarily. It gives very
plainly the idea of more or less tension as the earth
moves to or from the sun. As an evidence that Job
knew that the earth has no visible pillars, he had
made the statement that he "hangeth the earth upon
nothing." There is no variance, nor do these expressions vary from those made by philosophers.
They say "upon an imaginary line;" Job says "he
hangeth it upon nothing," "pillars thereof tremble."
As mind-helpers, tell me which is more illustrative.
The great Lecturer, in his preliminaries from the
whirlwind, began this subject thus: "Who is this
that darkeneth counsel by words without knowledge? Gird up now thy loins like a man; for I will
demand of thee, and answer thou me." "Stand up,
Job, like a man; answer me after the manner of a
man." Knowledge is the desirable thing. Then he
begins questioning Job as to earth supports. Job
xxxviii. 4-7: "Where wast thou when I laid the foundations of the earth? declare, if thou hast understanding. Who hath laid the measures thereof, if
thou knowest? or who hath stretched the line upon
it? Whereupon are the foundations thereof fastened? or who laid the corner-stone thereof; when the

morning stars sang together, and all the sons of God shouted for joy? "

"Where was thou when I laid the foundations of the earth?" There are two thoughts to which our minds are directed: that the earth has foundations, and that these were laid during some remote period in the past. God did this work, and so tells Job. Foundations differ from pillars in this: foundations are the groundwork, and are as firm as that in which they are laid, and always far more stable than the structure to be raised on them; pillars reach from these foundations directly to the thing to be upheld, and, as we said, are beneath the thing supported. The pillars have less strength than the foundations, and bear a relation in size and strength to the weight of the thing on the pillars. Every particle of matter in the universe is a stone in the earth's foundations. There is a plurality of foundations. To be sure, they do not occupy the same place, for then the earth could have but one foundation. Planted on every star in space is a foundation; from each of these a pillar rises to support the earth, while it sends back a pillar to each.

"Who hath laid the measures thereof? " There is an apparent ambiguity in this expression. What was measured? One of the two things mentioned in the foregoing topic. "Foundations of the earth." Foundations being used first and expressed in the plural, when compared with the topic that follows, inclines us to the opinion that "measures thereof" refers to the foundations of the earth. The things that support all matter have dimensions sufficient to give stability to the stupendous structure of worlds and systems built thereon. Again, the comparison is of such a practical nature that we can readily realize the intimate relation of matter and force or weight and support. Certain dimensions of foundations are necessary every time to support certain weights of greater or less height. The larger the house to be built, the greater the foundations; the less the house, the less the foundations required. The foundations are always laid first; afterward the superstructure goes up on these or on pillars rising from them. The same is true of the earth. This thought is made clear by many Bible expressions. For the present we cite you to Psalm civ. 5: "He hath founded the earth upon her bases." We give you the marginal rendering rather than the written text. Read the text. The earth stands upon bases that must have been laid somewhere outside and apart from the earth. The weight of the earth suggested certain bases. This created the necessity that the mountains be weighed in scales and the hills in a balance. Weight, and weight only, determines measures of foundations.

"Who hath stretched the line upon it?" Here reference is made to the foundation as the thing upon which the line is stretched. Gravity is influenced by two circumstances, and only two: weight and distance. Distance apart or removed has as much to do with the stones in foundations as does their weight. "The line." A definite line. The philosopher's line, and the same that David said went out through all the earth, is the one that was stretched upon the first foundations that stood upon the corner-stone that was laid before he made the stars.

The corner-stone, the first stone, is laid as a basis of
support for coming matter. Gravity, as a supporter
of worlds, is the corner-stone.

"Whereupon are the foundations thereof fastened?" On what now, Job, stand the foundations of
the earth? "On this stretched line." These foundations and this stretched line existed before the
earth, even before the sun, before our system was
created. David so says. "In them [these lines]
hath he set a tabernacle for the sun." These lines
existed, then, before the sun's tabernacle was set.
The foundations of the earth, these stones that support it, are the individual particles of matter
throughout space, each influencing precisely in proportion to its number of particles and its distance
from the earth.

"Who laid the corner-stone thereof?" Corner-
stone is the first rock of the foundation not of the
earth only, but of coming matter. The same is the
corner-stone of the earth's foundations. When this
was laid as to the earth's immediate coming the
morning stars and the sons of God shouted for joy.
The corner-stone of the earth's foundations for its
support is the corner-stone for the support of all
matter. This is gravity, the corner-stone of support.
From weight to weight the line finds its way to every
center and support till space is filled with golden,
purple, crimson lights from silver-burnished ceilings.

Judges v. 31: "Let them that love him be as the
sun when he goeth forth in his might." "Might"
signifies primarily and chiefly bodily strength or
physical power. Then the song of Deborah and Ba-
rak was that to those that love him, that they might

have a power or might like that of the sun, a light-
giving, a heat-giving power, and a power to impart
these. High above this is the thought of our work
-—viz., that it is a centralizing might of the sun as
potent in every respect as we believe that of the sun
is. This might is his strength to hold to himself
and draw after him planets, satellites, meteors, and
shooting stars without number. "As the sun when
he goeth forth in his might." The prayer was not
that they have a love as a standing, but a moving
sun, one full of power, motion, and activity, making
the law of love, the law of binding to, of leading on,
"Attraction." The law of love defines no acute angles. It is a plumb-line by which its votaries work.
It leads from heart to heart, center to center; in all
the changes it ever points there. The adoring subject moves round his center with his radius defining
his circle. This the most beautiful of all geometrical figures. The sun is here made to go forth. Astronomers tell us that he is making a great sidereal
journey, which in all probability will consume millions of years for him to complete. To us this is
comparatively a new theory; but it is so written in
the book of Judges, a published inspiration three
thousand years old. It was that old when Sir Isaac
Newton was born.

Isaiah xl. 26: "Lift up your eyes on high, and behold who hath created these, that bringeth out their
host by number: he calleth them all by names by the
greatness of his might, for that strong in power; not
one faileth." Lift up your eyes on high, and behold
who hath created these." What things are here spoken of as the created things? Only the things that

bringeth out their hosts, the leaders. What things
can we see with the eye when lifted to the starry
vault above? Suns, suns, suns, and only suns. The
prophet makes it so. The only visible things are
leaders, suns. "That bringeth out their host by number." Now we have visible to the eye, not through a
glass, suns; and we are told that each leads his host.
No better exposition of the theory of moving systems
can be found in all the learning of the world. "That
bringeth out their host." Bring—to carry, to convey,
to fetch from. Here a force is imputed to each sun to
convey a host. He created our sun, which leads its
retinue of worlds. He created all the suns that likewise lead out each its host. The power is given to a
material leader, that power with which matter is
endued.

"He calleth them all by names by the greatness of
his might." We said that might meant physical
power. Now we do not believe that it is a manifestation of great physical power in God to name these
stars, nor can we believe this any part of the thought
set forth. "He calleth them all by names." "Call"
means to summons. God created all these, and he
gave each the power to lead its host out. Now his
might is contrasted with the might not only of each
of these suns, but with all of them. "For by the
greatness of his might he summons each by name."
He says to our sun, "Send the shadow backward
round the dial of Ahaz," or, "Sun, stand still over
Gibeon," and it is done. This is God's strength, his
might.

"For that strong in power; not one faileth." You
observe that we omitted the italicized words in the

text. To correctly comprehend our last topic let us refer to a preceding topic and show that something else was implied. We deferred the other thought till we reached this part of our discussion. We said that God created all the suns; we had reference to the material of which these were made. Let us look steadily at this construction for a moment, and we will see beyond this a force, an implied creation also. "He created these, that bringeth out their host." He created a sun as leader. Beyond we see he created the force that carries, that leads and draws on its train, as we create steam or electricity. With the eye we see the engine drawing a great train, but the life of the engine is created first, and is within. "For that strong in power; not one faileth." These suns, endued with power, are strong; not one faileth. At his summons they obey, yet they have the bodily power to lead out their hosts. Now we can appreciate God's great power. Our sun has the power to hold to himself a train of worlds, to carry these with inconceivable velocities on an endless journey. He calls by name, "Sun, of the solar system, stand;" all the powers of the sun are broken, and it obeys. At the shining of his glittering spear it moves on.

"For that strong in power; not one faileth." Who is strong? Evidently these leaders. "Strong in power; not one faileth." Power is the thought, power is the thing that prevents a single one of this host from failing.

Isaiah xl. 12: "Who weighed the mountains in scales, and the hills in a balance?" Some one weighed the mountains, or the question should have been asked: "Were the mountains weighed?" Then

there was purpose for weighing the mountains and
the hills.   Yes; weight is only the force of gravity.
As the mountain poses in one pan of the scales, what
is laid in the other?   As a hill swings from one arm
of the balance, what swings from the other?   Not a
thing to be weighed, but an estimater of gravity for
the apportionment of matter to the ability of some
guiding or carrying force.   Here is a box car with a
capacity for carrying twenty thousand pounds.   The
car is loaded.   The force that drives the car along
the track must outweigh the force that would carry
the car and load to the center of the earth, or the car
would never move.   The mountains and hills were
weighed to adjust them to a supporting and a carrying force.   This is the central truth that supports
the theory of moving worlds and upon which they
hang in space.   The scales with one pound of coffee
on one pan are balanced or prevented from falling by
a pound of cast-iron on the opposite pan.   So with a
world, with mountains and hills that make up a
world.   "The solar system is a magnificent clock-
work of unfailing perfection.   All its stupendous
parts influence and are influenced by one another,
yet all move on in absolute harmony.   Every orb has
its magnitude set off by a scale, its materials
weighed in a balance, its distance measured by a line,
and its velocity regulated by an infallible law.   And
in this celestial machinery our planet has its place,
fitting therein as a wheel into a wheel in the works
of a chronometer."   Astronomers tell us that the
earth has not varied in its revolution the one-hun-
dredth part of a second in two thousand years.   How
fine must be that calculation that can retrospect two

thousand years and declare with definiteness that the earth has not made a variation so small as this! The one hundredth part of a second in two thousand revolutions, and each of these revolutions covering a distance of six hundred millions of miles at the clever speed of eighteen miles every second. We call that figuring. Says Josephus: "In the Wisdom of Solomon it is said of the luminaries, with relation no doubt to the miraculous standing still and going back, in the days of Joshua and Hezekiah: They have not wandered from the day that God created them; they have not forsaken their way from ancient generations, unless it were when God enjoined them by the command of his servant." Astronomy says that they have not varied. Solomon says, "They have not departed, unless it were when God enjoined them," not departed at all, not forsaken their way at all; no mention of even the one hundredth part of a second, not limited even to two thousand years, but all the years that have dropped between their creation and the days of Solomon. The other statement we denominated figuring; what shall we call this? This was before the world could figure. We can call it nothing but inspiration. Man is supremely blessed. He bears the image of God, he figures through gifts from God, and is the recipient of inspirations from him. Holding on to these great truths, let us notice the effect should this attraction cease. Philosophy teaches that the earth would fly off with headlong speed into the icy, cheerless regions of space. "It would be but the snapping of a cord, which, once broken, all the forces could not check its flight or bring it back into subjection."

14

So philosophers, looking on these unchanging forces, when in full harmony, have prophesied the probable results should the cord that holds our earth in its place be broken.

Isaiah xiii. 13, 14: "Therefore I will shake the heavens, and the earth shall *remove* out of her place. . . . And it shall be as the chased roe, and as a sheep that no man taketh up." Here God mustereth the armies of his wrath. The earth at some future period is to be made to lose its place and become as a chased roe, as a sheep that no man taketh up. No greater catastrophe could happen to this world in a physical sense. Here is a result emanating from a cause, we do not say similar to that given above, but is that in word, in its manner of production, and in the result itself. The simplicity of the illustration, together with its fidelity to the above fact, makes it wonderful. In his wrath he is to shake the heavens—not the earth, not the solar system, but all the systems. "I will shake the heavens, and the earth shall *remove* out of her place." We defined "shake" to move rapidly back and forth. Please notice the difference between the verbiage of Job and Isaiah. Now the heavens will rock; this motion will remove the earth, not in, but out, from the sun, from its own orbit. This will snap the line upon which the foundations of the earth are fastened and which holds it to the sun's tabernacle; cut loose from this, the earth will remove "out from her place," and shall be as a chased roe, and as a sheep that no man taketh up. Philosophy says that it would fly off with headlong speed into the cheerless, icy regions of space. If it moved out, we know that this would be from the sun.

The prophet says that it will be as a chased roe. If it is to be as a chased roe, then we can make a comparison showing the likenesses and detect the unlikenesses, if any. The roe is one of the smallest of the deer, and is the female. The sun we denominated the bridegroom; the earth, its bride—one of them, and also one of the least. The roe is the weaker, is less than the roebuck. The earth is less than the sun, is weaker in its attractive influence. The roe is noted for its elegant shape. The earth is round; the circle is the most beautiful figure. The roe is noted for its nimbleness; the earth is to be characterized by this. The roe makes its home in the mountains. When chased it flies to higher heights, to deeper gulches. The awful stillness that reigns in this region when sought alone fills one with an awe amounting to fear. The falling of a single leaf fills us with dread; the gentle rivulet that drops from a distant precipice awakens the belief that it is the tramp of some dangerous beast. The sun is long below the horizon, soon disappears, stars appear early, eminences stretch out long shadows where sunlight would be. These lonely and cheerless regions are the home of the roe. It betakes itself as far as possible from every human habitation. The earth is to be as a *chased roe*. This indicates a higher speed than usual; it indicates a wild, mad speed, treading along narrow, dangerous windings at dizzy heights or leaping from lofty precipices to great depths below, dashing against rocks and trees in this unguided flight. It is not making its accustomed rounds with genial companions on green grounds, by limpid streams. No; it is chased, pursued, and lost to all these. If the earth is tied to the sun by a cord, and if the earth sends out a thread to every star to hold it in its place, when the shake of the heavens is sufficient to move the earth out of its place, these flexible cords which tie it to the sun and stars will chase to their uttermost strength this fleeing earth as or like a chased roe in its ungoverned flight to the icy, cheerless regions of space.

"As a sheep that no man taketh up." Now it is made simpler. It is a stray over which no man has authority. Like the earth, no world will have an influence sufficient to hold it, nor a lawful claim to seize it. We see a comet; seemingly an uncontrolled, an unguided world, it flies away into the cheerless depths of space like a stray sheep. It darts into the very blaze of the sun, is out and gone again. Grappling forces can not or will not restrain it. This is a fair illustration of man when he loses his attraction for Him who is girded with power as the world is established. He breaks away from the light into the dark, cheerless regions of sin. No persuasions, no admonitions, no reason, can check him. He is an unbalanced stray on the world's social and moral stage. Again, what would be the effects should these ordinances fail and the rotation of the earth cease? Says philosophy: "Were the earth instantly stopped, enough heat would be produced to raise a lead ball the size of our globe three hundred and eighty thousand degrees centigrade. If it were to fall into the sun (not out from it), it would produce a thousand times more heat than its burning."

2 Peter iii. 10, 11: "But the day of the Lord will come as a thief in the night; in the which the *heavens*

shall pass away with a great noise, and the elements shall melt with fervent heat, the earth also and the works that are therein shall be burned up. Then all these things shall be dissolved."

"The elements shall melt with fervent heat." There are two opposing forces residing in the molecules of matter. The one expends itself in making solids, is called the attractive force, and is the subject of this chapter. The other expends itself in driving these matter particles asunder, is called the repellent force, and is heat. Ruin, seizing upon the true force, wraps the heavens in flames, consumes the earth and all the works therein. A great noise follows, announcing that the work of dissolution is done. Melted, its attractive force weakened.

"Then all these things shall be dissolved." Dissolve — to loose bonds. The fulfilment of this prophecy would be but the snapping of one of these cords. So the earth, as do all things, contains the very elements suited for the fulfilment of God's plan.

Psalm cxix. 90, 91: "Thy faithfulness is unto all generations: thou hast established the earth, and it abideth. They continue this day according to thine ordinances: for all are thy servants."

"Established the earth." Made it strong, durable, according to his laws, those laws that hold watch over the earth, that bind its particles to particles, and that tie it to the sun and stars, the law that keeps the floods from overflowing, the law that balances the clouds, that holds the mountains girded with power, the law that carries a falling body straight down to the ground. These are his serv-

ants. He has given them the care of every atom,
every grain of sand, every particle of matter in the
universe. These make the earth strong, these make
it abiding. "Everywhere in nature we find law in-
terwoven with every particle of matter. Nowhere
do we find chance. Every event is governed by
fixed laws. If we would accomplish any result or
perform any experiments, we must come into exact
harmony with the universal system. If we deviate
from the line of law by a hair's breadth, we fail.
These laws have been in operation since the creation,
and all the discoveries of science prove them to extend to the most distant star in space. The atoms
march in time, moving to the music of law. A crystal is but a specimen of molecular architecture built
up by the forces with which matter is endowed."

Let us follow these changes farther. Psalm cii.
25, 26: "Of old hast thou laid the foundation of the
earth: and the heavens are the work of thy hands.
They shall perish, but thou shalt endure: yea, all
of them shall wax old like a garment; as a vesture
shalt thou change them, and they shall be changed."
There are set forth in the text two ideas that we wish
to notice. We think these in full accord with the
teachings of astronomers and philosophers. All the
starry worlds are to perish, wear out, as a garment.
All of them shall wax old like a garment. The first
is a declaration that they shall perish. The second
tells how, by giving an example taken from the observations of every half-civilized, civilized, or enlightened household on the globe. It is to come
about in a manner simple to every understanding.
The great mysteries of the starry worlds find a solu-

tion suitable to the comprehension of the most illit-
erate mother in all the world. They are to wax old
like a garment.' See that old coat? Once it was
bright and new; the strength of the cloth was closely
scrutinized by cautious hands when the purchase
was made. The filling was picked from the selvage,
spectacles adjusted to examine the fiber, the chain
was passed upon. It was selected as the most durable, among its other qualities. The cutting and fitting was to a plan, for a purpose. The very best
thread was selected to hold it together. The very
best tailor joined the seams; it went from the shop
under a warrant not to rip. No ordinary force can
rip its seams or make a rent in it. But now these
cords that were the make-up of the cloth, that made
it strong, have lost their strength; rents are easily
made. The seams rip for want of strength in the
fabric. The time comes when its own weight can
not be sustained by these cords that once held it together as a great coat. So the heavens shall perish
when these forces are no longer able to hold all the
parts in place. These cords that run out to all the
worlds, from each to other, make the woof and warp
that clothes matter as with a garment. "Wax old
like a garment." Wax is a noun; a thick, tenacious
substance. In the Scriptures we find these phrases:
"To wax strong," "to wax feeble," "to wax hot," "to
wax old," "to wax worse." Tenacity is the idea set
forth in each of the above scriptural phrases, and
this, we think, is due to the word "wax" in part.
"To wax strong" is to grow in power or strength, as
wax approaches a consistency for greater tenacity.
The very thing about which we are talking, the

strength of worlds. "To wax warm" is to lose in part self-control, and thus approximate instability or a forgetfulness of self and self-surroundings. Warm wax loses some of its viscidity, its tenacity. "To wax feeble." Here is evidently a loss of strength. "To wax hot" tends to greater instability; its viscidity is barely above that of water. These worlds are to wax old like a garment; strength of cords gone.

"They shall perish." The earth and the heavens are the perishable things here spoken of. To perish is to be in a state of decay or passing away. It is said that if the heat of the sun were produced by the burning of coal it would require a layer ten feet in thickness, extending over the whole sun, to feed the flame a single hour. Were the sun a solid body of coal, it would burn up, at that rate, in forty-six centuries. "According to the theory of Laplace, the sun may yet give off a few more planets, whose orbits will not exceed its present diameter. After a time its heat will have all been radiated into space, its fire will become extinct, and life on the planets will cease." The heat of the sun is generally considered to be produced by condensation, whereby the size of the sun is constantly decreasing. If it is to go out in the heavens, what must be the fate of those worlds that are dependent upon it for light and heat? If our sun is fading, we conclude that the suns of the other systems are fading too. If these go out, the individual worlds that make up these systems will, like the earth and the other planets of our system, perish. The question above is no figure, but a stern fact. Mutation is written upon everything around us. Marble yields to the peck of time, brass and the harder metals bend, break, and dissolve under the fall of its noiseless strokes. The seas are not where they once were; the land is rising and subsiding. Suns, like untrimmed lamps, are going out from the deep above. The stars that we call constant, enduring, stars that have not varied from their appointed course since their creation, are to perish too. But they are to be changed as a vesture. How nice it is to tell us how the change is to come about! "As a vesture." When our garments become old and unfit for use we lay them aside and put on new ones— brighter colors, better fabrics. Then we conclude that space will be made more resplendent when these perishing worlds move again in new and brighter colors, that a new song will ring out from these renovated worlds, and the sons of God lift anew their shouts of joy.

Isaiah xxxiv. 4: "And all the host of heaven shall be dissolved, and the heavens shall be rolled together as a scroll: and all their host shall fall down, as the leaf falleth off from the vine, and as a falling fig from the fig tree."

"All the host of heaven shall be dissolved." "Dissolve" means to loose bonds. The bonds that make the hosts of heaven a unit will first dissolve. The work will begin with our system; then will follow the same results that would follow were the bonds of gravity loosed. At the creation of the first particle of matter in all the universe attractive forces drew them into worlds; gravity led these worlds into systems and directed the march of these through space, holding them in their appointed bounds. Now it is performing the last act in the drama. It is leading the *cortège* of worlds to one universal burial—down, down, as a falling fig.

"And the heavens shall be rolled together as a scroll." The heavens are the various systems that make the host. These are to be rolled together by systems. "As a scroll." How simple are the illustrations given by inspiration! A child can illustrate and comprehend many of the complex motions that baffled the wisest for thousands of years. "As a scroll." Take a sheet of paper (the longer the paper the better), mark the center, roll up the sheet till the center point comes round on top, now pass a pin through the center, extending through the plies in the roll, then as the center comes round continue marking till the scroll is complete. The point you marked for the center will still be the center. Unfold now your scroll and see with what arithmetical nicety you have marked these various stations. Their distances apart increase or decrease by a difference as invariable throughout the scroll as is possible to set off on a line with the finest dividers.

The systems will be clossed *en masse* "as a scroll." Then "all their host shall fall down, as the leaf falleth off from the vine." Now we can not be mistaken. The prophet is too explicit touching the how this dissolution is brought about. "As the leaf falleth off from the vine." He draws no foreign comparison; vines and leaves are scattered over all the world. Had he said the leaf of the coffee tree, the rubber, the banyan, the spruce, cedar, oak, or poplar tree, some, perhaps, would be shorn of an experiment. A leaf of the vine. "As the leaf falleth off." The leaf held

to the vine through all its life; its hold supported it
against gravity when it was young, tender, green,
and full of sap, and much heavier than at the time of
falling. Leaves are not severed from the stem by
their weight. The force that holds these to the vine
is weakened till it yields, then the leaves fall down.
These hosts do not fall down as a leaf falls down,
but they fall as the leaf *falleth off*. The snapping of
the force that sustains the hosts is just like the snapping of the force that holds the leaf, that frees it
from the vine. When once severed these go straight
down like a falling fig. They do not flutter through
the air like a falling leaf. It is not here like a
leaf shaken off by the wind nor one untimely severed
from the twig, but one ripe, having served its purpose, filled its mission, comes to the period of its
casting; the sustaining force, having served its purpose, gives up its charge, opens its hand, and a world
drops.

"And as a falling fig from the fig tree." This the
result that will follow when the hosts are loosed, dissolved. We hope that you will notice the difference
manifested by these two last illustrations, the act of
severance by the leaf, and the descent of the fig.
The tendency of all the worlds is toward each other.
Our moon, as it were, is falling toward the earth at
every point along its orbit; the earth, in turn, is falling toward the sun. The other planets and their
satellites are doing the same. The sun, with its retinue of worlds, is falling toward the center around
which it is moving and around which perhaps many
other systems like ours are revolving. And this far-
off center, accompanied by its systems, is sweeping

around another still more remote, yet having the same falling tendency.

"All their host shall fall down." The most pier-cing sight on a clear night may see six thousand suns, perhaps none so small as ours. Give each of these eight planets, and satellites equal in number to ours. The telescope increases the number of suns till they become marvelous. As our facilities for ex-amining the heavens improve, new suns come to us. Systems, constellations, themselves seem boundless. The force that has held each in its place, that pre-vented them from rushing together, will yield; dis-solution will have done its work. A mighty whirl-pool of systems and constellations will roll up till the center of all centers be the center of this scroll. As the hosts begin their fall, satellites drop down upon their primaries, primaries drop down upon their suns. Then will follow a rain of suns—blue, green, yellow, orange, and red—down, down, as or like a falling fig.

The law of gravitation was the direct result of ob-servations made on the falling of an apple. Newton said: "The force that drew the apple down to the ground is the same force that holds the worlds in their places; and, were this force severed, these worlds would fall together as or like the falling of an apple." Newton's demonstration was satisfac-tory to the learned. Isaiah says: "When the force that holds these worlds is dissolved then they will fall down as a fig falls down." There is no difference in the two illustrations. Newton illustrated the fall of worlds by the fall of an apple; Isaiah illustrated the fall of worlds by the fall of a fig. Had Newton,

in Isaiah's day, preached from our text the doctrine
of gravity as he did from the apple, the world would
have been as wise two thousand years ago as it is
to-day touching this doctrine.

After the ruin a great noise will follow, proclaim-
ing that the heavens have passed away. The songs
of the stars will have ceased. They will have no
voice, no speech, no language, no words. Their lines
will have returned from throughout all the earth
and their words from the end of the world. Emptiness and darkness will reign supreme. The forces
that controlled the mighty caravans in limitless
space will have wrought their missions; crouching
at the feet of Him who called them in his might and
whose servants they are, they become witnesses of
his faithfulness down all the ages. These are God's
servants; these minister about his house. When
communing with this force let us feel that we talk to
one of his servants, and let us feel assured that it will
tell us nothing but true and pleasing stories of its
Master, one perfect in knowledge. Jeremiah xxxi.
36: "If those ordinances [of the sun, moon, and
stars] depart from before me, saith the Lord, then
the seed of Israel also shall cease from being a nation before me forever." How impossible the departure of these forces from before him! They are
kept under his watchful eye, ever before him. These
keep the seas in place, hold the mountains, balance
the clouds, make the earth abiding, that it can not be
moved forever.

CHAPTER X.

MOTION.

Scientists tell us that nothing is absolutely in a
state of rest, that all things are in motion. They
define "energy" in a physical sense as the power of
doing work. It is, in general, something put into a
body by means of work. Ecclesiastes i. 8: "All
things are full of labor; man can not utter it; the
eye is not satisfied with seeing, nor the ear filled with
hearing." The truth of this and its conformity to the
teachings of to-day are too apparent to need a single
comment. We can not refrain, however, from calling attention to the last two clauses. "The eye is
not satisfied with seeing." This teaches that the
motions of objects we see around us do not satisfy,
but beget a spirit of investigation that carries us into
the hidden motion of matter, motions that the eye
can never see. The very fact that these visible motions have led men to seek and to find hidden motions in all the various forms of matter, and make

(222)

them say that light and heat are but manners of
motions and that temperature marks the velocity of
these motions, that among the molecules of matter
move the ethereal waves as wind in the branches
of trees, is a wonderful comment on the sayings of
the great preacher when we consider the age in
which he lived.

"Nor the ear filled with hearing." When the labors of matter are sufficiently violent to vibrate sixteen times per second our ears catch the vibrations
and we hear the low musical tone. As the vibrations increase the pitch increases till these vibrating
bodies swing back and forth nearly forty thousand
times per second. Our ear has distinguished each,
but now its gamut ends and stillness reigns, though
this cord vibrates on, forever increasing. Beyond
this our sense of hearing will not go. "The ear is
not filled." There are probable sounds in nature
that we never hear. These vibrating cords, as they
continue, present all the colors of the rainbow to the
eye and a sense of heat to the touch, through all
gradations of temperature. Thus is seen the inti-
macy of the eye and the ear and a suggestion of the
truth of internal senses that are too spacious to be
filled by even all the concomitant motions of matter;
that if these are ever filled that sufficiency will come
from science and sound too refined for our gross
senses.

"All things are full of labor." This means everything. To be full of labor is to be full of the power
of doing work, full of energy. To be full of energy
asserts the truth that nothing exists in a state of
rest. The air is filled with busy wings through sum-

mers and autumns; winter comes, these never-wea-
ried wings, though folded, are potent with the forces
that carry them on through all the modifications of
matter, more alive than when they transported the
body through its little instincts from flower to flower.   The animal kingdom seems never wearied in its
search for food.   Man is waked by the song of birds;
he rises and goes to the great business of life; his
ears ring with the clank of arms battling for a profi-
ciency, booming for a surplus, or cannonading at the
ramparts of luxury and ease.   The rivers keep up
their march to the ocean, the ocean is continually
heaving its mighty weight of waters on the shore.
The sun's heat is making light the vapors, these are
ever ascending from the ends of the earth, while
busy winds carry them all over the globe, and busy
currents precipitate these, and they take up their
march again for the sea.   Busy ocean currents plow
through every sea.   Some of them have velocities
much greater than any of our largest rivers.

Above the rush of all these winds and waters we
hear Solomon declare that he knows how the world
was made and that he understands the attractions
of the turnings; and David dispensing the great law
of gravitation and declaring that the sun had a motion which carries it and its retinue of worlds on
journeys of which we can form no conception.   Out
of the whirlwind, a vehicle of double motion, we hear
Him who made Orion and the seven stars bid Job answer him touching these motions that fill the earth.
High above the din of battle we hear Joshua exclaim:
"Sun, stand thou still upon Gibeon; and thou, Moon,
in the valley of Ajalon."   Thus is affixed the divine

seal to the motion of these worlds. Beyond these
we see busy worlds waltzing to their own merry music. Their ceaseless and never-ending motions
teach us the truth of the text that all things are full
of labor and that the earth bears its share in the
great cotillion of worlds. "It is a fine suggestion of
Humboldt's that if we could imagine those movements of the stellar universe which take place in long
periods to be compressed into a short space of time,
and were we endowed with telescopic vision to behold them, we should then vividly realize that there
is nowhere such a thing as rest. The stars, which
we term fixed, would be seen all in motion, constellations drawing together, clusters unfolding and
condensing, nebulæ breaking up, and universes melting away—motion in every part of the vault of heav-
en. Could we then be permitted to gaze into the living organism upon earth, plant and animal, we
should behold a kindred spectacle. The constituent
atoms in ceaseless movement, combining and separating, group dissolving and rearranging, and all cir-
culating in orderly and determined paths — movement in every point of the vital organism. Thus the
motions of everlasting suns, shot in radiant forms
across the universe, reappear in the movements of organic beings. The unity of the scheme is unbroken;
the harmonics of earthly life are but cadences of the
music of the spheres." Nothing is truer than that
all things are full of labor, that men can not tell it,
that the eye can not be satisfied with seeing nor the
ear filled with hearing. This brings us to consider
the real and apparent motions of the sun and our
earth and the many phenomena arising therefrom.

15

Job xxxviii. 12-15: "Hast thou commanded the morning since thy days; and caused the dayspring to know his place; that it might take hold of the ends of the earth, that the wicked might be shaken out of it? It is turned as clay to the seal; and they stand as a garment. And from the wicked their light is withholden, and the high arm shall be broken."

Let us first reconcile this term "wicked" as used twice in this text. This chapter is made up exclusively of questions. In it are found no less than forty questions propounded to Job. Strange to say, not one addresses itself to the wicked. Stranger still, there is not one but that is either directly or indirectly discussed in the literary schools of our own country. The first question asks about morning, the first part of the day; the second clause follows with the source of day, dayspring or sun; the third and fourth clauses are the purposes of the sun, while the fifth explicitly defines how these purposes are obtained; the sixth gives the relation of sun and earth; the seventh makes itself one of light by statement. In the thirteenth verse — "that the wicked might be shaken out of the earth"—can any one see how the wicked only are to be shaken out? Has that ever been done? Four thousand years have passed, and over half the world remains till this day in wickedness. But we do see and know that under the above conditions and through the motions there defined darkness is dispelled from the earth. In the fifteenth verse we can not see how the light of the sun can be withholden from the wicked especially, but we know that under the above conditions only can the light be withheld from the darkness that

gathers alternately about the poles of the earth.
There are two lights in the world: physical, the sun,
the center of the solar system; and Jesus Christ, the
spiritual Sun and center of our religious system.
"I am the light of the world." Did he mean physical light of the world? Most assuredly not. We
think that each of these lights is designed to teach
the other. From the sun flow all earthly blessings
and comforts; its fruit is the harvest of all our bodily
needs, and at the same time it feeds our senses with
all the various designs of the beautiful, falling alike
upon the just and upon the unjust. Our spiritual
Sun showers its harvests upon us till our spiritual
needs are met and till we become men, if we will,
built up by all its mysterious forces. Wickedness
is to the opposite of spiritual light precisely as darkness is to the opposite of physical light.

Proverbs iv. 19: "The way of the wicked is as darkness"—that is, the way of the one is brought about
as the way of the other. If we are turned from the
physical sun, we have night, are in darkness; so if
we turn from the spiritual Sun, we are in spiritual
darkness and are denominated "the wicked." If we
speak of physical light, we call its opposite darkness;
if of spiritual light, we term its opposite wickedness.
Without question, the topic under consideration is
one of physical light, light from a fixed sun, whose
purposes are set forth in the text. More, the term
"darkness" substituted for "wicked" will do no injustice to the word or thought, but will harmonize
these and add beauty to this most wonderful geographical dissertation touching earth motions, together with all the geography and the philosophy

and the astronomy gathered from these and prized by the world as its highest fund of human knowledge. The text will then be: "Hast thou commanded the morning since thy days; and caused the dayspring to know his place; that it might take hold of the ends of the earth, that the darkness might be shaken out of it? It is turned as clay to the seal; and they stand as a garment. And from the darkness their light is withholden, and the high arm shall be broken." This is no parable, no figure; is only spiritual so far as is the truth that God dispensed the sum of astronomical knowledge four thousand years before man conceived in his idle dreaming the least of the things told in the text. These are not broken passages, but one continuous argument by word and illustration, beginning where astronomers begin, making the same statements that they make, giving precisely the same illustrations as given by them, showing the same purposes and the same results. together with the exact how these purposes are attained.

We will examine the text in the order of its own divisions. The first clause introduces the subject as one of day and night. "Hast thou commanded the morning since thy days?" The second clause, the sun's place: "And caused the dayspring to know his place?" The third and fourth clauses are the purposes of the sun. The first purpose, that it [sun] might take hold of the ends of the earth;" second purpose, "that the darkness might be shaken out of it [earth]." The fifth clause tells how each of these purposes is brought about: "It [earth] is turned as clay to the seal." Each of these purposes is brought about by the same illustrative terms. In discussing this part of the text we will group these purposes separately with the manner of producing these separate designs. Then we will investigate this part thus: "That it [sun] might take hold of the ends of the earth." "It [earth] is turned as clay to the seal"—this the rotary motion of the earth. For the other motion, "That the darkness might be shaken out of it [earth], it is turned as clay to the seal." The sixth clause states the relation of earth to sun, motion, and rest, or the appearance to an observer on the earth as he watches the sun: "They stand as a garment." The seventh clause, motion of earth and sun through space: "And from the darkness their light is withholden, and the high arm shall be broken." In this arrangement of our topics we have given a general idea of the leading thoughts. We will follow with a strict word interpretation, and show that any other exposition of the above is impossible, and ours consistent.

DAY AND NIGHT.

"Hast thou commanded the morning since thy days?" Morning is the first part of day, and follows close on the last part of night. So night is implied in terms as strong as those that signify opposite conditions or day. "Hast thou commanded?" addressed as it is to Job must impress his mind with the truth of his supreme littleness and the fact that a something is able to exercise power or authority over the morning. "Command" literally means to send to, to send forth. These are the only literal meanings given by Mr. Webster. Then the morning is sent to,

and, secondly, the morning is sent forth. First, there
is nothing truer than that the morning is steadily
sent to the west every twenty-four hours, thus becoming a measure of the days. Second, there is
nothing truer than that the morning is sent forth,
out, abroad, and becomes a measure of the years.
These form the two motions of light over the earth.
The first, "sent to," flies on around the earth winter
and summer, remaining morning all the time. The
sun is not sent round, but morning. This dispenses
with sun motion as the cause of day and night.
Morning comes upon us; in one minute it appears fifteen miles west of us; in two minutes it is thirty
miles to our west; in one hour it is gone from us by a
distance of one thousand miles. So with every minute and hour during all the days and years the morning is "sent to" the west, which accounts for the apparent motion of the sun from east to west while the
morning is "sent to." It is, from December till June,
sent forth, minute by minute climbing higher, minute by minute spreading out, till March, when day
and night alternate during each revolution all over
the globe. The sun now seems to rise a little south
of east, and up he seems to climb higher, till June,
when his light falls far beyond the north pole, and
he is seen to our northeast. This is called, improperly, the sun's motion north. From June till December he seems to move in a direction toward the south;
minute by minute as the days go by he sends his light
in an opposite direction, till the sun in December is
seen again far to our south, indicating the extent to
which the morning is sent in that direction. This
is called, improperly, the sun's motion south. The

repetition of these light motions make the years as they go by. Thus the morning is "sent forth."

THE SUN'S PLACE.

"And caused the dayspring to know his place." "Dayspring," the sun. The pronoun "his" makes it a masculine noun. Astronomers call it a luminous body, because it emits light. Job's Lord calls it by a term which illustrates its office and at the same time makes it a stationary thing. It is the source of light and heat as a spring is the source of water supply. From it streams of light and heat pour forth into space in every direction. It is the world's never-failing fountain of light. The name illustrates all the needful and pleasing results afforded by the sun. It does this in its bounties which are so necessary to all life, animal and vegetable; it does this in the manner of its issuance from that body. There is in some respects a similarity of appearance. Newcomb compares the sun's appearance to a plate of rice soup. Willson's theory supposes that the sun is composed of a solid dark globe, surrounded by three atmospheres. The first is composed of a cloudy covering, possessing high reflecting power; the second is composed of an incandescent gas, and is the seat of the light and the heat of the sun; the third, or outer one, is transparent, like our atmosphere. That the spots are but openings seen in these atmospheres, made by powerful upward currents. From these light and heat pour forth. Did you ever see a boiling spring? See the small white pebbles that cover the bottom; see the smaller ones as they are borne upward by the rising current. I do not say that this has the appearance of a plate of rice soup. I leave you to say whether or not the spring resembles in its appearance Newcomb's given appearance of the sun. These outward currents of the spring pour through openings in the solid crust of the earth and flow off, unresisted, in every direction. Does this not resemble the issuance of light and heat from the sun? The illustration does not stop here. A spring is a fixed, stationary thing; we get its bounties by turning to it. So we get the light of the sun by turning to it. The whole earth, by the two motions turning and moving, gets the light of the sun. The same is true in a moral sense. Jesus Christ is the Dayspring from on high; everywhere we hear the entreaty, "turn." The sinner turns to him for the waters of life, for light and immortality.

"His place." The sun has a place, one that belongs to him. Astronomers and geographers—theorizing on the solar system, its motions, its light, and heat center, the seasons and years—first give the sun a special place, that he might do the things accredited to him. Job's Lord does this, and makes this the central truth upon which hang the two mights found in the text: that he "might take hold of the ends of the earth" and that the "darkness might be shaken out of it [the earth]."

Let us see how much depends upon "his place." Astronomically, the first work to be done is to determine the sun's place. When Kepler assumed the ellipse as the shape of planetary orbits, and had assumed the sun's place at the center, he followed the planet Mars in its course; but very soon there was a great discrepancy between the observed and com-

puted place as before. He assumed another hypothesis: he determined to place the sun at one of the
foci of the ellipse, and once more hunted down the
truth. For a whole year he traced the planet along
the imaginary orbit, and it did not diverge. The
truth was discovered at last, and Kepler announced
his first great law: "planets revolve in ellipses, with
the sun at one focus." "His place." This determined, the mystery was solved. How important to
determine the sun's place! How suggestive the in-
terrogation made to Job! There are two places, and
only two, and these situated so nearly alike that we
might say that there is in reality but one place for the
sun in this area of many quadrillions of square miles
where it could affect the two mights found in the
text, and that "his place." It turns up that the
stone of stumbling through all the ages becomes the
chief of the corner for astronomical knowledge, laid,
as sought and found by Kepler, the beginning of the
corner. The finding of the sun's place cost him seventeen years of unremitting toil. The importance of
this matter will be appreciated when we learn that
the decision of the learned world is that "this was
one of the greatest astronomical triumphs." Is it
not strange that Kepler should begin his researches
precisely where the great Lecturer began his discussion of earth motions? Something else depends on
"his place." It is observed that planets do not move
with equal velocities in different parts of their orbits.
These varying velocities absolutely depend upon "his
place." Kepler next set about to establish some law
by which these varying velocities could be computed
and the place of the planets determined. His re-

searches led him to his second law: "A line connecting the center of the earth with the center of the sun passes over equal spaces in equal times." It affords a certain means for calculating the velocity and for locating the exact place of any planet. There is still another thought connected with "his place" in our discussion that makes it still interesting when we consider that it too is dependent upon "his place." It was found that certain relations existed between the times of the revolutions of the planets about the sun and their mean distance from that body. Again Kepler hunted it down, and gave us his third law: "The squares of the times of the revolutions of the planets about the sun are proportional to the cubes of their mean distances from the sun." Speaking of these laws, Mr. Steele says: "These constitute almost the sum of astronomical knowledge, and form one of the most precious conquests of the human mind." Before Kepler the world had its theories, some of them hundreds of years old. The sun either had been awarded no place or had not been found in "his place." Vain gazers had looked upon the earth as a center about which the sun and all the stars move. Kepler, finding "his place," moved the world's observatory to it, and marked out planetary orbits with precision, computed their velocities, computed the times of their revolutions, and gave a law by which we are enabled to locate the planets. When he saw the secret and found the truth he exclaimed: "Nothing holds me; the die is cast; the book is written, to be read now or by posterity, I care not which. It may well wait a century for a reader, since God has waited six thousand years for an observer."

Reader, it does look like the sun rises and sets; the earth seems to be the center around which all else revolves. That could not be, and the sun have a place. The world saw this deception, and determined that these move about the sun in circles, and that the sun is situated in the center. This later conclusion was for a while accepted, and the theory accounted for on the ground that the circle was the most beautiful figure. Were this true, we would not attach so great importance to "his place," for then things would be just what they seem. But the fact that these move in elongated circles, with the sun stationed at one end, offers high reasons why it should be a leading question in Job's recitation. This is a peculiar place. In our opinion this question, its importance in researches along this line, its position in the discussion, give the very strongest proof of divine inspiration. In this matter, like all others, God has his way; those who find him in his way and work must come to his way. Had the world given the Bible that importance due to it from the time of the writing of the text, it would have saved itself a shameful record of its foolishness and the folly of men for thousands of years, trying to go another way, subjecting all things to fancy, and imputing to it reason. I make this bold statement: that Kepler absolutely sought the answer to Job's question as though propounded to him. "Kepler, dost thou know the sun's place?" He was seventeen years answering this single question. More, every discovery along all the lines of our advancement has been reached in a manner and in terms, and dispensed in a manner and in terms, very similar to a Bible-suggested procedure and in Bible terms. Before we close this discussion we will present you with a Bible illustration drawn from the text, and demonstrate to your satisfaction each of the laws given by Kepler.

"Caused . . . to know his place." "Caused calls his mind to the truth when given to him, and mine to it as now investigating, that a something was the cause that made the sun "to know his place." Then we live in a cause world, surrounded by causes that make suns know and hold their places. How logically are we led to the desired truth! Job, did you cause the sun to know his place? Were you the sun's teacher? Do you even know his place? Has he a place? These thoughts led to investigation; investigation found "his place" under Kepler; while "cause to know" was reserved for Isaac Newton. "Cause." Mr. Webster says that the root of this word coincides with that of castle, caste, etc., which expresses a driving, that which produces an effect. The effect here is "to know his place." Then from its own term we develop the truth that force taught the sun its place. This drops it into the lap of philosophy. Force impelled the sun to take his place; force holds him in his place with irresistible grasp. From effect we go to cause; this we call law. All matter is under law. It yields with such willing obedience that a sense of knowing is imputed to it. Here we have a globe a million times larger than our earth, held in his place, yet moving on, showing a childish obedience to every impulse, and that so promptly that his acts and motions say that he moves from an apprehended wish of that which controls. He does this with such a promptitude and such an exactness that we impute to him a knowledge of knowing his place as to position and his place as a worker, that he might do the things, the very things spoken of him in the text. Each planet that circles about him performs all its motions with a regularity and with such undeviating certainty that it seems endued with capacities of perception, of knowing its place. The very atoms that compose all matter, while too small to be seen by the most powerful glass, yet each, through the forces that drive it, is thus caused to know its place in all its diversified chemical unions. At one time we see these atoms rush into an embrace sweet and close, as if drawn by a fitful knowledge of experienced love. We see others, nitrogen and hydrogen, even in a receiver together exemplifying a sense of bashfulness or cold sullenness, stand off like two pouting, timid children. But when caught up together in any substance they seem to become more affable and to form for each other an attachment powerful and strong; for the very instant that the substance is dissolved and they are liberated from this union, they then combine and form a product truly their own. This is so uniform, so certain, that a chemist knows the result that will be produced by a union of these elements before they are combined. He knows how these atoms will act; he operates with them as though they were intelligences. So potent is the thought that our chemists call it "chemical behavior." If these little atoms are caused to know their places, we must not wonder at a sense of knowledge being imputed to the great sun. We see it in all the wide field where forces are doing work. Could we instantly create matter and

as instantly drop it from our hands, like the oldest
forms, it would go straight to the ground. It would
obey the law of gravitation as promptly as the oldest
rock or metal. Matter will do the same thing under
the same conditions and the same surroundings
every time. Every change of conditions and surroundings will produce corresponding changes in its
acts. We watch this modification under the slightest force or the slightest change of surroundings till
we are persuaded that matter is, to say the least of it,
semisentient, especially when we affix "caused to
know." Scientists admit as much when speaking of
the stars. "Those far-off lights seem full of meaning
to us could we but read their holy message; they become real and sentient, and, like the soft eyes in
pictures, look lovingly and inquiringly upon us. We
come into communion with another life, and the soul
asserts its immortality more strongly than ever before." "The heavens declare the glory of God; and
the firmament showeth his handiwork. Day unto
day uttereth speech, and night unto night showeth
knowledge." We live surrounded by worlds of matter, matter full of meaning, teaching, talking matter.
These teach the great law of causation, which is the
thought of God himself. "Caused to know his
place" is the theme of the great singer in his sub-
limest of all songs. These definitions and explanations bring us now to consider the earth's daily motion, or its motion on its own axis. We will first present you with the statements of geographers touching these motions. We propose to show from our
text all the statements presented by geographers
pertaining to the earth. They teach that there are

eight major planets stationed at different distances
from the sun, and that these revolve each on its own
axis, producing alternations of day and night, in
many respects similar to ours; that the days and
nights differ in length each from the others. Some
have more light and heat than others. All differ in
their seasons and the length of their years. They
travel in different orbits, with different velocities.
The sun's position relative to these makes these dif-
ferences. That planet nearest the sun moves fastest, has the smallest orbit, and consequently the
shortest year. That planet most remote from the
sun has the greatest orbit, moves slowest, and consequently has the longest year. This is due to a difference in distance from the sun. The earth rotates on
its axis from west to east, completing its revolution
in twenty-four hours. When our eastern horizon is
depressed below the sun we say that the sun is rising; when we are wheeled directly under the sun we
say that it is noon; when our western horizon is being elevated above the sun we say that the sun is
setting. We thus attribute our motion to the sun,
and say that it rises and sets. Let us illustrate this
motion by the spinning of a top. Let us imagine the
top as not standing perpendicularly on the floor, but
slightly inclined. Make a spot on the side of the top,
and if it does not revolve too rapidly you will observe the spot moving into sight and as rapidly moving out of sight as the top turns the spot to and from
your eye. Now your eye was supposed to be in the
sun's place. Suppose your eyes were fixed where the
spot is and you could see the sun, you would experience all the phenomena of a rising, a noonday, and a

setting sun as the top turns your eye to, under, and from the sun. The United States is but a small spot on the globe. We imagine the globe standing on the south pole, leaning slightly as it spins round like our top. The United States comes round, bringing the sun to our sight, and we say that the sun is rising; the earth moves on till we are brought directly under the sun, and we say that it is noon; the earth moves on, and as the sun is passing from our sight in the west we say that the sun is setting. These changes, you see, are brought about by earth-motion. This motion alone would make the sun appear to rise and set all the time precisely in the same place, and make our days and nights of the same length forever. The earth has another motion, one about the sun. This motion gives to the sun the appearance of moving north or south. In December the sun seems to rise far south of east and west points; till June, on each succeeding morning he seems to rise farther north than on the preceding morning, when his rays fall far north of east and west points. These are the bounds of his apparent movement. This sun-motion, like the first, is also a deception, and is due to the motion of the earth. These changing positions of the earth produce corresponding changes in the length of our days and nights and in the temperature on the earth. These make our seasons. One cycle of changes is the measure of a year. The two purposes of lighting and heating the earth are, like the two motions, simultaneous and continuous. So, when speaking of the heat ray the light ray is not to be neglected or forgotten, nor are we to neglect the heat ray when talking of the light ray. They come together. This

brings us to consider the rotary motion of the earth,
or its motion on its own axis, from revelation. When
we have made this motion plain we will define each
term used and show ours the only interpretation possible.

"It [the earth] is turned as clay to the seal."

"Turn" has two meanings, and only two: to turn as
a wheel, and circular motion. These correspond to
the two motions of the light, sent to and sent forth.
The first of these is the rotary motion of the earth,
that motion that allows the light to be sent to the
west, and the motion that we are now considering.
The second is the other earth-motion, motion in a circle, the one that allows the light to be sent forth or
abroad, while it is being sent to the west at the same
time. This motion we will consider presently.
These two motions of the earth are simultaneous
and continuous, warranted by the text. So, when
considering its rotary motion, its circular motion is
not to be forgotten or neglected, nor are we to forget
or neglect its rotary motion while considering its
circular motion. These two motions produce the
changes of light and heat positions on the earth.
"It [the earth] is turned." A positive declaration
that the earth turns. More, it implies force, for the
earth is purely passive. "It is turned." It does not
turn, but is turned. And the very how is given in the
simplest language, at the same time naming a very
common instrument that will illustrate this how.
"As clay to the seal." Or like clay to the seal. Seal
is not the instrument, but the writing on that instrument. So it is not the turning of the clay, but the
turning of the writing made on the clay by the seal.

16

Then the earth is turned as the writing of a seal is turned when transferred to the clay, or the same transferred from the clay to the seal. Take a stick of printer's type, which is set up as the writing on a seal, get a piece of clay, and you are supplied with everything necessary for illustrating transfer of motion as seen in the sun when compared to the earth. That motion of the sun, when transferred to the earth, transfers the turnings we see in the sun to the earth and makes it real earth-motion, as the writing of the seal is turned when the writing is transferred to the clay. Your clay is before us and also your stick of type. You observe that the letters of your type are inverted and turned about; you observe also that you read from right to left instead of from left to right. The whole presents a confusion, at least to one not experienced in reading type. Make an impression on the clay with your type; now the letters are all erect, and we read from left to right without any confusion. If the writing is turned as this motion is transferred, then the direction in which this writing is read is the direction of this motion of the earth. Let us now apply our illustration to the rising of the sun. We say that the sun rises. Let us prove, according to the statement made to Job, that the earth turns and produces the phenomenon of day. Let us set in type across the sun the clause, "It is turned," just as it would stand were we going to use it as a seal (see Sun, Fig. 1), arranging it as to coincide with the earth's equator when brought into contact with the earth. Examine this seal reading: the letters are inverted, the right side of each letter is turned to the left, and the left is turned to the

right; you read the clause from right to left, at the
same time you feel a sense of confusion. Apply
now the earth to the sun as clay to the seal, and the
turning attributed to the sun will be as the turning
of the clay to the seal. Job's Lord says that the earth
is turned just this way. We said that it was the
turning of the writing that illustrates the turns of
the earth. Now the letters on the earth are erect,
and are read from left to right or from west to east.
Then the earth turns from west to east, that the
morning may be "sent to" the west. In this reading
there is no confusion. It is intelligible, and teaches

Figure 1.

o Observer's position. He is supposed to face north.

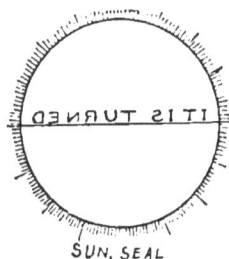

real earth-motion and the direction of that motion.
The confusion found in reading the seal writing
illustrates that confusion that hid the real motion
for four thousand years. This was the stone of
stumbling through all the ages. All earth-motions,
when compared to the sun or stars, are practically
illustrated in this way. Star maps and the survey-
or's common flat compass are examples. Even a
map of the earth's surface partakes of this in a
measure. In learning the cardinal points I am
told to face the north; then my right hand will be
toward the east and my left toward the west, and my

back will be toward the south. My face takes a position with reference to a star, north star, while my right hand, my left hand, and my back are but a species of seal writing coming from that star. I have a star map, and I wish to locate some particular star. If the star is in the north, I face the south; if the star is in the south, I face the north. Each time I elevate the star map above my head and look upward at it. The map is a seal; I place it above the thing to receive the impression. A surveyor's compass is an instrument for guiding us along the lines of a survey or for marking new lines. The old line is traced and the new one determined with reference to the north star. Toward these our needles all point (variations excepted). Let us examine the compass. It has a shape similar to that of a seal. Its use resembles the use of a seal in that it makes an impression which is to the reverse of the writing on the compass. If I wish to trace a line anywhere between north and east, I set my compass with the star on the face toward the north and wait for the needle to come to a state of rest and pointing directly to the star. I turn the compass to the desired direction. When I look at my compass I see that I have turned toward W for west, instead of toward E for east. So the motion of the compass was just the opposite to the letters on its face. E is where the geographical west point should be, while W for west is where the geographical east point should be. I elevate the compass above my head with its face downward and the star on the compass toward the north star, and each of the letters takes its geographical place. The compass would make it the motion of the star, applying it as seal to the clay or the line, and it becomes line turns east. Starting at the equator, I follow the needle till I have gone sixty miles; now the north star has risen one degree above the horizon; when I have gone another sixty miles, I see this same star two degrees above the horizon. As I advance this star seems to rise higher and higher, till I stand directly under it. My own motion made this star rise on me, as the earth's own motion makes the sun rise on it. No other illustration is so simple, so illustrative, nor any other apparatus so cheap. "It is turned as clay to the seal." It was this idea, and this alone, that carried Copernicus through his demonstration and afforded proof of the deceptiveness of this motion. Then the rising and the setting of the sun are not due to sun-motions, but due to the motion of the earth, which is transferred in the same manner that a correctly written clause on the earth would appear on this sun were it printed there from this earth writing as a seal. This brings us to consider the first purpose of this turning as clay to the seal.

"That it [the sun] might take hold of the ends of the earth." Then the earth is turned as clay to the seal, that the sun might take hold of its ends.

"The ends of the earth." The equator is an imaginary line passing around the earth from east to west midway between the poles. This line marks the center of the torrid zone. The northern limit of this zone is twenty-three and one-half degrees north of the equator, and is marked by the Tropic of Cancer. The southern limit is twenty-three and one-half degrees south of the equator, and is marked by the Tropic of Capricorn. The sun never rises north of

Cancer or south of Capricorn. Geographers say that
the sun always rises and sets within these bounds;
that the sun holds to this region amid all the changes
of the earth. It only remains for us to show that
this region marks the bounds of the ends of the earth.
First, it is a literal truth. Within these bounds lie
the northern end of Australia, the southern end of
Eurasia, the northern end of Africa, the southern
end of North America, the northern end of South
America, and the numerous islands of the Pacific; or
the southern end of the eastern hemisphere and also
the southern end of the western hemisphere. The
former shows that one end of each individual land
mass was in these bounds; the latter form, indeed,
the ends of the great land masses of the earth. "That
it might take hold of the ends of the earth." No
sun ever rose north nor ever set south of these ends.
Secondly, it is a geometrical truth. The extremity of
the longer side of a thing we call its end; the length
of its shorter side we call its breadth. The equatorial diameter of the earth is twenty-six and a half
miles longer than its polar diameter. Then the extremity of its longer diameter must mark one end of
the earth, while the extremity of the shorter diameter must mark the breadth. The earth is rather tur-
nip-shaped, with the torrid zone along the bulge.
The expression says "ends." Three hundred and
sixty degrees make a great circle; the equator is defined as such a circle. If we allow one diameter for
each degree along this great circle, the earth would
present to the sun the ends of three hundred and sixty diameters each twenty-four hours. Allow it a diameter for each two minutes of longitude, each

twenty-four hours the earth would present to the sun over ten thousand ends. Proverbs xxx. 4: "Who hath established all the ends of the earth?" They are many. Thirdly, it is philosophically located by Bible statement. Psalm cxxxv. 7: "He causeth the vapors to ascend from the ends of the earth." One end of each of the great land masses contributes its influence to this result. David uses a term express- ive of plurality, "ends," and locates them with a pre- cision that no geographer can excel; and his state- ment is an example of the truth that the sun does take hold here. Job xxviii. 24-26: "For he looketh to the ends of the earth, and seeth under the whole heav- en; to make the weight for the winds; and he weigh- eth the waters by measure. When he made a decree for the rain, and a way for the lightning of the thun- der." "He looketh to the ends of the earth." He ex- pects this part of the earth to make the weight for the winds. It is true that the ends of the earth are the birthplace of the winds, the source of that general circulation that blows all over the globe. It is also true that one end of all the great land masses con- tributes to this result. This process began when he made a decree for the rain and a way for the light- ning of the thunder. Along this line of central stoves there is no frost, no snow, no ice, except in high, elevated regions or from other local causes. Here the heat does its work of sending up the vapors, and by the same act invites the winds to scatter them over the earth. Had David said that the vapors as- cend from the torrid zone, or Job that he expects the torrid zone to make the weight for the winds, it could not have been more explicit.

"Might take hold." "That it [the sun] might take hold of the ends of the earth [the torrid zone]." We have shown you that the sun rises and sets continually within these bounds. Then, aside from other proof, the text affords sufficient proof that the torrid zone is the bounds of sun-motion, for the part held to by the sun is this zone, whether called ends or not. This is the sun's astronomical position. The sun was caused to know his place for this, as the first of two purposes mentioned in the text. Let us now see how this act of taking hold is philosophically executed. "The molecules of the sun are in rapid vibrations; these set in motion waves of ether, which dart across the intervening space with the velocity of light, and, surging against the earth, give up their motion to it, the earth. These surging waves, arrested by the surface of the earth, their motion is converted into heat. Pounding on the end of a wedge with a maul makes the end of the wedge warm. This warmth is the product arising from the motion of the maul being instantly arrested by the wedge or the motion of the maul setting up motion in the wedge. Bend a wire rapidly this way and that to break it, and the resistance to its moving particles produces heat enough to burn the hand. Heat is the parent of motion and *vice versa*. Resistance is the enemy of motion, but the parent of heat. The surface of the earth offers the resistance. Here the ethereal motion sets up motion, and here the earth literally takes hold of this motion and arrests it. If it is the motion of the sun coming to the earth and establishing that motion in the earth, then the earth literally takes hold of the sun. "Take" and "hold"

means to stay. In the torrid zone it is always hot.
The reason offered is that the sunbeams fall perpendicularly on this region all the year. The sun was
caused to know his place that it might take hold of
the ends of the earth—that is, the ends of the sun's
central diameters might meet the ends of the earth's
central diameters, that, like the motions of the maul
on the wedge, these solar strokes, falling perpendicularly all the year, would make the heat of the sun
hold to the ends. The bounds of continuous heat are
limited to the ends. Then the conclusion is that it
does not stay in other regions as it does here.

"Might take hold." "Might." The leading idea
of this verb is power or possibility. If the peculiarity of the sun's place is to afford the sun a possibility
to do the things accredited to him in specified
bounds, then we conclude that from no other position
could the sun possibly give us the days and nights,
the seasons and zones, such as we now have. "It
[the earth] is turned as clay to the seal," "that it
[the sun] might take hold of the ends of the earth."
Now the turning of the earth is such that it might
present its equatorial diameters to the sun; then it
must turn these diameters in a way that the sun
might reach them, for he can not move, he has a
place. As he takes hold only along the line of these
central diameters and through the motions of these
diameters, then the earth turns to the sun to produce day and from it to make night. There is a liberal interpretation that we offer.

"That it might take and hold." The spectrum ex-
hibits three classes of rays: heat, luminous, and
chemical rays. These rays during all the ages have

been falling on the earth. They have played a very important part in working the changes found in the earth. They tear down and build up, they destroy and make alive. Traces of their first work remain to this day. Not one sunbeam has ever fallen upon the earth and returned to the sun or stars. Its form may be modified. A sunbeam may be a worker in the torrid zone to-day, sending up vapor; this, wrapped in the crystal spray, on the wind rides and flies, it may be, to some fertile valley, some elevated plain, or some chilled mountain top, there throws off its garment to bless the valley, enliven the plain, or cap the mountain with snow; then enters another field of labor. Its cycle will only end with the death of terrestrial motions. "Geologists count the world's growth from remains that were built up from these forces. In the laboratory of the leaf, forests were built up, sun-forces garnered. These carried their mines of reserved force to the earth. Coal is but crystallized sunbeams, fagots of force ready to impart to us at any moment the heat of some old carboniferous day. The oil-well spouts not alone unsavory kerosene, but liquid sunbeams, the garnered store of a geological age. As we warm ourselves by our fires or sit and read by our oil or gas lights, how strange the thought that their light and heat streamed down upon the earth ages ago, were absorbed by grotesque leaves of the old coal forests, and kept safely stored away by a divine care in order to provide for our comfort!"

"Hast thou commanded the morning since thy days; and caused the dayspring to know his place; that it might take hold of the ends of the earth? . . .

It is turned as clay to the seal." The real motion of the clay (earth) is transferred to the seal (sun), and there it is truly apparent motion.

NOTE.—"It Is turned." If the letters of these three words should stand on the sunbeams as they would on a seal, inverted, and the words transposed; then they would fall with the same significance on each of the planets alike, and each would interpret this reading as clay to the seal. Now there are ten planets. So there are ten letters in these three words. These three words make a complete sentence. It is used with an obvious antecedent: each of the planets as addressed by the sun becomes subject. Thus in our written language we have a system of words representing our solar system. More, this system becomes an illustration of its motions, the direction of these motions, the combination of its parts, their relations, the unlikes that made them into bulks, and the attractive influences that hold them to one common thought, or purpose, as manifested by similarity in every respect. Out of the eight letters composing the words "is turned" five are initial letters for five of the planets: i and s, for Mercury (the Greeks called it "The Sparkling One"); e, for Earth; s, Saturn; u, Uranus; n, Neptune.

YEARLY PATH OF THE SUN THROUGH THE HEAVENS.

We hope you will observe the potency of this transfer of motion as expressed both by Copernicus and Job and as manifested in the heading given above. It is not meant to discuss here the yearly path of the sun through the heavens. Astronomers do not know which way this great movement is directed, nor do they know the center about which this movement is made. It is the yearly path of the earth through the heavens that we intend talking about. Geographers head this topic in the same way, and then they make their demonstrations and illustrations say that the earth is the moving body. This is the result of that

peculiar manifestation of motion seen in the sun and
stars. Wonderful, wonderful the expression "it is
turned as clay to the seal!" By it the mystery that
shrouded these motions is made childishly simple.
There is another correspondence that revelation observed—that is, the order in which these topics are
discussed. Geographers discuss first the daily motion and then the yearly motion of the earth, and
that in the same chapter; and by the use of the same
illustration is each motion demonstrated. Revelation does not vary from this in the least. These illustrations show and mean precisely the same thing.
Copernicus tells how this motion is, and tells how
the deception is brought about. Job tells the same,
and makes the very statement an illustration, and
the only illustration possible for the story of Copernicus. By no other method is it possible to paint
transfer of motion save by the seal and clay. It is
said that our Bible has no science in it, no terms expressive of scientific thought. Let us see. These
motions of which we are talking engaged the minds
of Copernicus, Kepler, Galileo, and Newton. Touching this thought, Mr. Steele, in speaking of the laws
Kepler evolved from these motions, says: "They form
one of the most precious conquests of the human
mind." Now we have the statements of each, we
have the illustrations of each, we have a full understanding of the facts as given by each. Now aline
Job along with these learned men above, place each
back to back with Job. Then tell me, on the honor
of a man, which is the taller. You can't deny the
fact that you see in Job the look of Goliah, while in
his hand you see the sling of David. No science in

the Bible? Bosh! It is the mother of science; it is
the father of science; it is a compendium of all
learning, all knowledge, all wisdom crystallized. If
Copernicus can use an illustration to show that the
motion of the sun is only apparent, that it is a deception, that the earth simply revolves on its own axis to
produce day and night, and then use the same illustration to show its yearly motions about the sun,
and make us say that instead of the sun moving
north and south, as it certainly appears to do in summer and winter, the earth simply moves back and
forth around it—if, I say, Copernicus can do this,
then we feel authorized by scientific example to say
that the course laid down to Job is no departure. It
is more satisfactory, since the same thought is to be
illustrated, and no new applications. This brings us
to consider the second division of our text, the motion of the earth about the sun.

"Hast thou commanded the morning since thy
days; and caused the dayspring to know his place;
. . . that the darkness might be shaken out of it?
It is turned as clay to the seal."

The first object was the presentation of its ends to
the sun to produce day and night. While this motion is continuous, another motion is added that does
in no way change the direction of these ends. Having defined all the terms used in the text, except
"shake," we propose to examine it at this time.

"Shake." This is a household word. It finds its
use in every family circle throughout the English-
speaking world, from the five-year-old child to the
aged man or woman, each alike. While every one
might not be able to give Mr. Webster's definition,

yet each can do more: he can illustrate it. Curious
to say, each will give the same illustration. Hand
a child something to be shaken. This should be done
in a way that the child realizes a necessity or that he
should not think it a joke or quiz. Hand him a small
bottle (the smaller the better) containing a liquid,
and ask him to shake it for you. Observe closely the
motion of his hand. Take the bottle and shake it
yourself, and as you shake it watch very closely the
motion of your hand. When you have done, draw on
paper the figure described by the moving hand, and
you will have evidently the picture of a "shake."
Let us now compare Mr. Webster's definition of this
word to the picture of your shake and the manner
of making it, and see how nicely you have illustrated
its meaning. "Shake, to cause to move rapidly one
way, then another." This term was used to illustrate to Job how the earth moved to rid itself of
darkness. Now we have two motions: one way, then
another. It takes both to get the darkness out.
"One way;" this gets the darkness out, but must do
more, or the motion, "then another," would not be
necessary. "One way" relieves the darkness at one
quarter, but admits it to the opposite quarter. "Then
another" relieves the earth of darkness, and then the
former opposite quarters have exchanged light and
darkness. The definition justifies our expression,
"opposite quarters." Darkness participates in the
shake, as it also moves back and forth. The limit of
"one way" is the limit to the greatest light in one
quarter, while the limit of "then another" must be
the limit of the greatest light in that other quarter.
As the shake was a chase after darkness, then in

truth the greatest darkness must be always to the greatest limit opposite the greatest light. If this earth-motion "one way" be its motion north, "then another" must be its earth-motion south. If one be its motion east, then the other must be its motion west. Mr. Webster prefixes "caused to move." The sun was caused to know his place for purposes. Now the earth is caused to move rapidly one way, then another, to accomplish the very purposes for which the sun was fixed. Then which moves? Let us now speak of the three rays of the sunbeam. In the earth's lesser motion we spoke of the heat ray and those rays that produce the changes in matter and are termed chemical rays. Now we speak of the light ray, a thing that does not stay, a thing very unstable, that comes and goes with a shake. In the first we looked at the heat and chemical rays apart, as presented, yet a combination. The combination is manifest by "that it [sun] might take hold"—all the virtues of a sun. The same may be said of the light ray. While it is a part of the combination, we here consider it apart from the others. "That the darkness might be shaken out of the earth," not the ends only, but the whole earth. (See Fig. 2.)

The observer sees the sun rise far to the southeast December 20. At this time the center of the sun is in a line with the tropic of Capricorn and the center of the earth. Each morning the sun seems to rise a trifle farther toward the earth's north pole. The cause of this apparent sun motion is a real motion of the earth toward its own south pole. This apparent motion of the sun, the real motion of the earth, continues till the sun has apparently moved from A to B, its position June 21. Now a line connecting the center of the sun and the center of the earth passes through the tropic of Cancer. During these six months the sun has never risen south of Capricorn or north of Cancer—a proof that during this half of the year the sun's center falls continuously upon the earth's center and takes hold of its ends. From June 21 the observer watching the setting sun sees it at C, far to the northwest; each evening he sees the sun set a trifle farther toward the earth's south pole. This apparent sun-motion is due to a real motion of

Figure 2.

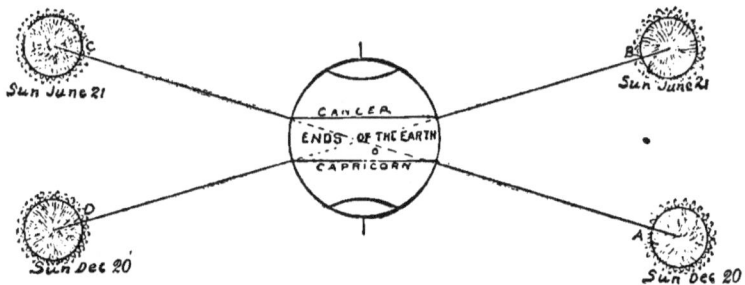

o Observer's position. The center of the sun from its opposite position ever holds to this point.

the earth toward its own north pole. This continues till the sun is seen far to the southwest December 20, never setting north of Cancer or south of Capricorn. This completes the earth's yearly journey about the sun. These sun-motions are due to earth-motion in an opposite direction to the sun's apparent motion.

In winter we have all noticed that the sun seems to rise and set low in the south (see Fig. 2, sun's position December 20), considerably south of east and west points. As spring and summer advance he seems to

rise higher and higher, or farther north, each morning, till he reaches the sun's position June 21 (see Fig.
2), when his rays fall on the north side of our dwell-
ings or north of east and west points. This motion
of the sun north is only apparent; the real motion of
the earth south produces this deception. This motion can be justly interpreted only as the writing on
the seal to its impression in the clay. Copernicus
transferred this motion of the sun to the earth, and
termed it "transfer of motion." Such is the explanation given by the learned world to-day. Let us apply
Job's method and see if we can not prove the deceptiveness of this motion equally as well, and at the
same time prove the very direction of this motion,
and offer a simple illustration, one easily understood, easily retained. In our first illustration we
showed the earth's movement on its own axis with
reference to its east and west points. Now we talk
of the earth's great motion about the sun, its motion north or south, with reference to a fixed sun.
In other words, we are illustrating the sun's apparent motion north. We now look upon this machine as we would a map, and see just what we
mean when we say that the sun moves north or
south. When we say that the sun moves north we
mean that it appears to move in the direction of
the earth's north pole, and when we say that the sun
moves south we mean that it appears to move in the
direction of the earth's south pole. So with all our
illustrations. First let us suppose it to be the 20th
day of December, and we see the sun in the east, as
shown in Figure 2. From this point the sun, as we
say, begins to move north. (See Fig. 3.) Let us set

17

in type along the ends of those sunbeams that come
to the earth our clause "it is turned," just as the letters would stand when affixed to a seal. As the
earth passes under each of these letters, each leaves
its impression on the earth till "It is turned" occurs
across the torrid zone as you see in Figure 3. This
shows that the motion of the earth was such as to
depress its south pole. Then, instead of the sun
moving north, the earth simply moves south. "That

Figure 3.

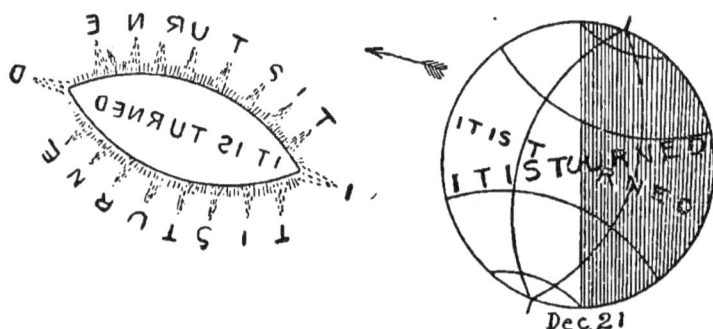

The earth rotates on its axis from west to east. This is indicated by the correct reading along the earth's equator. The
earth's motion about the sun is also from west to east. This is
indicated by correct reading across the Torrid Zone from southwest to northeast. The impressions of these words, we suppose,
were made on the earth from the seal-writing as seen on the
sun and also on the sunbeams that fall on the earth's orbit.

the darkness might be shaken out of it [earth]."
"It is turned as clay to the seal." Now the earth
has moved "one way." At this point (Fig. 4) the
earth begins, "then another way," to complete the
shake. Now you see the darkness is at the south
pole and light at the north pole. The relation of
earth and sun is just the reverse of that seen December 20. The earth, in reality, begins to move north,
that the darkness might be shaken out of it. The

earth returns to the beginning, passing on an opposite side of the sun. D marks the sun's center on
the earth; so in reverse order each letter in turn as
it passes the sun's center on till the earth comes
back to her position December 21. The same visible
finger as seen in the direction of the reading is an
index to its motion; thus the earth moves back as
before. "To cause to move rapidly one way, then
another." This can not refer to points in space

Figure 4.

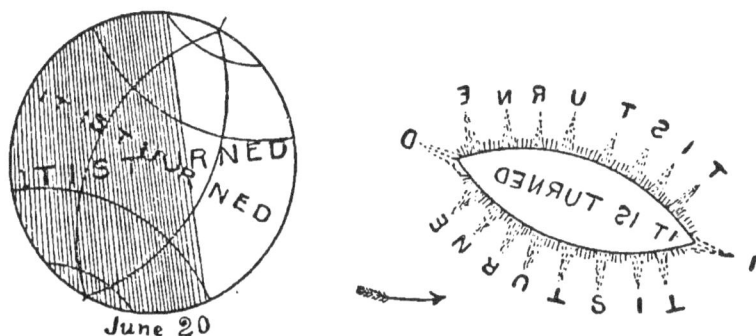

June 20

The earth has now reached her greatest distance from the
sun, and at this point turns to retrace her steps. Should we
drop each letter from the earth as the sun's center reaches it,
we observe that the letters would be dropped in reverse order
to that which was observed in placing them in position, and the
journey would end at the beginning, and all the letters be
dropped.

so directly as to a central something about which
this movement is made. How beautifully does this
account for the apparent motions of the sun, and
how truthfully do they award these to the earth!
"To cause to move rapidly one way, then another."
The earth moves at a mean velocity of eighteen
miles per second, many times faster than a cannon-
ball travels. So we are given an idea of its velocity by the text. Let us now illustrate the three

laws of Kepler. We will begin by presenting you with a picture of your shake. If the earth travels the line of a shake in its rapidly moving one way, then another, then its orbit will be an ellipse as your shake is, and the moving force appear as marked by the sun, not the center.

Let us now present you with a Bible text that will fully and simply place before you a shake, that you

Figure 5.

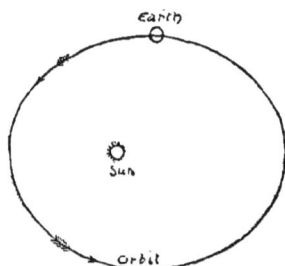

SHAKE.

Figure 6.

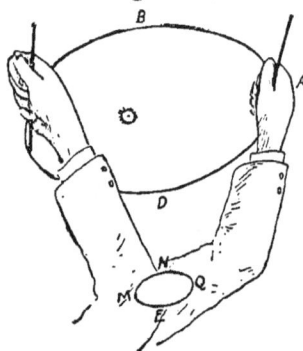

THIS YOUR SHAKE.

Isaiah x. 15: "Shall the saw magnify itself against him that shaketh it?" This is an illustration so simple that no cut or engraving can improve. See the motion of the saw in the hand of him that shaketh it. The motion is back and forth, and the figure elliptical, unmistakably seen in the moving hand. The above illustration represents Mr. Webster's definition of a shake. We, without an illustration, lay by it a practical example of this shake given by Isaiah.

may see what it is and how made, together with the figure described by the thing being shaken; and more, that you may see just what a Bible meaning of the word is. Isaiah x. 15: "Shall the saw magnify itself against him that shaketh it?" We have a saw in hand; we place the opposite end, or near that end, of the saw on the timber to be sawn. We push the

saw from us, it cuts more and more as we approach
some point; from this point, not from the center, it
cuts less and less. Or we will say that at some point
between the beginning and the ending of the stroke
a maximum of work is done. To this point the descent of the saw is gradual and uniform; from it the
ascent is equally so. This point, perhaps, is nearer
the hand. Then the saw is lightly lifted, not designed to cut, and brought back to the beginning,
thus completing an ellipse. So back and forth the
saw moves rapidly. The power is applied at the handle, does work at the points of the teeth. The plane
of the ellipse made by the saw is parallel to the blade
of the saw. Now take the set of the saw-teeth, and
you can measure their inclination to this ellipse,
or, which is the same, measure their departure from
the perpendicular saw-blade. The motion of the
saw will vary so uniformly that its very sound as
it flies back and forth enables one skilled in its use
to locate or determine at any time just where in
this ellipse the saw is, whether going or coming.
To the sawyer there are points of less labor and of
more labor; these occur uniformly in the same parts
every time. It also has at regular intervals an increased or decreased velocity. Watch the motion of
the sawyer's hand as it flies back and forth, and you
will have a figure of the earth's orbit, an ellipse.
This also illustrates Kepler's first law: "Planets revolve in ellipses with the sun at one focus." Let us
make the shake according to directions, and then so
picture it as to include the hand and arm; one is the
thing shaken, while the other is the force or that
which causes the hand to move rapidly back and

forth. (See Fig. 6.) Stand up and take a pencil in your right hand, letting one end extend a little above the clinched fist, while the other extends below. The fist will represent the earth, the ends of the pencil its poles.* Put out your hand, just as you would were you going to shake the pencil. There! you see that your pencil is not perpendicular to the floor, but inclined. I leave you to estimate at what angle; measure and see. Now say, on the honor of a man, is the pencil inclined more or less than twenty-three and one-half degrees from a perpendicular? Astronomers call this the obliquity of the ecliptic. Let us now locate the moving force. This is at or about the elbow. Now as we make this shake watch the pencil and see if it does not remain parallel to itself during each shake. Notice the direction of the fist. See if it does not uniformly vary its velocity in different parts of the ellipse. Notice also the relation that the elbow, the location of the moving force, sustains to the plane of the ellipse, and you will observe also that the hand does not move in lines parallel to the floor, but gradually rises in one part of its orbit and as gradually descends in the opposite part.

---

* If the pencil represents the earth, the thumb and four fingers the five outer planets; the thumb is Mars; space between thumb and first finger, position of planetoids; first finger, Jupiter; middle finger, Saturn; ring finger, Uranus; little finger, Neptune; or clinched fist represents the earth, the flat circular spaces on top the fist, the north polar region. The space below, the south polar region, while the four fingers represent the two temperate and the two torrid zones. The line of the lower edge of the little finger, the antarctic circle; the little and the ring finger, tropic of Capricorn; the middle space the equator; the space between second and first finger, the tropic of Cancer; the upper line of the first finger and the thumb, the arctic circle.

Now make your shake vigorously; move the fist rapidly back and forth. Did you notice that when the hand came to C it swept so hurriedly around that the increased motion caused the hand to articulate with the wrist, bringing the hand nearer the elbow at this point than at any other? If the shake be made with the left hand, it will only reverse the motion and change the location of the force to the opposite focus of the ellipse. These answer the two positions, the only positions tLe sun can have to give us the days and seasons such as we have. Let us now point out the features of your shake that are so strikingly similar to those made by the earth in its motion about the sun. The inclination of the pencil was about that maintained by the earth's axis, and is called the inclination of the earth's axis. The elbow, or moving force, was situated nearer one end of your ellipse. This is true of the sun, and is termed one focus, or the sun's place. As the hand swept around the pencil remained parallel to itself in every part of the ellipse. This is true of the earth, and is termed parallelism of the axis. The fist changed its direction at every point; the earth does the same. You observe that the hand did not travel with uniform velocity throughout, but in some parts faster, while in others it traveled slower. There was a constant uniformity in this particular. Where the hand traveled slowest it will ever do the same as it comes to this part of the ellipse. Where it traveled fastest it will ever do the same with each repetition. The earth does the same. The hand did not move in the same plane, but gradually rose in one part and as gradually descended in the other. The earth does the same. These latter are called nodes. The articulation of the wrist brought the fist nearer the moving force at one end of the ellipse. The earth at the same point in its orbit is brought with greatly increased rapidity nearest the sun. This is termed its perihelion distance. At the beginning of the shake the arm was extended; then the fist was at its greatest distance from the moving force. So the earth at the same point in its orbit, June 20, is at its greatest distance from the sun. This is termed its aphelion distance. A line from the center of the force at the elbow, were it light and heat, will rise and fall on the pencil or fist, and the fist will experience all the changes of light and heat that the earth does in its motion about the sun. (Compare Figs. 6 and 7.) Let us now compare the changing velocity of the fist to that of the earth in a similar part of its orbit. From A the earth starts slowly, increasing in velocity till B is passed, when its motion is partly against gravity or sun attraction; this has a tendency to check its motion. At C, or near C, the centrifugal and centripetal forces balance, and the earth turns more toward the sun, then shoots off with increasing velocity. To this point the earth has been rising, when now the center of the sun falls on Capricorn, far south of the equator. Let us now follow the hand this far. The hand, starting at A, moves more slowly here than at any other points along the shake. It increases, as you perceive, till B is passed; it slackens as it approaches the point of articulation, or C; as this point is reached the hand comes around with a jerk, and starts back with greatly increased velocity. All this time the hand has moved gently up-

Figure 7.

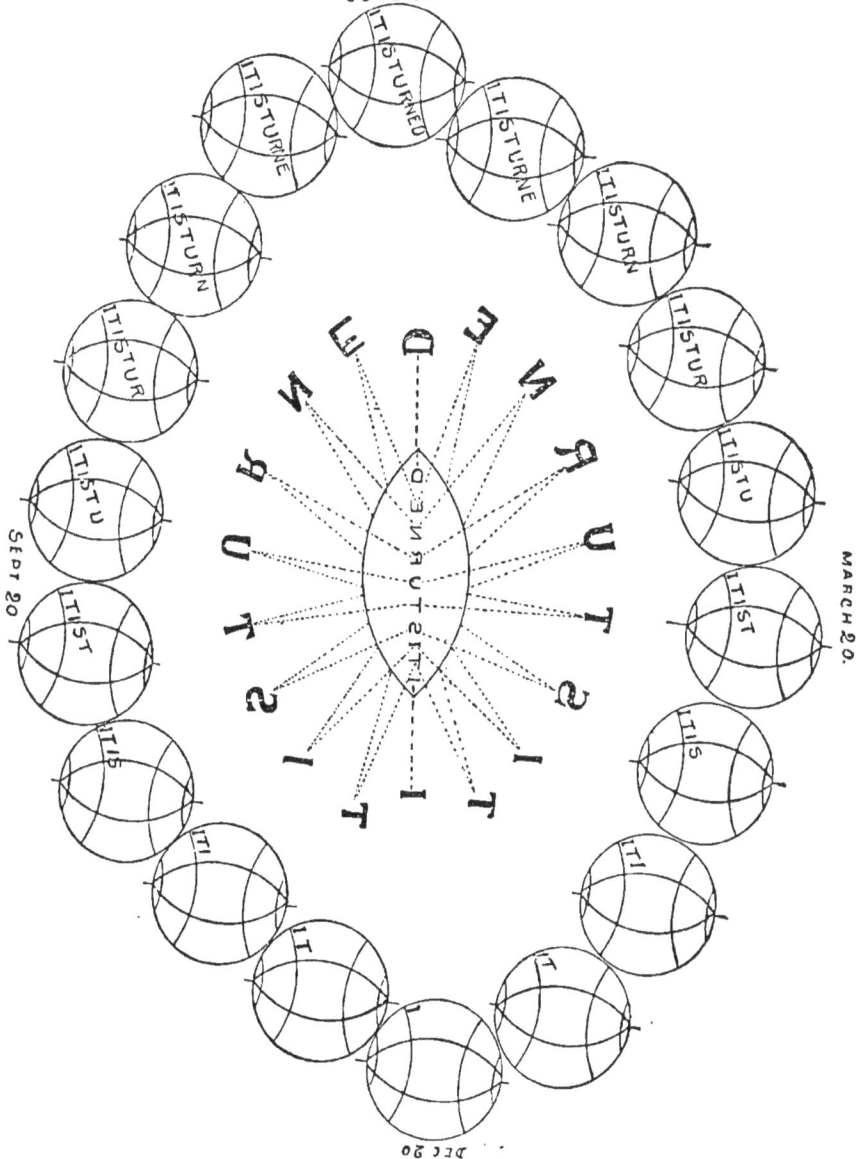

Figure 7 beautifully and truly illustrates the apparent northward and southward motions of the sun, and shows conclusively that this motion is due to real earth-motions and in an opposite direction to that awarded the sun. A backward reading on the seal, a correct reading when applied to the clay. It not only illustrates the above, but it will enable us to determine at any time the earth's position in its orbit, and the exact time of sun-rising for any day in the year. December 20 the sun rises and sets with its center directly over the tropic of Capricorn, 27° 27′ south of the equator. It never rises or sets south of this line. From this point it begins its apparent northward journey, and continues it till June 20. During this time six months have passed and the earth has moved over one hundred and eighty degrees of its orbit, and the sun's center has appeared to move over forty-seven degrees, or across the torrid zone, the ends of the earth. Had we set up a line of stakes December 20 marking the direction of the sun-rising of that day, and for each twenty days thereafter had arranged a new line marking its position when rising, on till June 20, each of these lines of stakes will give the earth's position in its orbit for each twenty degrees. And had we arranged our line of stakes across the torrid zone, between each would have been five and two-ninths degrees of latitude. We can dispense with the stakes. If we will keep Job's seal and his sentence in our minds, the individual letters will answer as stakes, and we will be able to determine any or all the questions pertaining to earth-motions, whether it be its daily or yearly motion. We can determine questions pertaining to its light and heat. More, the time will come when from this seal-writing of Job's, the sun's direction, the distant center about which it moves, and the period of its year will be told. The seal-writing around the sun's disk and along its equator are the letters of the sentence from which the true motion is to be found. The letters of this sentence are arranged with reference to east and west points as the sun's daily risings and sittings are noted here. We place these letters as they would occur when fixed in a seal. You observe that our sun resembles the picture of a seal. The letters on the sunbeam are projections of the letters of the seal; and each is thrown out and appears on a line that connects the centers of the earth and the sun. From these as our stakes, we propose to explain the real motion of the earth, and the direction of that motion about the sun. The truth sought here, as in the daily motion, is found between the seal and its impression. It is the hows and whys of the turnings found when we compare the letters, their arrangement, the direction of the reading of this combination that makes the seal, to the letters, their arrangement, and the direction of the reading of the combination found in the impression. December 20 the sun's central ray falls on Capricorn. Our first stake is I. This is thrown out on the sunbeam and falls on Capricorn. When the earth has moved twenty degrees along its orbit, we come to T. This is projected by the sunbeam till it appears as though coming from the sun's center it falls five and two-ninths degrees north of I, our beginning-stake. Now this stake would not fall north of the previous one, unless the sun moves north or the earth moves south. From T the earth moves twenty degrees, when I appears as though coming from the sun's center, and makes its impression five and two-ninths degrees north of T. Where is this motion? Again the earth moves forward twenty degrees, and we reach "S," our fourth stake; it leaves its impression on the earth, as the previous ones, five and two-ninths degrees north of I. Twenty degrees more, and T is reached, and half the letters that make the words of the seal are passed. This, you observe, makes its impression, allowing the same interval as before, within half a space of the earth's center, or near the equinox. Now we know that when the earth moves forward ten degrees or within about ten days, the equinox occurs. The earth moves on as before till the remaining letters (stakes) are passed, and their impressions left upon the earth or till June 20.

We have said the direction of the reading made upon the earth by this sun-seal was the true direction of the motion; that the impression was always on the thing that moved. The impression is the only intelligible truth. Now we have, "It is turned," written on the earth and along that line, which connects earth and sun centers, below or above which the sun never rises or sets, exemplifying the truth that the sun takes hold of the ends, and only the ends, of the earth.

The earth holds out the statement that "it is turned." Now this is written from southwest to northeast, exemplifying the truth that this motion of the earth about the sun is eastward. The first stake was set in the southwest, and each north of the other till the last one was set in the northeast. Then to deposit

these letters each north of the preceding ones, the earth must
have moved down an incline, thus depressing the south pole
below the point when at I, the beginning. To this point the
letters have been deposited singly and at regular intervals.
This illustrates the truth that the earth at every point in its
orbit is on *turn.* Here the full declaration, "It is turned," is
made. Here the earth, which has for some time been moving
from the sun, makes the turn that must start it on its course to
the beginning. If to this point the earth has been moving
down an incline, one that depressed its south pole, its return
must be up the incline and tending to elevate the south pole.
Our stakes will occur in reverse order as we watch the sun during the next six months apparently moving south. At this point
the sun's central ray projects D, which falls on the tropic of
Cancer. When the earth moves twenty degrees we drop D,
and you observe that E is projected to fall on E. As the
earth moves on we have at each stake passed dropped off a
letter as we approach the beginning. You observe that, in
dropping these letters, each letter dropped was south of the one
previously dropped. As the earth moves toward the north its
center at each stake is elevated till it passes north of the sun's
center, and till the sun's center falls again on Capricorn. Then
this motion of the earth must be in a direction to elevate the
south pole, and hence accounts for that southward motion attributed to the sun. The daily motion of the earth we have
omitted here, as this has been fully explained.

---

ward. Now the lower edge of the ring finger is
brought about on a line with the elbow. The earth
moves from C, increasing its velocity till D is passed,
for the reason given above; then it more slowly approaches A, the beginning. This motion was down
the incline till the center of the sun falls on the
tropic of Cancer, far north of the equator. The
hand moves from C, increasing its velocity till D is
passed, then decreasing as A is approached. This
motion is down the incline, till now a line from the
elbow falls on the upper line of the middle finger,

the two middle fingers illustrating the torrid zone.
During the continuance of the shake this part of the
hand is held to the moving force, or the moving force
never rises above or below these fingers. Make the
shake often, and you will experience in some parts a

Figure 8.

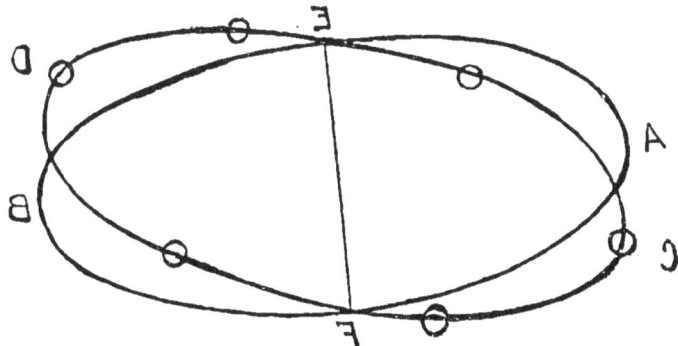

AB an ellipse laid on a plane. Incline it till it takes the position CD. Along this incline the hand is supposed to move
while making the shake. The earth is supposed to move along a
similar incline. Along FDE the hand rises above the fixed plane.
The same is true of the earth. Along ECF each descends below the fixed plane. The point F is called the descending
node; E and F joined by a line make the line of the nodes.
Should the shake be made by lowering or elevating the hand,
or in any possible way the shake can be made, all the foregoing
phenomena of earth-motions will manifest themselves. Turn
the above figures round till A comes where B is, and B takes A's
place, and then the figure will conform to our shake. That is
the node. It will not change the illustration if the hand rise
or fall from D to C.

sense of ease, while in others you experience a sense
of resistance. Take a heavy weight in your hand,
and move the hand along the line of your shake, then
these points will more readily be noticed. This motion of the hand up and down the incline given above
illustrates the nodes (see Fig. 8)— the former the

ascending; the latter, the descending (see Fig. 9). My arm measures from the pencil to the point of the elbow about twelve inches. The wrist articulation to be true would move the hand toward the elbow about two-fifths of one inch, making this perihelion where the lower end of the pencil approaches nearest. Again, the elbow described a small circle; by measurement we found the circle

Figure 9.

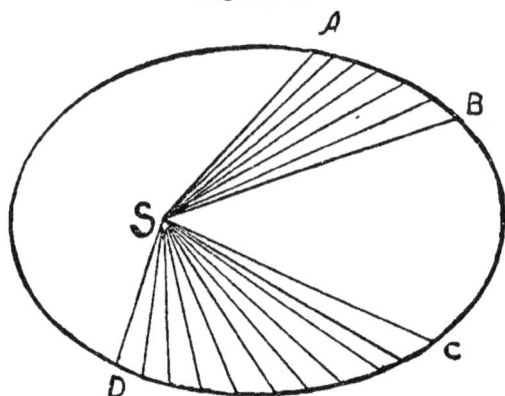

KEPLER'S SECOND LAW.

The hand in going from B to A moves very slowly, and from D to C very rapidly; yet the space enclosed between the lines SB and SA is equal to that inclosed between SD and SC. "A line connecting the center of the fist with the center of the elbow passes over equal spaces in equal times."

to be about one-fourth the size of the circle made by the moving hand. The sun is said to move through the heavens with a velocity equal to about one-fourth that of the earth's velocity. The elbow and wrist are both hinge joints, suited only for back and forth movements. The arm is a lever of the third class, suited for rapid motions rather than for great strength. Let us see if we can deduce from our shake Kepler's third law: "The squares of the times of revolution of the planets about the sun are proportional to the cubes of their mean distances from the sun." I said that my arm was twelve inches long. Suppose this length represents the earth's distance from the sun, and your arm, a much longer one, represents Mars's distance from the sun; your arm would describe a larger circle and with less velocity, consequently requiring a longer time for the hand to move around. Then the square of your period (the time that it takes you to make your shake) is to the square of my period (the time that it takes me to make my shake) as the cube of the length of your arm is to the cube of the length of my arm. In our shake you perceive that the hand did not follow each time the precise track made by the preceding one. The points of resistance and those of acceleration are influenced in a measure. So, due to the attraction of the planets, the earth's orbit is undergoing a slow change of position. It vibrates backward and forward, each oscillation requiring a period of ten thousand years. So the earth, in each of five motions, together with the track along which these motions are kept up, participates in the two motions, back and forth. Every periodical recurrence must be produced by a back and forth movement of the earth. Let us now give this term a liberal interpretation. "Shake," to agitate. This is the general and the practical meaning in every-day use. Should the earth move steadily and without other motions than even those we have mentioned, it would not fill fully our liberal meaning of "shake," for it would not furnish our minds the idea of agitation. The earth has a motion of rotation upon its own axis lasting a day, a motion of translation about the sun continuing for a year; it also has one motion upon its axis accomplished in nineteen years, and another which is only accomplished in twenty-five thousand eight hundred and sixty-eight years. It also has a fifth motion with the solar system through space, which may require millions of years. All these combined make an agitation, a shake according to our practical notions of a shake. From this liberal interpretation of this term let us see the liberally interpreted results that follow. The lengths of our days and nights are constantly changing, from the equator to the poles, from days and nights of but a few hours' duration to days and nights lasting six months. This apparent irregularity is beautifully expressed by "darkness shaken out," sometimes more, sometimes less. The same may be said of the earth's varying temperature from burning to frozen zones, and the fluctuations in the zones outside the torrid, sometimes more, sometimes less, till the seasons are scattered along the line of the shake. So, while to Job illustrations of those visible motions were given, in the Word are found those invisible and intangible motions that intricate calculations and continued observations assure us do exist.

MOTION AND REST SYSTEMATICAL.

"It [earth] is turned as clay to the seal; and they stand as a garment." It is the last of these two clauses that we wish to notice here. We present you with the entire verse, that you may see the dependent relation and the close connection of the thoughts. Geographers, in discussing the motions of the earth and the sun, maintain this order—viz., the rotation of the earth on its axis, its motions about the sun, motion and rest. Then they group earth and all with the sun as a center, and move the whole around some more remote, higher center. When we have discussed the last three topics in this geographical order, which we will do, you will see that the order as given to Job is no departure. This must strengthen our interpretation and make the statements to Job a direct gift of inspiration.

"They stand as a garment." "They," the earth and sun. These are the only parties mentioned as participating in any way in these motions, whether real or apparent. "Stand," to be placed, to have a certain position. Then the earth and sun are placed, have certain positions. How simple! It reaches a clothes-wearing world of every clime, every tongue, learned or unlearned. "As a garment." The position of a garment in its relation to the body is the position of the earth or any planet in its relation to the sun. Our investigations then consist in noticing the relation of garment and body. This will teach us the astronomy of our system and most beautifully distinguish absolute and relative motion, and afford positive proof that rest is only relative. When we rise in the morning we put on our garments and go forth legitimately for a day of activity. The body is the center, and each garment is made to surround it or some of its members. If the garment surrounds the body, then the body to it becomes the central moving force. If it surrounds the arm, a dependent of the body, then the arm is the central moving force of that garment or that part which surrounds it. So

18

with the head, leg, foot, or hand. Each garment has
its sphere and stands in its place. So the sun is the
central force or body about which the earth and the
other dependents circle. As eyes, ears, arms, and
legs are dependents of the body, so the sun has its dependents. Every man, in decency, is the center for
as many garments as there are major planets gathered about the sun. He goes forth with all these
garments properly adjusted. At first they were
made in conformity to certain laws for cutting, and
then adjusted by the law of ease and comfort to the
motions of the body, all of which was designed before even the material was seen or selected. These
planets go forth properly adjusted. They were
made in conformity to certain laws of weight and adjusted to a law of weight and motion, all of which
was designed even before the material existed.
These planets keep their places in the march of the
sun through space. I go over the fields, still my
garments have not moved from the positions given
them in the morning. As I go, the eye peeps up at
the hat and sees it in motion, which is determined by
the houses, trees, and other objects that it passes.
This we call absolute motion of the hat. I reach up
my hand to determine what changes the hat is making from the position given it in the morning. It
stands just as it did when I placed it on my head.
The eye said that it was in absolute motion, and
proved it by the houses, trees, and other objects.
The hand said that it had not moved. The buckle
was still on the right side, the brim was in every respect as when first adjusted. This we term relative
rest—that is, the hat held the same position relative

to the various parts of the head that it did at first. While the eye was making its observation on the hat it was impossible that the eye could perceive its own motion. The hat looks down at the shoe and sees it in motion, which is determined by the objects passed on the way. This is distinguished as absolute motion of the shoe. The eye sees, however, that the shoe has not changed its position relative to the various parts of the foot. While it was in absolute motion with the body, it was in a state of relative rest with reference to the parts of the foot. The sleeve sees the arm in motion, while it to itself stands. The arm sees the sleeve in motion, while it to itself stands. The whole system was in absolute motion, while each to the other stood. Then they (earth and sun) stand as a garment. The earth sees the sun rise and set, while it to itself stands; both are journeying as body and clothes.

TEACHES SYSTEMS.

Every man and his clothes, as they go forth, make a miniature system. The relation of planet to sun is as close and as dependent for motions as garments to the body. If "they stand as a garment" affects both alike, then planets and sun go forth a system, and the sun must have the same or similar motions that the earth has, for the earth stands to sun as sun stands to earth. Parts of a garment have no special independent movement; if detached, would be as motionless, as lifeless, as a cast-off garment. "Stand" has two significations: either meets the relation separately or collectively. In one sense it signifies to be in a particular relation—that is, the garment en-

circles the body or a member of the body. The planets encircle the sun, while satellites encircle a planet,
a member of the body. Again, it signifies "to support." The cords and lines that make a system
strong are the great doctrine of gravitation, attraction. "In them hath he set a tabernacle for the sun,
which is as a bridegroom coming out of his chamber,
and rejoiceth as a strong man to run a race." His
boast is that of a strong man leading a company
that stands as a support to each other. For the purposes of each and all the relation is as close as the
meshes of the cloth, and as strong, but no stronger,
in proportion, than the cords and threads that make
a garment. Their dissolution is prophesied to come
about like the wear of a garment and their renewal
as the same. "They shall wax old like a garment; as
a vesture they shall be changed." This still holds up
the idea that they are not only enduring a similar
wear, but that the effects on each are the same, and
that the change will come on many, "they;" that as
a garment affects all systems as one grand, moving
army, each dressed in its own habiliments, yet the
whole moving on as one great central body, while
systems, individual members, having about them
their parts of a special garment, move in harmony
with the whole, as a hat, shoe, or sleeve. From this
we may determine what other suns are doing. There
are other bridegrooms leading on trains where love
guides and governs, as they turn "as clay to the seal,
and stand as a garment."

"And from the darkness their light is withholden,
and the high arm shall be broken."

It is evident from the construction that the

thoughts expressed in the above topics are closely related in some way to the thoughts expressed by the preceding topics. It is evident, also, that part of this peculiar lecture to Job begins with the twelfth verse and closes with this, the fifteenth, verse. If our interpretations heretofore are just, then we would expect this to be a continuation of the same geographical thoughts so closely followed by Job, and would naturally expect an explanation as found in the sun's motion through space, accompanied by the earth and the other members of his train. Let us offer the reasons afforded by the text.

"And from the darkness their light is withholden." First we will notice a few of the individual terms. If we can understand their true significance, this will afford light sufficient to guide us, at least, along a suspected direction. "Their light." This must refer to the light of the earth as well as to that of the sun, for these are the only bodies mentioned in this lecture. Does the earth shine? It is hard for us to believe that the earth is a star. The stars that we see are bright and full of motion, while to us the earth is without brightness and seems destitute of motion. "At the very beginning of astronomical researches we are to consider the earth as a planet shining brightly in the heavens and appearing to other worlds as a star does to us. God alone could have said "their light" when including the earth with the sun, and that four thousand years ago.

"And from the darkness their light is withholden." The light of the sun and the earth is withholden from the darkness. No one will think for a moment that this darkness is confined to the earth or special places or special things on the earth. This is as un-reasonable, and more so, than to say that it referred to the dark places on the sun, for we do see dark spots on that body. The earth now affords light. The text intimates that the earth-light and the sun-light are the same light, otherwise, perhaps, it would have been written "their lights." The earth reflects the light of the sun, one and the same light. "With-holden" means to keep back. Then this is kept back from the darkness somewhere. According to the laws of light, their light fades this side the abyss of darkness lying between our system and the fixed stars. Within this space, perhaps, our sun moves, manifested by "and the high arm shall be broken."

Arm is a limb of the human body which extends from the shoulder to the hand. Mr. Webster ob-serves that if the Latin word signifying arm was di-rectly from the Greek, the term had reference to a joint; "and the high arm" had reference to the high joint of the arm or the joint connecting the arm with the shoulder. Then the arm will articulate here. The hand and arm have furnished the instruments for illustrating the previous motions of the earth, together with the seal, which is a hand-manipulated instrument. The shake was made with the forearm by hinge movements. Now "the high arm [upper joint] shall be broken." "Shall be broken." All the motions of the earth are simultaneous and con-tinuous. These motions, from the least to the great-est, were in their order (their purposes given) told to Job. The earth "is turned as clay to the seal," that the sun might take hold of the ends of it; it "is turned as clay to the seal," that the darkness might

be shaken out of it. They stand all the while as a
garment. Now, in connection with all these, the
declaration comes, "And the high arm shall be
broken," another motion added. On ball in socket,
full freedom of motion in a circle shall carry fingers,
hand, wrist, elbow, satellites, planets, sun, round a
higher, grander center. Isaiah xl. 12: "Who hath
measured the waters in the hollow of his hand, and
meted out heaven with the span?" The waters of the
earth are a handful. The bounds of the solar system were circumscribed by a span. The diameter of
a span is the distance from the end of the thumb to
the end of the middle finger. This measurement, applied to the muscles of the arm, reaches to about the
socket in the shoulder, the upper joint. "His going
forth is from the end of the heaven, and his circuit
unto the ends of it." As these sweep round their
light is withholden from the darkness that fills the
chambers of the south and the emptiness over which
the north is suspended.

NOTE.—When the true direction of this great sidereal journey
is determined, it will be found closely allied to our shake; its
direction will conform to the angle and direction taken by the
arm as the high arm breaks, to the angle made with the shake.
We face the north, the hand moves from east to west, which is
the reverse of the earth's motion. If the shake is kept up, as
the arm breaks at the elbow, the sun-motion would be less than
perpendicular to the shake.

Job, in reply to Bildad, made some uses of the term
shake, and for purposes similar to the preceding,
which we shall notice here. We offer these as addi-
tional proof of the correctness of the preceding interpretations. Job ix. 4-10: "He is wise in heart, and
mighty in strength: who hath hardened himself

against him, and hath prospered? Which removeth
the mountains, and they know not; which overturneth them in his anger; which shaketh the earth out of
her place, and the pillars thereof tremble; which
commandeth the sun, and it riseth not; and sealeth.
up the stars; which alone spreadeth out the heavens,
and treadeth upon the waves of the sea; which maketh Arcturus, Orion, and Pleiades, and the chambers
of the south; which doeth great things past finding
out; yea, and wonders without number." We have
given seven verses, yet all are included in one sentence, which rehearses more than a dozen of his wonderful acts of wisdom and strength, each of which is
a positive declaration. It is not our purpose to investigate each topic here. "He is wise in heart, and
mighty in strength." Thus Job introduces him; then
he follows with performances that require both wisdom and strength. He removeth the mountains, he
shaketh the earth out of her place, he commandeth
the sun and it riseth not, he sealeth up the stars, he
spreadeth out the heavens, he maketh Arcturus,
Orion, and Pleiades and the chambers of the south.
This is no parable, no figure, but simply a statement
of wonderful acts. We will review these briefly.

"Which removeth the mountains, and they know
not; which overturneth them in his anger." Mountains are upheavals made by great and violent forces.
The thought is one of anger, fury, rage, done by nature's great repellent force. So in reality were the
mountains made. Our observation in reading the
Scriptures is that when a thing is done to inanimate
objects, and these are said to know it not, we have
found it consistent to impute the act to violence,

some irregular force, some act outside the regular operations of the forces. And when to inanimate objects a sense of knowing is imputed, our observation holds good that the act is in accordance with law; and "to know" manifests a willing disposition to implicitly obey. Inanimate objects, like animate, like man himself, are under law. Violence produces irregularities, a sense of knowing not what they do. This can not be otherwise. Violence is resistance to forces acting in obedience to law, or these forces made terrible in executing the law or carrying out a decree. This is physically, socially, morally, true. These latter triumph every time. There is no motion they do not control, no uprising in matter they can not assuage. Arcturus makes his flight through space many hundred times faster than the fastest cannon-ball, yet is guided with perfect security. Were all the planets, satellites, and suns in space to revolt, the revolt would be put down, these unknown worlds reduced to obedience, led back to their stations and put on duty again. We see this truth in all the affairs of life. If I lift anything, I do this positively against gravity. I hurl a stone through the air, every inch is resisted by air and gravity till this stone is brought to a state of rest, to a sense of knowing its place. Obedience exemplifies a sense of knowing.

"Which shaketh the earth out of her place." Then the earth moves, moves back and forth, rapidly. Then in the same sentence follows the true philosophical result: "The pillars thereof tremble." "Pillars"—what are these? Where situated? How many? What makes these tremble? A pillar is

that which sustains, upholds. Pillars are always
situated beneath the thing to be sustained or supported or upheld. Pillars of the earth—let us see
how they are placed beneath the earth and uphold it,
and what they are in this sense. The earth is a globe,
the center of which is its lowest point; every other
point is above this. Then the pillars that uphold the
earth must be situated at the center of the earth.
The earth, then, is round. Who would think of
placing pillars above the thing to be upheld? Office
of these pillars: All bodies are drawn toward the
center of the earth, not because of any peculiar property or power in the center, for all we know, but because the earth, being a great sphere, the aggregate
effect of the attraction exerted by all its particles
upon any body exterior to it, is such as to direct the
body toward the center. The total amount of attraction exerted by the earth upon bodies exterior to it is
the same as though that force were all concentrated
at the center. Every particle of matter in the universe sends a pillar to help uphold the earth. These
tremble. "Tremble," to shake involutarily. This
is surely a shaking subject. This is an involuntary
act; not the will of these pillars, but an edict from an
earth that moves back and forth. These pillars
tremble, the earth's foundations tremble, these pillars that come from every particle of matter in the
universe tremble. These are forces that make the
universe a unit. Then these tremble, and not volun-
tarily, but are forced to do so, as these particles move
toward or from each other. Gravity acts as a tense
spring. As the earth moves from the sun this spring
bends more and more, retarding its motion, till it

reaches a point beyond which it can not go; then the earth turns, and the bent spring brings it back. This is the involuntary shake, the swinging back and forth of the forces that make the earth abiding while being shaken out of her place. "Tremble" beautifully illustrates the vibrations of a spring. These vibrations are long or short, as the tension slackens or is increased as the earth moves from or toward the sun. "Which shaketh the earth out of her place, and the pillars thereof tremble." Why connect these clauses so closely? Why make the latter so directly dependent upon the former? (See "Influence of Gravitation.")

"Which commandeth the sun, and it riseth not." The preceding topic was a positive statement that the earth moves. Now we have the positive statement that the sun does not rise. Job is not now illustrating the deceptiveness of motion when applied to the sun, but he talks about these motions as they really occur. The earth moves; the sun does not. The sun never rose one single time, nor ever will. "He commandeth the sun, and it riseth not." A cold, stubborn fact. Does this accord with the statement made to Job: "and caused the dayspring to know his place?" What do you say?

"And sealeth up the stars." Notice how closely this clause is joined to the one that preceded. "He commandeth the sun, and it riseth not," fixes the seal on the stars. It does this and no more—no rising sun, no rising stars, no standing earth around which sun and stars revolve. The text setting forth earth-motions, found in the preceding part of this chapter, exemplifies this truth, and accounts for the deceptions that obscured the truth found in our present topic. The very instrument that was used to illustrate these motions, or rather their deceptiveness, now seals the motion of the stars.

"Which alone spreadeth out the heavens." The act of moving the earth back and forth, joined with the truth that the stars are fixed, to us spreads out the heavens, which refers to these acts. The stars that rise on the 22d of March have passed behind us and out of sight on the 21st of June, like oases on the desert. New ones rise, twinkle awhile, and pass out of view. Those that rise on us in September tell us that we are three hundred million miles from our starting and as far from the ending. The stars are fixed mile-stones along the earth's track, as familiarly known to astronomers as are the stations along our great thoroughfares to the engineer that has watched them so often with great interest.

Job xii. 22: "He discovereth deep things out of darkness, and bringeth out to light the shadow of death."

"He discovereth deep things out of darkness." "Discover," to uncover, to lay open to view, to disclose. "Deep things," that which is profound, not easily fathomed. These mysterious things out of darkness are to be laid open. These are the trophies that man will win when he has made himself master of the situation at the poles of the earth. The motions of our earth, the winds, meteorological conditions of the atmosphere, the planets, their satellites, aurora, electricity, the sun, and stars, when viewed from this land of darkness, man will discover that which is profound, man will soar to a new height in

all things, showing himself to be only a little lower
than the angels.

"And bringeth out to light the shadow of death."
The shadow here spoken of is the earth's real shadow, that, by its own motion as it moves from the sun,
settles alternately about the poles. (See "Frigid
Zone.") This shadow as borne by the earth to the
sun, the place of the shadow, is brought to light—no
sun-motion, but earth-motion. Jeremiah xiii. 16:
"And, while ye look for light, he turn it into the
shadow of death, and make it gross darkness."
There is that transfer of light from one pole to the
other spoken of before. Read the entire verse. This
is a figure; yes—but a figure of what? The real motion of the earth to or from the sun. Amos v. 8:
"Seek him that maketh the seven stars and Orion,
and turneth the shadow of death into the morning."
Here it is numbered among his wonderful works
among the stars. It is the same story of a turning
shadow to the morning, to the sun.

Astronomers tell us that in some mysterious way
the motions of our system are connected with the
seven stars. Some think that we journey around
this cluster. This, in all probability, is one of the
deep things to be discovered out of darkness. Let
us interview Solomon on these motions. Wisdom of
Solomon vii. 17, 18: "For he hath given me certain
knowledge of the things that are, namely, to know
how the world was made, and the operation of the
elements: the beginning, ending, and the midst of the
times: the alterations of the turnings of the sun, and
the change of seasons: the circuits of years, and the
positions of stars."

We will review this text briefly, adopting Solomon's topical order as he gives them.

"For he hath given me certain knowledge of the things that are." Solomon says that "certain knowledge" is given him. This is the theme of this book. The work of our lives is to demonstrate the truth of God's gifts of inspiration. To Solomon it was not knowledge acquired by study, but knowledge acquired by gift. We have in his statement before us evidence of the fact that it was a gift, for he talks about truths of which the world was absolutely ignorant two hundred years ago—yes, fifty years ago. This knowledge is only limited to the things that are, that now exist, everything.

"To know how the world was made." "Make," to form of materials. Then he knew how the world was formed of materials already created. Then he follows in close connection with "the operations of the elements." That can not imply other than that the world was made from elements by their operations, action, or effect. Now an element is the last result of chemical analysis, that which can not be decomposed by any means now employed. An atom is the last result of mechanical division, and is called an element because it is the first principle or minutest part of matter. This world was made of these elements. By their operations molecules are formed. Molecules unite and make bodies. Solomon says that he knew these operations to the making of this world. Then he was a profound chemist by gift. To be that he must know that all matter is composed of indivisible atoms; that atoms of the same element have the same weight, but in different elements they have different weights; that the combining numbers represent these relative weights; that all chemical compounds are formed by the union of different atoms. Let us see how the worlds were made by Bible statement. This will, in a measure, justify our interpretation. Hebrews xi. 3: "Through faith we understand that the worlds were framed by the word of God, so that things which are seen were not made of things which do appear."

"Through faith we understand that the worlds were framed." Faith is a gift; that is the way it came to Solomon. Let us look at it in a physical sense. "The worlds were framed." That means that things were put together, that the world is a framed structure made of invisible atoms, mechanically put together. Now let us see if all our knowledge of chemistry is not based on faith alone, and that from the things we see. "A molecule of water is so very small that a total of eight billions of these molecules is barely visible in the best of modern microscopes. A molecule of water contains two atoms of hydrogen and one of oxygen. Now if these atoms were of the same size and could be separated, and if all the atoms of either the hydrogen or oxygen, or one-third of the total, could be collected, it would then form a bulk too small to be seen in the most powerful glass. Still, there are more than two and one-half billions of these water particles. Then you must accept chemistry by faith. An atom is invisible, intangible, tasteless, and without odor.

"The beginning, ending, and the midst of the times." The elements are indestructible, their operations invariable. The laws that governed their action in the beginning will do so to the end and through the intervening time.

"The alterations of the turnings *of the sun.*" The phrase "of the sun" was not found in the original. This affords proof that the learned world at the time of the revision thought that the sun turned, rose, and set by its own motions. It does not take even close observation to determine that there was no omission at all. That there might not possibly arise any mistakes as to the character of the knowledge given to Solomon, he particularizes and introduces the particulars by "namely."

"The alterations of the turnings." Both are written in the plural. Alterations of turns of this world. His knowledge extends to this world only. Then the turns of this world alter. This world has five turns, three on its own axis and two through space; one of the latter about the sun and the other with the sun as he pursues his journey. While alterations of turns beautifully applies to many directions of turns, it at the same time illustrates circular motion combined with its rotary motion. As it turns from west to east the turn that carries it through space is altering all the while. These alterations of turnings are the very things that give us our seasons and years. He follows this with our result given here.

"The change of seasons, the circuit of years." The fact that Solomon should so arrange these topics that when given the most rigid or the most liberal interpretation they teach the philosophy of the earth's motions and their results—days, seasons, and years —affords proof of an inspired insight to earth-motions. The fact that alterations of turnings do produce these effects, and that Solomon should say so, is enough to convince one of a high inspiration.

"And the positions of stars." The connection will show you that this too is a result brought about by the same cause that produced the seasons and the circuit of years. The turns of the earth alone develop the positions of the stars. To the earth they are mile-stones, as truly fixed as are the mile-rocks along our great thoroughfares. As the earth rotates it covers or uncovers the sun and stars. These are found in the same places day after day, night after night. When our western horizon is elevated above the sun we see the stars precisely where we saw them on the preceding night, while they may appear further east, west, north, or south. A change of this world's position makes this apparent change in the position of the stars, while the position of the stars every time determines the amount of this change. Again, as the earth moves along its orbit new stars come into sight. These are seen to rise higher and higher on each succeeding evening till they pass out of sight behind us to rise no more for a year. Like trees and mountain peaks that rise on us in our travels, we come to each in turn, we pass them, and they fade from sight behind us. The stars we see over our heads on the first night in January have disappeared in the west by the 1st of April. New stars appear; in a few months they are gone, like passing mile-stones along our thoroughfares. New stars rise and set till the year ends. The new year is marked by the visitation of the stars that marked its advent before. The same stars that were beacons to guide the earth in its course in former years will offer the

19

same gentle luring through coming generations. Our signs, together with the regularly returning influence wrought by the stars over the conditions of earthly matter, find a system in the fact that we return to the same star clusters day after day, month after month, till the year ends, and to be repeated as the years repeat their periodical return.

We mark the positions of these stars and call them by name. Thus it is that the earth's motion around the sun as a center explains the various aspects of the heavens in summer and winter skies. Says Mr. Steele on the position of the stars, under the head of "Value of Stars in Practical Life:" "The stars are the landmarks of the universe. They seem to be placed in the heavens by the Creator not alone to elevate our thoughts and expand our conception of the infinite and eternal, but to afford us, amid the constant fluctuations of our own earth, something unchangeable and abiding. Every landmark about us is constantly shifting, but over all shine the eternal stars, each with its place so accurately marked that to the astronomer and geographer no deception is possible. To the mariner the heavens become a dial-plate, the figures on its face set with glittering stars, along which the moon travels as a shining hand that marks off the hours with an accuracy that no clock can ever rival. Standing on the deck of his vessel, far out at sea, a single observation of the sun or stars decides his location in the waste of waters as accurately as if he were at home and had caught sight of some old landmark that he had known from his boyhood. In all the intricacies of surveying the stars furnish the only immutable guide. Our clocks vainly strive to keep time with the celestial host. Thus, by an evident plan of the Creator, even in the most common affairs of life, are we compelled to look for guidance from the shifting objects of earth up to the heavens above."

Thus we close the discussion of the rotation of the earth on its axis, together with its motion about the sun, as given by inspiration. How nicely do these accord with the scientific theories touching these great movements! There is one difference noticed in the manner of setting forth such theories and their special illustrations: Man discusses one subject with many long sentences, and every time the illustrations are a kind of separate side-show that accompany, rather than form a part of the big circus; while inspiration discusses many great questions in a few short sentences of well-selected words that are living illustrations, illustrations that talk. These go to our faith, give it new hopes, and breathe into us anew the breath of life. We should worship Him who made all things and has given evidence that he is perfect in knowledge by his simple and lucid explanation and illustration of things the world has so recently learned. We should revere that science which accords with his word, for it is God's own way of work, his mode of making visible his thoughts. Scientists must no longer claim the honor of being the first to find the deception produced by these motions, but to place it where it belongs. It was told to Job more than three thousand years before their first conceptionist was born. Scientists should boast that their theory is in harmony with Bible teaching. Let us boast because we live in an age when science, if it does not draw its theroies from the Bible, so closely imitates them by example and well-defined truths that we know these theorics are settled upon the rock, indisputable truths, no longer weapons in the hands of the enemies of the Bible, but living witnesses, testifying to its truths. Let the decision of the world be what it may to-day, like Kepler, we can well wait a hundred years for an adherent, since God has waited four thousand years for an expounder.

God's covenant was with day and night, physical, or light and darkness. (See "The Earth Is Round.") There the philosophy of the movements of light and darkness are more minutely noticed.

To Whom Is Honor Due?

If to Cæsar, then give it to him without stint; if not, then withhold it from him and give it to him who is deserving. Astronomy is the oldest of the sciences. "The study of the stars is as old as man himself. Many of its discoveries date back of authentic records amid the mysteries of tradition," so we are told. These are silent touching earth-motions. The Chinese tell us of a conjunction of four planets and the moon twenty-five hundred years before Christ. They show records of an eclipse of the sun that were made 2127 B.C.; yet they show no records, do not pretend to have them, have no tradition, no intimation of these earth-motions older than the middle of the sixteenth century. The Chaldean priests were astronomers. Alexander found at Babylon, 331 years B.C., records reaching back nineteen centuries. These records say nothing about

earth-motion. The Chaldeans divided the day into
hours, invented the sun-dial—divided the day into
hours without knowing the cause of day. Seven
hundred years B.C. Thales, the Grecian philosopher,
taught that the earth was round; that the moon received her light from the sun; introduced the division of the earth's surface into zones, the theory of
the obliquity of the ecliptic, and predicted sun-
eclipses—yet he saw no moving earth. One of his
pupils taught that stars were suns and that the planets were inhabited. To this one the earth stood, had
no motion. These men were noted for their oppor-
tunities and astronomical knowledge. Their names,
like stars of immense orbits, have risen on every succeeding generation, have gone down on none. Many
of them traveled over the known world, and spent
an average life in search of knowledge. Astronomy
was the great prize. No country, no people, no man,
ever told them that the earth moved. Five hundred
and fifty years before Christ Pythagoras, astronomers say, conceived that the earth revolved on its
axis, and that he was the first man that ever even
conceived such a thing. Copernicus, about the middle of the sixteenth century, a little over three hundred years ago, taking up the theory (only a theory)
of Pythagoras, by a demonstration established the
truth of its motion. Such is the highest claim of the
scientific world to this discovery. This was a century after the discovery of America. Many of our
towns and cities are witnesses coming up from that
period. What a rebuke to Bible-readers! It had
been dispensed to Job more than a thousand years
before Pythagoras was born or four thousand years

before Copernicus demonstrated the truth of earth-motions. Job, as a man, had not ranked among philosophers, as far as we know, nor have we any knowledge of his having visited any nation or country in search of knowledge. Imagine the difference as you go backward from the middle of the sixteenth century three thousand years or more. It would be but going backward from a bright dawn into night, thicker, thicker, denser still as we put the years behind us on our journey back to the age of Job. From a human standpoint, all the disadvantages of age and opportunity were his. It did not depend upon these. It depended alone upon inspiration; for, as we have shown, the world knew nothing of it for ages after the days of Job. If it depended upon inspiration, then, too, it being found in the Bible, would give the preference to this book, and hold it out to us as the great book of inspiration, one through which God talks to us of his wondrous ways. Notice the striking difference between these men. The first that we mentioned came recommended as learned searchers after knowledge, but Job comes and is introduced as one that feared God and eschewed evil. What would have been our *status* to-day in astronomical knowledge alone had the world taken up the theory dispensed to Job so long ago? The answer is apparent: we would be three thousand years in advance of our present standpoint.

CHAPTER XI

Who We Are, and What We Are—Man—Assets of His Wealth —Circulation of the Blood—Spinal Cord—The Body before and after Death—After Death the Body Is to Be Broken Up by Physical and Chemical Forces and Scattered—Will Be Collected When the Earth Gives Up the Dead—Faith.

WHO ARE WE? WHAT ARE WE?

We head this division with two questions. The answers to these questions involve the creation, formation, and establishing of the earth and all things therein, animate or inanimate. We are sons and daughters of a great Creator, of a great King, who, during his own life, has given to us by will all things that we see around us, together with all the invisible forces that attend on matter. That we were in his thoughts before the least of these was created, and that these are all specified in a will made directly to us, see Isaiah xlv. 18: "For thus saith the Lord that created the heavens; God himself that formed the earth and made it; he hath established it, he created it not in vain, he formed it to be inhabited." We call your attention to the order of the principal words in the text. "He created," brought into existence the materials of the heavens, all the systems. From this he formed, gave shape to the earth; then established, made solid, made it strong in its place. The purpose was that it might be inhabited. If we look at the convenient things around us, or if we consider that all of our earthly needs, temporal gratification, can find a full enjoyment from these forma-

(295)

tions, we can not but say that we see design, and the
text declares a Designer even from the beginning.
Man, by a special deed of gift, is made heir to all.
Psalm cxv. 16: "The earth hath he given to the children of men." What a gift! Fifty million square
miles of land and three times as many miles of ocean.
This is not all: the same will bequeaths one hundred
and fifty thousand plants and herbs. Genesis i. 29:
"I have given you every herb bearing seed, which is
upon the face of all the earth." Nothing reserved.
Botanists tell us that there are one hundred and fifty
thousand. Zoologists say that the earth is as rich in
animal as in vegetable life. These, together with all
the fishes of the sea and all the fowls of the air, land,
and water, are given to man. Genesis i. 28: "Have
dominion over the fish of the sea, and over the fowl
of the air, and over every living thing that moveth
upon the earth." Air—the very thing needed most,
needed oftenest, the very thing without which he
must die—surrounds him on all sides. The base of
a column of air twenty-five thousand miles in circumference and fifty miles high stands upon his shoulders. How abundant, how convenient, how press-
ing the claim, when we know that he must breathe
several times every minute, inhaling about one hundred cubic inches each breath! Yet his demand can
not exhaust nor even lessen the supply of this storehouse which is placed at every one's door. Then it
is swallowed without an effort on his part; not la-
borious, but pleasant. Its own pressure would drive
it into the mouth. This is also specified in the deed.
Isaiah xlii. 5: "He giveth breath unto the people
upon the earth." There is another gift, higher still,

the one that distinguishes man above all of God's
works: a spirit. Man alone has this, so far as we are
told—something more refined than matter, a living,
imperishable something — a spirit. Isaiah xlii. 5
says that he giveth breath unto the people upon the
earth and spirit to them that walk therein. There
is another, still more excellent, specification found
in this will: these spirits of ours are susceptible of
gifts of understanding, knowledge, and wisdom.
Job xxxii. 8: "There is a spirit in man: and the inspiration of the Almighty giveth them understanding."
With these spirits, which are susceptible of endless
expansion under the gifts of inspiration, God makes
man the consummation, the end, the object of all the
creations in the earth or the starry worlds, and fits
him to rule over these and more. The very forces
lodged in all these—in the sunbeam, in ascending vapors, in the winds, in the latent energies of the
waters, in the wily lightnings, and in the ordinances
of the moon and stars—are his by lawful conveyance.
The specification in the will hands all over to him as
an intelligence capable of dominion. Psalm viii. 6:
"Thou madest him to have dominion over the works
of thy hands; thou hast put all things under his
feet." This text was to David a prophecy. We behold its fulfilment; we realize as a truth what was
to David three thousand years ago only the kiss of
inspiration. In this high estate man finds himself
crowned with glory and honor. The animal world
withdrew from the contest in remote ages in the
past. The forces with which nature is endowed are
one by one kneeling at man's feet to take his burden.
"These results are of the mightiest import. The dis-

coveries of gravitation, of oxygen, of the circulation
of the blood, of vaccination, anesthetics, and photog-
raphy, the invention of the mariner's compass, of
gunpowder, the printing-press, the chronometer, the
steam-engine, and the electric telegraph have constructed human relations. They are steps of advancement in which the whole world is moving. But
great as are the material revolutions which they
have produced, they have a more momentous signifi
cance as a first glorious fruitings of the growth of
knowledge. They are witnesses of what can be accomplished by the earnest, persevering study of nature. They are prophetic of a new dispensation of
the intellect, of a wider and nobler culture, in which
the living universe of God shall neither be contemp-
tuously passed by nor assigned an inferior place in
courses of study." The Bible is a gift full of gifts
and giving from Genesis to Revelation, and givings
that we realize from the cradle to the grave, givings
by hope without end. What a Giver! what gifts!

These spiritual eyes are opened upward to other
treasures, that are specified in a new deed, from one
lawfully seized and having the authority to covenant
new gifts, equal in all respects, to that authority to
convey lands and tenements. It tells him that he is
to fall heir to another world, unmeasured my miles,
whose riches and glory exceed the riches and glory of
this as far as the heavens are above the earth. How
many good things have we heard in life! O, most
excellent things have we read, have we listened to!
Our great social enjoyment is in talking, hearing,
writing, and reading. We are able to express ourselves vividly to the understanding of our friends in

descriptions of the things around us. But this is a kingdom and country of free mansions, where the common people wear crowns, upon whom is shed a glory too boundless for tongue or pen to describe, as endless as immortality with all that it means. Such is the limit as specified in this new deed.

Let us return now to our analogy or comparison. Revelation teaches that the human family all sprang from one man and one woman. This is a question about which so much has been said that we will give one quotation simply to keep our line, and then pass to other features. Quackenbos, speaking of the origin of the English language, says: "Celtic was itself an offshoot from the Hebrew or Phenician tongue. Thus etymology, as well as profane history, confirms the account given by Moses of the peopling of the earth from one parent family." Then we have two living witnesses besides revelation bearing witness from every age that man is of divine origin. With the authority of revelations, of profane history, of the etymology of our own tongue, we shall speak of him in this light. We will begin with him before he was, fall in with him where he is, and follow him, hand in hand with his philosophy, to the grave, where his philosophy, as perishable as he, shall wither with him. But a new philosophy, clothed like him with immortality, shall, with the strong grip of the Lion of the tribe of Judah, raise him and put skin and flesh upon the dry bones and bid them live to breathe a new air. to walk in fields of new philosophy, unalloyed by the errors of the old. Nevertheless, one of the lions of infidelity, after having dissected man and dog, pronounces them one and the same. Be this true or false, Solomon underlies even this with a pleasing hope. Ecclesiastes ix. 4: "For to him that is joined to all the living there is hope: for a living dog is better than a dead lion." We will try to show in the proper place a very great anatomical difference; at present will only leave you the saying of the prophet Isaiah (xxix. 16): "Surely your turning of things upside down shall be esteemed as the potter's clay: for shall the work say of him that made it, He made me not? or shall the thing framed say of him that framed it, He had no understanding?" Let us carry our comparison into the domains of physiology. Psalm cxxxix. 14: "I will praise thee; for I am fearfully and wonderfully made: marvelous are thy works." How strong are the three modifying words, "wonderfully," "fearfully," "marvelous," as used in speaking of this complex machine, man! Let us see if physiology will so testify. "The human body is composed of six kinds of material: bone, cartilage, fiber, muscle, nerve, and fat. There are two hundred and twenty-six bones in a full-grown person—sixty in the head, thirty-two in the trunk, the upper extremities each contain thirty-two, making sixty-four; the lower extremities each contain thirty-one, making sixty-two; there are eight other cap or pan-bones. There are over five hundred muscles in the human body." Let us examine the trochea. "This divides into bronchial tubes, which lead into the lungs, and continue to divide into very small tubes, upon which cluster the air-cells of the lungs like grapes upon the stem, only they are ultimately so small that there are supposed to be six hundred millions of them in the lungs." The heart: "This mar-

velous little engine throbs on continually at the rate
of one hundred thousand beats per day, forty million
per year, often one billion without a single stop. If
it should expend its entire force in lifting its own
weight vertically, it would rise twenty thousand feet
in an hour. During a life such as we sometimes see
it has propelled half a million tons of blood, yet has
repaired itself as it has wasted during its patient, un-
faltering labor." O how that would shake my faith
had revelation said it! How thankful I am that my
salvation does not depend upon my believing this!
This story, like faith, "is the substance of things
hoped for, the evidence of things not seen." I am of
the opinion that revelation has never called us to believe, unaided by any evidence, questions more stupendous than when we are called upon to accept
many of the scientific theories of the day. Often,
as we try to take in some of these great theories, our
faith is shaken by whisperings: "Go slow! go slow!
the world's wisest philosophers taught with pride
some very foolish theories, and they were kept alive
by the world for more than a thousand years." The
real physiologist can not but place his hand upon his
mouth, his mouth in the dust, and exclaim with the
Psalmist: "I am fearfully and wonderfully made!"

The heart is the organ that starts the blood on its
tour of the body. Out of the right ventricle it is
forced to the lungs, there it is cleansed, the impuri-
ties taken from it, and in their stead stimulating
properties from the air are taken in for the uses of
the system. It then returns to the heart to be forced
to the various parts of the body for the uses of the
body. The left auricle receives it as it filters in,

bright and pure, from the lungs; out of the left ventricle it is forced to the remotest parts of the body.
The right and left ventricles are open avenues leading from the heart, through which the blood is forced.
One, as we have said, directs its flow to the lungs;
the other, throughout the entire body. Proverbs iv.
23: "Keep thy heart with all diligence; ror out of it
are the issues of life." This entire chapter is filled
with beautiful parables. "Keep thy heart with all
diligence." It is a vital organ; out of it are the issues of life, issues more than one. From it are the
open gateways of life. The ventricles. "Issues of
life." The blood issues from the heart. Blood is
only liquid flesh. A long time ago Plato said that
the blood was the food of the flesh, the life of the
flesh. Leviticus xvii. 11, 13, 14: "For the life of the
flesh is in the blood; . . . he shall even pour out
the blood thereof, and cover it with dust. For it is
the life of all flesh." So if Solomon had said, "Keep
thy heart with all diligence, for out of it are the issues of blood;" it could not have been more intelligible, for the blood is the life, and the very thing that
comes through the heart. I am told that this is a
figure; if it is, then a figure of what? Take it spiritu-
ally, it is a figure beautifully illustrating the circulation of the blood. The blood is the life of the
flesh. Then, in a physical sense, our life continually
goes from the heart, carrying strength and life to the
body; as continuously it is sent to the lungs to be
purified and revivified. So, in a spiritual sense, the
life we get goes from the heart (figurative of the
physical propelling motor) to build up the spiritual
man; all the time the heart is sending its current to

the fountain of life, there to be renewed and purified, preparatory to being sent to the spiritual man. Take it physically and it is a type of those moral, life-giving streams that issue from the heart—the one to build up life; the other that issues, goes out, for life, affording a tangible·pulse in fruit, daily walk, and conversation. To make it a figure only strengthens our position. We are taught that chemical combinations liberate muscular force. This is always done at the expense of muscular tissue. The muscles most active are quickest destroyed and oftenest renewed. The labors of the heart are more incessant than that of any other organ, consequently it is oftenest worn out, oftenest rebuilt. It throbs on day and night, as incessantly when we sleep as when · awake. We are further taught that our hearts are burned up and replaced every thirty days. The prayer "Create within me a new heart" is as true in a physical as a moral sense. "A heart of flesh" places it as a physical change of heart. Proverbs xvi. 9: "A man's heart deviseth his way." Compare Proverbs iv. 23: "Keep thy heart with all diligence; for out of it are the issues of life." If a man's heart deviseth his way, the heart of some deviseth to them the way of death. But "out of the heart are the issues of life." We can not accept the clause "out of the heart are the issues of life" only in a physical sense. How could a man devise in his heart the way of death, and life issue from this workshop of death? Like our other expression, this is a figure, and finds a solution only as we compare our physical transformation to those of our spiritual. Thus the circulation of the blood is taught.

Ecclesiastes xii. 6: "Or ever the silver cord be loosed, or the golden bowl be broken, or the pitcher be broken at the fountain, or the wheel broken at the cistern."

"Or ever the silver cord be loosed." The silver cord is the spinal cord. Sever that, loose it from its connection, as done by hanging and many other ways, and death ensues. The nerves, as is the spinal-cord, are called silver cords, from resemblance to silver threads. The golden bowl is the vessel that holds the brain.

"Or the pitcher be broken at the fountain." The peculiarity of a pitcher is its spout. The object of the pitcher is to hold a liquid designed for immediate use. The spout is affixed to conveniently and surely conduct the contained liquid into its channel of use without loss and the inconvenience of having it trickle down the sides of the pitcher. The heart has four chambers, and these are termed ventricles and auricles. The ventricles receive the blood from the auricles as a pitcher receives water from the cistern. The right ventricle, as a pitcher's spout, directs the blood, starts it to the lungs. Returning from the lungs to the heart, it runs into an open cistern, a momentary stop, and then enters the left ventricle; from this it is poured or starts again as a spring or rivulet, makes the tour of the body, and returns to the heart. Then to break the pitcher at the fountain would be to break it at the spout, and its further use as a pitcher is marred. So, to break the circulation at the ventricles impairs these, the fountain stops, and death ensues. If these remain intact, and let the auricles fail to fill their functions, fail to fill the pitcher, then too death ensues. Here the blood has completed its tour of the body and has returned to the starting.

"Or the wheel be broken at the cistern." Had Solomon said, "Or the circuit be broken at the cistern," he would not have been more explicit. We said that there is a physiological difference between man and dog. We grant that all hair is hair, whether from man or dog; that all bone is bone, whether from man or dog. The former is but a covering, a protection for a something, the covering a very nothing; the latter are but sills, sleepers, joists, and rafters—framework of a house, in which something lives. This framework is nothing but iron and rock. The life is all. "The blood is the life." The blood is composed of a thin, colorless liquid, filled with red disks or cells. These cells vary in size in the different animals, and man has a cell in size peculiarly man's. These cells are so small that it would require thirty-five hundred, laid side by side, to measure an inch; it would take eighteen thousand, placed one upon the other, to make a column that high. One of these little red disks from human blood is only about one two-hundred-and-twenty-billionth of a cubic inch. Then the difference between man and dog is great enough to be detected in one two-hundred-and-twenty-billionth of a cubic inch of blood, whether of man or dog. So conclusive is this that the testimony of blood is taken before the courts. A murder had been committed, the deed was done with an ax, after which the ax had been carefully cleansed. In the eye of the ax, between the metal and the handle, a small quantity of blood was found. This answered
20

for examination and the conviction of the murderer. See this same silent particle, so small that its story must come through some magnifying-glass to reach the perception of judge and jurors. It uttered one sentence only: "I am human blood." The story was not gainsaid, its veracity not questioned. On this testimony a man was hung. Tell me the sum of the difference.

THE BODY AFTER DEATH.

It is not our aim to intentionally spring a mooted point nor to arouse a controversy, but to shun both. As for the resurrection of the body, that is nothing more to me than where I shall get the next draught of air or the next suit of clothes. If new bodies are fashionable, then I'll have a new one; if we take the old ones again, none will be out of style or fashion. We should not let our minds go far enough to speculate on our garb in heaven. It surely is enough that we spend so much of our earthly lives thinking of what we shall wear here. You will be clothed free, my brother. The subject of this chapter has been the theme of skeptical chemists and philosophers to the injury of the Christian religion. These are the questions that we are hunting for. In this instance it will spring a question upon which the Christian world is not agreed. If we should shake up any on this matter, be sure that that is no part of our business, and that we will give you something to think about worth far more than any benefits coming from an argument as to what we shall be. The great question is: "What are we now?" The teaching is about this: When I die, the elements of my body broken up by chemical forces and dissolved, are scat-

tered at the grave's mouth, absorbed by the air, carried away by the winds, or taken up by the vegetable kingdom as food for it; or these elements, absorbed by the air are breathed by countless numbers,
and then go to build up new bodies for other men,
beasts, etc.—that is, the elements of my body after
death may go to make bone, muscle, and flesh for
myriads of men, beasts, fowls, insects, and reptiles.
These die, and these again are dissolved and again
scattered. The grasses that have absorbed elements
of dead bodies are eaten by the animal kingdom until
our dust is so widely diffused over the earth that it
will be impossible to collect them on the great day.
Therefore there can be no resurrection of the dead.
So our religion is vain, is nothing. Some have looked
upon this with fear, have doubted, trembled, fell—
doubted for want of light, trembled for lack of wisdom, fell for want of strength. It mattered not
whether they were believers in the resurrection of
the body or not. This startling fact deters many, no
doubt, in the very outset of their researches. We
will say for the comfort of those already at ease and
to dispel the cloud from those who doubt and to
equalize the circulation of those who tremble and to
lift up the fallen that neither infidels, chemists, nor
philosophers are the authors of this doctrine, that it
is as plainly taught in the Bible as any other doctrine. Other doctrines have given rise to many opinions from the great abundance of testimony touching
them. This one comes in few terms, about which no
dispute can arise. How passing strange that the
stone of stumbling was broken and the stronghold of
infidelity stormed thousands of years before their

adherents were born! The teachings of chemistry are that matter is persistent in space—that is, no two bodies can occupy the same space at the same time—and that it is persistent in time—that is, it is indestructible. There is no evidence that in the course of nature or by any of the operations of art matter is either called into existence or annihilated. It may be changed from state to state thousands of times without the smallest loss. A pound of ice converted into water or steam continues to weigh exactly a pound. When fuel is burned or water disappears by evaporation or our own bodies are resolved into earth and air it is only the migration of matter through the cycle of natural transformations. Forms alone are destroyed; matter remains imperishable. How closely are life and death linked together! Oxygen, the thing that life needs most, oftenest is its deadly foe; it would destroy all organized beings, and, pursuing them to the tomb, decompose and dissolve their structure, carrying back their elements to the quiescent mineral world. When we die, our bodies, under physical forces, are broken down to the molecule. Chemistry completes the liberation of atoms by splitting the molecules, thus separating the very elements themselves. These separated elements are unlike the compound which their union forms. Hebrews xi. 1-3: "Now faith is the substance of things hoped for, the evidence of things not seen. For by it the elders obtained a good report. Through faith we understand that the worlds were framed by the word of God, so that things which are seen were not made of things which do appear." We challenge the learning of the world

for a better illustration of the atomic theory. We
challenge the theologians of the world for a better
illustration of what faith is. Faith is a substance
as is a grain of salt. Faith is the evidence of things
not seen—this grain of salt is only visible, tangible
evidence of unseen atoms. "Through faith we understand that the worlds were *framed* [by word],
. . . so that things which are seen were not made
of things which do appear." "The worlds were
framed," were put together, built up of unseen
things. It is believed that these invisible atoms
have shapes and that compounds are in a measure
determined not by the atoms that make them so
much as by the manner in which these atoms are
brought together. The worlds were truly *framed;*
no other word in our vocabulary can take the place of
this one! Not our world only, but worlds—all are
framed in the same way. "According to the faith of
the old alchemists the earthly elements were ruled
by the magical influence of the stars. It was a prophetic dream, and has been fulfilled in the consum-
mate researches of modern science, which has given
us a true *celestial chemistry.* The spectrum of the
stars has its bands of absorption, and Mr. Ruther-
ford, of New York, has discovered a coincidence between several of the dark lines of Arcturus and those
of the sun, these lines being possible indications of
the chemical conditions of their sources. The light
of the stars also contains a positive chemical energy." "So that things which are seen were not made
of things which do appear."

Bodies are of two kinds, according to their make-
up of invisible elements. These are simple and com-

pound. Compound bodies are such as can be decomposed or separated into simpler parts or elements. Simple bodies, on the contrary, can not be thus separated. Water is a compound, and can be resolved into two invisible gases, but neither of these can be again decomposed. Water is not made of the things that do appear; these things are invisible. Brass may be separated into copper and zinc, but no one has yet been able to obtain from these anything besides copper and zinc. Atoms are but invisible bricks, stones, lumber, metals, sands, that are framed together, making all the forms of the many substances that we see around us. Our earth, with its three kingdoms, all the planets, our sun, all the suns and systems, were framed of these. The "things which are seen were not made of things which do appear," not made of visible things; atoms do not appear. Faith is the beginning, the corner, of the Christian survey. Now the great apostle tells us that through it, using it as an illustration, we are taught how the worlds were put together. Like nature's vast laboratory, our inward, invisible, indestructible elements are framing us as living stones for that spiritual building, that house not made with hands, eternal in the heavens.

The atomic theory is as plainly taught by the apostle as by any work on chemistry. He tells us how the worlds were framed, how these invisible things were put together. David is equally as accurate and simple in illustrating their separation. He says that it is like the splitting of wood.

Let us see if faith is not the foundation as well of the business world.

FAITH.

It is a curious fact that while so many object to or even think the question of faith foolish when used as the power of God unto salvation to every one who will accept it as such, quite all the business of the United States is one, absolutely so, of faith. Here is my check on the bank at Dallas for twenty-five dollars. This check is a substance, an evidence to my banker, for the thing you hope for. You present this check, and the banker counts out to you twenty-five dollars. Be these paper, silver, or gold, they are in no respect like the check. A draft is a written order of one person or company upon another for payment of money. The form of a draft is: "Thomas Jones, at sight pay to the order of the First National Bank of Comanche, Tex., eight hundred (800) dollars, value received, and charge to the account of James Knox. To Tom Jones & Co., Nashville, Tenn."

Will Mr. Jones pay these eight hundred dollars and charge same to James Knox? This is a question of faith with Mr. Jones. I go to a bank of discount to borrow money. Faith in the security alone will pass the money through the window to me. The Comptroller's report shows that ninety-four per cent of all our business is transacted thus. It is a transfer of credit, based alone on faith. This does not depend upon wealth every time, but something higher: absolute faith in the man, together with his ability to pay. A stock exchange is an association of brokers and dealers in stocks and other securities. United States bonds are but notes secured by the government. Our legal-tender notes, greenbacks, are but promises to pay on demand. So the fundamental doctrine of the Bible is the foundation of commercial intercourse, home and foreign.

To the Christian "faith is the substance of things hoped for, the evidence of things not seen;" to the world faith is the substance of things expected, evidence of things not seen. The difference is the difference in the meanings of "hope" and "expectation." Hope is a desire of some good, with at least a slight expectation of obtaining it; it expects a good desired; it originates in desire. Expectation is founded on some reasons which render the event probable. Hope is directed to some good; expectation is directed to good or evil.

Let us return to the text. Psalm cxli. 7: "Our bones are scattered at the grave's mouth, as when one cutteth and cleaveth wood." Here the two changes that our bodies undergo at the grave's mouth are illustrated by the chopping and the splitting of wood. "As when," just like. These two changes define well the domain of the two forces that are working all the changes we see around us, as well as the thousands that we can not see, but can realize with certainty are going on. The former, "as when one cutteth" wood, illustrates the physical change, a change that does not destroy the properties of matter, but separates into single or individual properties or parts, the molecule. The cutting of wood into individual sticks does not destroy its identity. This stick cut off is in every respect like that from which it was cut. The flesh drops from the bones; these break under weight; their crumbling weakness can no longer sustain, till each particle is cut and severed from the bulk. The severed particles hold with powerful grasp all the former properties of the body. Philosophy has done its work, leaves the completion or further dissolution to the maul and wedges of the chemist, and then retires from the field.

"As when one . . . cleaveth wood." The wood-chopper's sticks are turned over to the man of the maul and the wedge. When he is done, a load of rails is the result. He has destroyed the identity of the stick, but not the individuals that make it. Chemistry takes the individual particles as philosophy left them, and finishes the separation by splitting these particles and giving their several atoms to the winds as they call at the grave's mouth for them. Psalm ciii. 16: "For the wind passeth over it, and it is gone; and the place thereof shall know it no more." Job xxx. 22: "Thou liftest me up to the wind; thou causest me to ride upon it, and dissolvest my substance." Wherever the wind blows it carries these dissolved substances, to be deposited here, yonder, wherever chance or determination may direct. Isaiah xxvi. 19: "Thy dead men shall live, together with my dead body shall they arise. Awake and sing, ye that dwell in dust: for thy dew is as the dew of herbs, and the earth shall cast out the dead."

"The earth shall cast out the dead." By this act the dead are not to rise, but shall be cast out. "For thy dew is as the dew of herbs." This is the how cast out and the purpose. It becomes dew for herbs, will feed these, showered as gently upon them as fall the dews of heaven. We have them now in the winds and herbs. Are they rebreathed? Job xxi. 33: "The clods of the valley shall be sweet unto him, and every man shall draw after him, as there are innumerable before him." "Draw," to inhale, to take air into the lungs. Johnson says that "it expresses an action, gradual or continuous, and leisurely."

These dissolved elements are showered as lightly and gently upon the herbs as the dews of heaven that nourish them. So these herbs are devoured by the beasts or wither and throw these elements back again to earth and air. This is the channel for the bones that were scattered at the grave's mouth and lifted up by the winds. How are these elements preserved, kept up with, followed through all their intricate changes? There is a bookkeeper that charges and credits us as we draw upon the world or transfer its bounties to other claimants. In the sequel of this chapter we wil' give you some extraordinary bookings from the practical matters of life as startling in proportion to the ability of these bookkeepers as is the great question of which we are talking. Psalm cxxxix. 15, 16: "My substance was not hid from thee, when I was made in secret, and curiously wrought in the lowest parts of the earth. Thine eyes did see my substance, yet being unperfect; and in thy book all my members were written, which in continuance were fashioned, when as yet there was none of them." Let us step aside with one remark. Were revelation only a fable gotten up by man, it would have looked more manlike to have left out these stupendous flights of faith that tax even the minds and hearts of those who see the beauty of holiness and feel the touch of a gentle hand at every turn in life. To speak well of their ability shows doubly the foolishness of such a policy. Now would it not seem an easier matter to book, take care

of, and collect these scattered elements than to book
them when as yet there were none of them? Most
assuredly so. We have followed man, hand in hand,
to the grave; philosophy and revelation have scattered him there precisely alike; but here his philosophy must perish with him. We will bridge the
chasm from the rock of ages and show him up as he
shall be when the winds return to him these bor-
rowed elements. Thus he is rushed with rashness to
impute as an impossibility to God a question that
man can not philosophically account for. He measures the work by his own capacity, looks for a theory
in his own philosophy. The one is as vain as the
other is foolish and weak. As revelations have settled the first part of this great question satisfactorily
to philosophy, philosophers shall be made the richer
by adhering to the great truths of revelation. Job,
David, and Isaiah stood hand in hand with scientists and declared with them that our bodies are
scattered at the grave's mouth, chemically split into
atoms, there assume new forms, build up new molecules in the vegetable kingdom, are breathed and rebreathed, and will continue until the earth shall
cease to "cast out the dead." It would seem unjust
for us to introduce new witnesses now; it might
weaken the chain of testimony and furnish grounds
for criticism. If our witnesses have deviated by a
hair's breadth from the teachings of philosophy, let
the world challenge them. The witnesses that went
down with philosophy came to the stand and testi-
fied at their own instance. Let us look at the character of these witnesses. One is the breathings of a
man whose property had all been swept away, whose

person was afflicted with a most painful and loath-
some disease, his children taken from him, and he in
sackcloth and ashes; one is a prophet of high re-
pute; the other is a most opulent and powerful
king.   Here is the testimony brought from the extremes of society.   The man of the greatest misfor-
tunes, the humblest station, says: "I know."   The
great king upon his throne declares that "he shall
bring me up."   Between these two greatest extremes
rests the hope of all flesh.   These are the extended
arms of the compasses that circumscribe all humanity.   There is one nice feature that we notice in the
testimony of these men: they speak for self.   I may,
by inference, conclude that if these men are to be
thus resurrected then I shall too.   Let us attain the
point beyond every inference and say, as did Job, "I
know that I shall see God," and with David, "He
shall quicken me."   Such are the characters of the
men that we propose to introduce again, men of unimpeachable characters.   The law of evidence is that
when a witness or witnesses testify without hesitan-
cy to facts that we can demonstrate, that we know to
be true, we are bound to give them full faith and
credit touching questions of which we have no other
means of finding out or methods for demonstrating
their truth.   This testimony is the more valid from
the fact that these men were left free to make these
statements or let them forever rest.   They were not
pressed by public sentiment for ends of profit, nor
were these questions shaped to suit a then existing
theory of science.   Psalm xvii. 15: "As for me, I will
behold thy face in righteousness: I shall be satisfied,
when I awake, with thy likeness."   My own likeness,

the reflected image of thyself, the very likeness with which I was created, for then I was like him. "So God created man in his own image, in the image of God created he him; male and female created he them." Psalm lxxi. 20: "Thou, which hast showed me great and sore troubles, shalt quicken me again, and shalt bring me up again from the depths of the earth." The very me that had seen great and sore troubles, the same me that went into the depths of the earth, this very me shall he quicken again; the identical me that had been quickened before shall be brought up. Psalm xvi. 9: "Therefore my heart is glad, and my glory rejoiceth: my flesh also shall rest in hope." With David the gladness of heart is not all, the rejoicing of his glory is not the end, but "my flesh also shall rest in hope." He saw beyond these scattered elements unity; he saw hope, an easy, resting, patient hope for the flesh. Isaiah xxvi. 19: "Thy dead men shall live, together with my dead body shall they arise. Awake, and sing, ye that dwell in dust: for thy dew is as the dew of herbs, and the earth shall cast out the dead." "Dead men shall live, together with my dead body shall they arise." Our bones may be scattered at the grave's mouth, may be carried away by the winds, become life-giving dew to herbs, these herbs, together with all flesh, going back to the earth; the earth finally "shall cast out the dead." Let us again bring up our witness from the land of Uz, he who stood hand in hand with science in discussing the higher laws that control the universe, that rotate the earth on its axis, or lead it in an elliptical path around the sun. No question has he ever asked so pointedly or answered so emphatically as this one. Job xiv. 14: "If a man die, shall he live again?" Job xix. 25-27: "For I know [no doubt in Job's mind] that my Redeemer liveth, and that he shall stand at the latter day upon the earth: and though after my skin worms destroy this body, yet in my flesh shall I see God: whom I shall see for myself, and mine eyes shall behold, and not another; though my reins be consumed within me." Job answers the very question: "Mine eyes shall behold, and not another." "Although I may have breathed particles from all the bodies in the land of Uz, though my bones be scattered at the grave's mouth, though they go away with the winds, though thou dissolveth my substance and it becomes as dew to the herbs, though every man draw after me as I have drawn or breathed of those before me, the Book-keeper—who understands all the entries, single and double; one whose perspective pen made this entry, 'Thine eyes did see my substance, yet being unper-fect; and in thy book all my members were written, which in continuance were fashioned, when as yet there was none of them'—he it is will follow these scattered fragments till the earth cast out the dead. Then he will give me back my own eyes, and not an-other's. He booked my eye before it was, gave it to me when it is, charged the world with it, payable when the earth shall cast out the dead. In the final settlement I am to be trusted with the very same eye that had loved to scan the heights and depths of its own native land, to mark out her rivers and far-off seas, that speculated upon the starry worlds above; the same eye that had with delight marked the cattle and herds on a thousand hills; that overlooked the

greatest prosperity in all the land of Uz; the same
eye that had shed rivers of tears when wrung by the
severest affliction; that frowned indignantly upon
the upbraiding Shuhite and his coadjutors; the same
eye that sought out the causes it knew not—with this
eye am I to see God, when at the latter day he shall
stand upon the earth, the first-fruit of his reappear-
ing."

Let us now look at some of the mammoth corporations of to-day, examine their books, and see if the
practical bookkeeper does not have questions as
complex, proportionate to the ability to solve. There
is a large business corporation of which two hundred
million dollars constitute the capital or business
body. Stocks and bonds are bought and sold, discount and premium adjusted, interest and brokerage
settled. The year closes, the books are balanced,
and twelve million dollars are the profits. Making
the account accurate to one-ten-thousandth of a dol-
lar, and counting each one of these an atom, we have
two trillions of atoms invested; the open avenues of
profit have drifted in one hundred and twenty billions more, making a total of two trillions, one hundred and twenty billions. Now in so vast a business,
where the sums handled are so large, these money
atoms may profitably and tangibly be reduced one
hundred times smaller, yet many times larger than
an atom of the human body. This would give us two
hundred trillions. In this business, during the year
two hundred trillions of these little elements have
flown through the coffers; if two entries are made,
then four hundred trillions have been noticed by the
pen. In all the changes and transfers the books

must show the very day each of these elements came
in, from whom, and for what purpose. Not one
leaves without the notice of the bookkeeper; the date
of its departure, to whom it went, and for what purpose, the books must show. The man who has never
been one hundred dollars ahead revolts at the idea of
one man following so closely and so accurately after
these little elements which revelation and experience both teach have wings. So with the man that
has made but small spiritual investments; yet it is
so. This moneyed omnipotence numbers the hairs
upon the head of every atom; not one of its spar-
rows, much less an eagle, falls without its notice.
It speaks railroads into existence, creates banks,
blows upon the seas the breath of life that animates
every ocean with mighty keels. By telegraph and
telephone it makes all the cities on the continent
stand on and occupy the same space. It is the center of gravity around which all the planets, great and
small, together with their satellites, revolve. If it
does not give heat and strength to these, it affords
an example for mimicry to all. Every corporation
swings around this as a great center. It gives to a
nation's currency its value, sustains its declining
credit, and controls its revenues. This is man. How
unreasonable the story, yet how true! God began
his man speculation many thousand years ago on a
small scale. In purpose this speculation suffered
the same fluctuations of gain and loss, premium and
discount. Not one human frame of all God's creation contains the number of atoms this business body
does. This business body may have had several
clerks. David says: "In thy book all my members

were written." All the laws are his clerks, book-keepers, servants, and these book the incoming and the outgoing atoms as they fall within the province of a particular law. The one seems to me no more difficult than the other. But I am told that our living bodies are continually changing, that none of the elements I possessed ten years ago are now mine. Science teaches that; perhaps it is true. My neighbor, who is a physician, had the smallpox twenty-two years ago. According to the theory of taking on new bodies every seven years, he is now on the third since he was afflicted with this disease. Every year makes him older, still the marks are there. To me the strangest of all is that he tells me he has waited on several patients with that disease since he had it, but has never taken it again. Has he, in his taking on new bodies, managed to breathe particles of bodies that had been infected before? I had the measles several years ago. I may have a new body, yet every time I take cold I am annoyed by the same unpleasant taste contracted by the measles. One says that he could take the measles but once, then afterward he is safe against that disease. If I lost by having this disease, I gained the knowledge of knowing that I am to have it no more. The same is true of many diseases. Yet no truer than the theory that I shall die but once. That is a vaccination against every ill, every contagion, every infection, even the one that began in the garden. It will leave no scars, but do away with those that now exist, and I shall look upon another death as my physician looks upon the smallpox. Thus, amid all our boasting, we find many strange "hows"

21

and "whys." Because we do not understand them makes them none the less true. There is thought to be a strange sympathy between a living body and a lost member of that body, one for which we can not account. It falls beyond the reach of every known law and baffles our reason till we thrust it from us as a problem that we can not solve. If there is a sympathy between the living man and one of his lost members, who can tell the depth of that sympathy when we come to separate from or lay in sleep all our members? Near Smithville, Tenn., lived a lad who was employed in a sawmill. He had the misfortune to have one of his arms wrenched from the socket at the shoulder. For the first few days his rest was not less than might be expected from so severe a hurt. After this his pain grew intense; he complained of his hand hurting, that buried hand. It would be impossible to picture here the pains, the agonies, as they were told. At that time I lived within ten miles of the scene of the accident. Every drug that had the power of allaying pain was given, but to no effect. On examining the buried arm the hand was found to be clinched till the ends of the fingers were imbedded in the palm. The hand was straightened and redressed, and it is said that the pain ceased. The parties that told this were unimpeachable. They stated that there could not have elapsed more than a minute between the time of straightening the clinched fingers of the lost hand and the cessation of the pain. Within six miles of where I lived at this time there was a man who had the misfortune to lose a leg. The doctors were called to allay the pain in a buried foot. Physicians were summoned from many miles away to relieve, if possible, that intense pain in a lost and buried foot. The accident entailing the loss of an arm, related above, happened not more than fifteen miles from the residence of this man, and this strange precedent suggested the propriety of examining the lost foot. On taking it up it was found that the box in which it had been buried was too small, and that the foot had been pressed rather tightly into the box. The moment it was taken out the sufferer found ease. This story was told by as good people as the county contained, and I am personally acquainted with all the parties. These circumstances, having fallen under my own observation, lead me to say that, though strange, there must be a potent sympathy between the living body and one of its lost members. How far this sympathy will go, or how long it will last, I am unable to say. That such a sympathy does exist, many people believe.

CHAPTER XII.

Joshua at Gibeon—The Miraculous Standing Still of the Sun, and the Stoppage of the Moon—The Foolishness of the World's Theory Touching This Miracle—Joshua's Knowledge Exceeded the Knowledge of the World Till the Nineteenth Century—Is Not Inferior to That—A Physical and a Spiritual Miracle—The Unsolved Question Solved—Light the Cause of Planetary Motion.

JOSHUA AT GIBEON.

Joshua x. 12-14: "Then spake Joshua to the Lord in the day when the Lord delivered up the Amorites before the children of Israel, and he said in the sight of Israel, Sun, stand thou still upon Gibeon; and thou, Moon, in the valley of Ajalon. And the sun stood still, and the moon stayed, until the people had avenged themselves upon their enemies. . . . So the sun stood still in the midst of heaven, and hasted not to go down about a whole day. And there was no day like that before it or after it, that the Lord harkened unto the voice of a man." Joshua commanded the sun to stand. For this he has become the subject of severe criticism from certain characters. It was stated in an infidel paper some years ago that if Joshua had been inspired he would have known that day and night were not due to sun-motion, but to earth-motion, and that he should have simply commanded the earth to stand. Is it not wonderful that Joshua never thought of doing this? We learn two things: God's plan differs from man's, and that man's vanity is sometimes as limitless as space and still more empty. The foolishness of such criticism is the more apparent when we consider how

(324)

little man knows about the sun and how recently he has acquired that little. This very sun-motion of which Joshua talks was not known; no motion was accorded to the sun till the nineteenth century, except that foolish notion that the earth was the center, and that the sun rose and set by its own motion, producing the phenomenon of day. Even now (1893) it is not known which way he is traveling, the extent of his orbit, the length of his year, nor the center around which he is moving. We are astonished that any man, even a New England editor, should offer suggestions as to how this matter should have been accomplished. He reminds me that Phaethon, long ago, did not get all the foolish presumptions. Ovid gives an account of one, Phaethon, that earnestly besought of Phœbus and obtained the right and government of the winged horses for a day. The horses are led from their lofty stalls vomiting fire. The sounding bits are added. The advice given to him is to spare the spur and use the rein. This audacious boy seizes the thongs and occupies the light chariot with joy, and the race begins. A want of weight in the driver makes the load light. The horses that draw the sun perceive this and leave the way early. The sun moves in other tracks. Phaethon becomes alarmed, and regrets that he ever touched the paternal horses. He drops the reins, and the horses roam, rushing this way and that without law. Fields are scorched and trees burned, cities catch fire from the nearness of the sun, people and nations are burned to ashes, rivers and oceans are dried up, and ruin is the result. So we think that man's capacity may be large to suggest or his foolishness blind him to un-

dertake, but weak and small when he comes to exe-
cute such gigantic deeds. Joshua knew that the sun
had this onward motion and more. David taught it.
Habakkuk testifies that they did stand still, and that
afterward they moved on. Josephus says that the
day was lengthened at or about this time. If that be
true, there should be no cavil over the "how" it was
performed. The question is: Was it done? Revelation and history say: "Yes." If this took place at
the command of Joshua, the simplest of us know that
the power to do these things was not Joshua's.
Then, if not his, whose was it? How was it done?
Why was it done? These are questions that we propose to answer.

1. It was purely a miracle. The fact that the sun
did stand still and that the moon did stop at the
command of Joshua makes it a miracle. Josephus
says that the day was lengthened at or about this
time. On the same page you will find a foot-note
that apologizes for this miracle. God help us that
we may never become so weak as to offer an apology
for his miraculous works or to try to bend them to
suit our little theories! We are glad that he has at
various times wrought these wonders above the arm
of every law, beyond the field of our philosophy. We
believe that they were necessary at one time, were
great helps in the early lessons of faith. But the
foot-note says: "Whether the lengthening of the day
by the standing still of the sun and the moon was
physical and real by the miraculous stoppage of the
diurnal motion of the earth for about half a revolution, or whether only apparent by aerial phosphori,
imitating the sun and moon as stationary so long,

while the clouds and the night hid the real ones, and this parhelion, or mock sun, affording sufficient light for Joshua's pursuit and complete victory, can not now be determined. Philosophers and astronomers will naturally incline to this latter hypothesis." If I were either a philosopher or an astronomer, I would resent this. You see that this gives neither light nor relief. This apology grants it a miracle still. All that I can see in this is that it robs this miracle of its grandeur by substituting a less one in its stead, implying that God is not able to do so great a thing. To admit a miracle possible does away with the idea of a limit to its exercise. This aerial phosphori phenomenon, occurring at the command of Joshua and disappearing with the accomplishment of his plan, makes it none the less complex, and the miracle is made a mockery by substituting in its stead both a miracle and a deception, for then the great and good Joshua either practised a willing fraud or was an accomplice in the matter, neither of which is either just or consistent with common reason. It was purely a miracle wrought over the sun and moon. To me this implies an interruption or rather a suspension of law not to be accounted for by any mode of reasoning consistent with our philosophy. If philosophy accounts it consistent, then it drops from the list of miracles. Philosophy can not deduce from this a law nor measure it by her now existing laws. Then we are left only to say that it is a miracle; that the whole is sealed in the Word, and can never be philosophically understood by man, and can be employed by God only, whose servants these ordinances are.

2. How it was done. "Sun, stand thou still upon
Gibeon; and thou, Moon, in the valley of Ajalon,"
was the order; and the report that followed was,
"And the sun stood still, and the moon stayed, until
the people had avenged themselves upon their enemies." This is all that we know of the physical
how. The time may come when we will know.
Some have ridiculed Joshua's apparent lack of
knowledge in issuing this order. Now we want to
show that as far as the connection could permit
Joshua manifested as much knowledge concerning
the sun and moon as we know to-day, and much more
than was known one hundred years ago. Where did
he get his information? Not from the world surely,
for it knew nothing about it. Ask your mind this
question again and again, and living water will come
forth. This is the smitten rock that watered Israel's
hosts, and so will it water you. But we are examining Joshua's geography in this how it was done.
"Sun, stand thou still." We have shown in another
place that the sun has two motions. That is the
teaching of astronomy. It has an onward and a rotary motion. Now had Joshua simply commanded
the sun to stand, would that imply more than a forward motion? Most assuredly not. Is it not pre-
sumable that he would have said: "Stop, sun?"
Why put the still to it, if it had only one motion?
To illustrate, I say to a friend as he passes: "Stop!"
He checks his onward movement. Suppose that I
wish to make a discrimination in some fine feature,
one that requires that he should be motionless. I
say: "Stand still!" I put the "still" to it to check not
the forward motion, but certainly those lesser bodily

motions. The evidence that Joshua understood that
the sun had both a forward and also a lesser bodily
motion is manifested by the command issued by him
to that body: "Stand," stop moving forward, be still,
motionless. Another evidence that he understood
truly the motions of these bodies is that the order
was not given to the moon as to the sun, and the report that follows justifies both Joshua and this conclusion: "And the sun stood still, and the moon
stayed." The sun has a forward motion and a motion on its own axis. To have commanded the sun
simply to stop would not of necessity, so far as we
know, have stopped its lesser motion. The moon
has only a forward movement in reality. The moon
presents to the earth the same hemisphere all the
time. The result of this is that when the moon has
passed around the earth it has made one rotation on
its axis. Now comes the nice feature in Joshua's inspiration. To command the moon to stop, to stand,
without putting the "still" to it, would of necessity
stop every motion that the moon has. The world's
wisest men could not have made this discrimination
three thousand years after the days of Joshua.
Joshua speaks to the Lord in the sight of Israel;
with uplifted hand he bids the sun stand still and the
moon stay, motionless, breathless, pulseless, and see
the accomplishment of God's plan and purpose, the
fulfilment of his promise, the seed of Jacob laying
hold on the promise pledged by an oath, now sealed
by the greatest miracle that can be wrought over
the matter of our system. We have our conjectures
on mysteries, while we can only look upon a miracle
with a strange sense of awe that comes from the re-

gious beyond the law and its philosophy. If we think it strange, Isaiah made it none the less so. Isaiah xxviii. 21: "He shall be wroth as in the valley of Gibeon, that he may do his work, his strange work; and bring to pass his act, his strange act." Speaking of these luminaries and this miracle, we are told how the work was done, thus: "They have not wandered from the day that he created them: they have not forsaken their way from ancient generations, unless it were when God enjoined them by the command of his servant." They were enjoined by God through his servant. "Enjoined" is a legal term, and means to forbid judicially, to direct a legal injunction, to stop proceedings. This admits that the motions of these luminaries are in conformity with and in obedience to law, and that by a due course of law they were stopped; that man, the appointed instrument, served the writ, and that God, their Creator, issued the writ. Then it could not be even a violation of law. Injunctions are common papers that may be issued by any and every court in the land. These, when served by the appointed authority, become barriers to the proceedings of the highest courts in the nation. Still the law is not violated, but the thing is done in conformity to the law. Joshua's plan was not only lawful and a success, but the most beautiful and the grandest. Through the injunction in his hands he measures arms with the greatest force known to us, and the parent of all our forces. There was no possible chance for this foolish phosphori theory, nor a deception in any part of this performance. It would have been no miracle in the eyes of that people to tell them that the earth stopped its rotation. They did not know that it had this motion; they believed it stood, and even till the middle of the sixteenth century it was not known that the earth turned on its axis. If we look at the man plan, we see the man object: to make a fight, conquest, slaughter, only for the end attained by dominion, man's glory. God's plan was as far above this as was his object above man's object. It was done for the sake of the miracle, and not as a necessity for the accomplishment of God's purpose. To have stopped the earth by direct order would not have appeared as a miracle in the eyes of friend or foe. Leaving man's bloody ambition out, to have stopped the earth would not, at the present, be the true scientific engineer's method for lengthening the day. We know that liability to danger made security by its being a miracle. Then liability to danger, wreck, or ruin is not to be weighed in the matter. Let us see which is the better plan, to stop the earth or the sun—I mean from an engineer's standpoint. In the first instance the earth bears the whole shock; in the latter, the shock is distributed by an opposite relation being maintained by each, if the forces that hold these worlds in their places have anything to do in controlling their motions. To stop all, the shock, if any, is borne alike by each particle composing our system. To illustrate: Take a steam-boiler able to sustain a pressure of one thousand pounds per inch. Apply the fire, and the steam generates gradually. As gradually the force is distributing itself; every inch is bearing its equal part of the pressure. The hand on the steam-gage registers a thousand pounds. This is done with perfect safety to the boiler and to all within its range. But suppose that one square inch is to sustain the tremendous pressure of all the inches, and that suddenly; then comes a rent, a crush, a catastrophe. But, instead, suppose that the engineer draws the fire; then the force or pressure leaves each inch alike, till the pressure is all gone, when the engineer says, "Engine, stand still!" and all is motionless. He lays his hand on the force, when he withdraws that which begets this force. The pressure leaves each inch alike. In the first the relation of each inch was one of equal pressure; now the relation of each to each is the same. In other words, the relation has not been disturbed; the force is dead to all alike. Again, he applies the heat, the steam rises, and the gage indicates a thousand pounds pressure. He opens the throttle, and the engine begins its motion. By this motion the pressure is drawn, every inch contributing its equal share to this moving force. The ponderous drive-wheel is revolving hundreds of times per minute, while the piston flies back and forth with each revolution. All this time the pressure per inch remains the same —that is, each inch bears the same strain. The moving of one lever stops the whole machine. The central force is cut off from that which it moves. Again, the force accumulates in accordance with its law of equal distribution. The engineer is able to stop its motion with a very high pressure without danger. To stop any one wheel beyond the drive-wheel or the throttle would endanger the whole machine. Joshua addressed himself to the sun, the center of motion, the repository of all our forces, the throttle of our system, and stopped the whole machine—the true philosophical course. This miracle was not done under a bushel nor in a manner to produce doubt or unbelief, nor was it in any way a deception; it swung out from the sun, was visible to all the world. It did not in appearance conflict with the then existing theory that the sun rose and set by his own motion, thus producing day and night.

"That he may do his work, his strange work; and bring to pass his act, his strange act." What was strange about this miracle? Certainly not the bare fact that it was a miracle; Israel had been seeing miracles every day and night for forty years. It was his spiritual food. It did not consist in the fact that he would stop the sun to lengthen a day, for to them this was the true course. To him there was nothing strange about it. I speak of this as it seemed to them. Isaiah denominates it a strange work and a strange act. The work and the act were strange ones; the appearance of the work, the purposes, and the results were not strange, but the very act. If it was dependent upon the theory of this day, then the act was a strange one; had it depended upon the theory of that day, now it would be a strange act. Based upon the theory of to-day, to-day's process would have stopped the earth; then it is still a strange act. That does not affect it in the least; the procedure was lawful; the world says that the day was lengthened, and the purposes of the miracle were accomplished. There is more: we do not think that anything was made older, neither the world, man nor beast. We hinge the thought on the idea that it was not a necessity, but a miracle of wonderful stoppage—not of worlds only, but of time. We believe that when we shall see the inhabitants of the other planets they will tell the story of this great event. Were they in it? How much, I do not know. I do know that the sun, moon, and earth were involved; that the sun is the parent of all our forces. This assures us that all the sunlit planets of our system saw and felt and realized the stoppage in the father and leader of these motions. We said that nothing was made older. The earth and sun move on; each sustains to the other the same relation that it did before—the season could not advance; the year continued just where the suspension left it; the dial that proclaimed twelve when the stoppage took place showed it to be twelve the moment these bodies moved on. This could not have been so had the rotation of the earth alone ceased, for the year would have been lengthened. "Sun, stand still," hold back the forces that move those that are dependent on thee for motion. All motion died in the earth as well as in the sun and moon.

It was a miracle to friend and foe alike, these the two purposes: to strengthen Israel's faith and to terrify Israel's foes. Before we speak of the direct purposes of the miracle let us show that, as is commonly thought, the object was not to lengthen the day to give Joshua time to avenge himself upon his enemies: this would make it a necessity. God was in the battle, and there are no necessities to him that would force him to prolong a day, no condition so straitened as to press him for time. The thought is blasphemous or pure profanity. What in the text seems an intimation of the purpose is dispelled by a closer examination. The Bible affords nowhere an intimation that the purpose to lengthen the day was that of time to do this work. All the attendant circumstances in the lesson, the construction and the individual words, attest the correctness of this view. Joshua had taken and destroyed Ai as he did Jericho and her kings. Gibeon had made peace with Israel. Five kings of the Amorites had united and gone up to smite Gibeon because she had made peace with Joshua. The men of Gibeon, alarmed at this, sent to Joshua, at Gilgal, to come speedily against the kings of the Amorites. Joshua ascended from Gilgal, he and all the people of war with him, and all the mighty men of valor. "And the Lord said unto Joshua, Fear them not: for I have delivered them into thine hand; there shall not a man of them stand before thee." In the name of good sense, why lengthen a day to slaughter a people already delivered into the hands of Joshua? "Not a man of them shall stand before thee"—then lengthen a day to fight such a foe? stop the sun and moon to hew these down? Again: "It came to pass, as they fled from before Israel, and were in the going down to Beth-Horon, that the Lord cast down great stones from heaven upon them unto Azekah, and they died: they were more which died with hail-stones than they whom the children of Israel slew with the sword." Now with Joshua and all the people of war and all the mighty men of valor to fight an enemy bound and delivered, also the Lord to rain down stones upon them, then want a day to be prolonged for this purpose? How foolish the idea! If that was the idea, why command the moon to stand, in order to lengthen a day of cloudless sunshine, and that at noon? This is sufficient proof to convince a reflecting mind that this order was not issued to lengthen the day to make the fight. "He said in the sight of Israel, Sun, stand thou still upon Gibeon; and thou, Moon, in the valley of Ajalon." "In the sight of Israel." This is where the performance took place. Why? We said that this was one of the objects of the miracle. This would require a rehearsal of God's dealings and promises toward Israel for hundreds of years. It began with a promise made to Abraham and repeated to Jacob five hundred years before this. The beginning of this journey was wrought through miracles; all along the route of the sojourn in the wilderness miracles were wrought: flocks of quail were driven by the winds into the camp; from smitten rocks gushing streams broke forth; manna was rained continuously, which was their bread; a cloud rested upon the tabernacle by day, and a pillar of fire gleamed from it by night. These constituted, in a very great measure, the spiritual food of Israel; they were as necessary to spiritual constancy as was the manna to a bodily support. Miracles were object-lessons, without which we believe Israel's hosts would have very early returned, even to the taskmasters in the brick-kilns of Egypt. Now we come to the end of the journey; the land of promise is reached. The whole course has been signalized by miracles that might soon be forgotten, as these pertained only to Israel; the greatest of them could only live as a part of the history of the children of Israel. The end is now reached. The whole is to be signalized by a miracle that shall make this day more illustrious than any other day that pre-

ceded it or shall ever come after it. While done in
the sight of Israel, yet it is not limited to a sect, but
to heathens alike; nor is it limited to a nation or nations, nor is it limited to the earth: the moon and
sun pause submissively to the Arm that had made
itself bare so often in reaching out spiritual food for
his people. It was the greatest miracle ever wrought,
the accomplishment of the highest undertaking, the
fulfilling of a promise, a seal of Joshua's acceptance
with God. It was done also to strike terror to Israel's enemies. Ecclesiasticus xlvi. 6: "And with
hailstones of mighty power he made the battle to
fall violently upon the nations, and in the descent [of
Beth-Horon] he destroyed them that resisted, that
the nations might know all their strength, because he
fought in the sight of the Lord, and he followed the
Mighty One." What a sermon was this preached by
the sun and moon! It fell upon Greek and Jew
alike. In this all the nations saw the great strength
of Israel, and accounted for it on the ground that
"he fought in the sight of the Lord, and he followed
the Mighty One." In this is seen the secret of every
success, whether it be the little passionate temptings
that assail us in private life or a contest in which
nations with great armies are called to the field.
"In his sight." We are made bold in following the
Mighty One, and we will surely triumph. The van-
quished look upon it with wonder and astonishment,
and realize that a power is behind it all. What must
have been the feelings of Israel's foes as they
watched a poised sun that delayed the darkness,
which perhaps they expected would hide them from
the sword of their enemies? What were the feelings

22

that filled the hearts of Israel's hosts? Then faith
and fear were the whys that were rendered for this
miracle.

It was a military command, a second miracle.
"And there was no day like that before it or after it,
that the Lord harkened unto the voice of a man."
That the sun stood still and that the moon stayed
at the command of Joshua did not make this day
wonderful; it simply made this day longer than
other days. The thing that distinguished this day is
found alone in the fact that God "harkened unto
the voice of a man." "Harken" means to observe,
to obey. The text makes it wonderful that the Lord
should obey a man. Now take the connection, omit-
ting the parenthetical clause, "in the day when the
Lord delivered up the Amorites before the children
of Israel," and the truth of the text is clear: "Then
spake Joshua to the Lord and said in the sight of
Israel, Sun, stand thou still upon Gibeon." He
spoke to the Lord and said: "Sun, stand thou still."
The party addressed is the party that obeyed. "The
Lord God is a sun and shield." He is the one that
harkened unto the voice of a man. He, at the command of Joshua, stood still on the field of Gibeon.
This fact alone made this day wonderful. . Now, behind the screen, we see him, as leader of Israel's
hosts, stop at the command of a man. We remember
that after Joshua had crossed the Jordan he circumcised all the male children of Israel. On their departure from Egypt all were circumcised. Those
that had been born on the way had not been circumcised. While in camp here at Gilgal they kept the
Passover, and other ordinances were attended to.

Joshua v. 13, 14: "And it came to pass, when Joshua
was by Jericho, that he lifted up his eyes and looked,
and, behold, there stood a man over against him with
his sword drawn in his hand: and Joshua went unto
him, and said unto him, Art thou for us, or for our
adversaries? And he said, Nay; but as captain of
the host of the Lord am I now come." Here he asserts his captaincy to Joshua. If he appeared to
others on this occasion, the text is silent. In our
text under consideration Joshua spoke to the Lord
and said in the sight of Israel. Here we think he
manifested himself. Luke i. 80: "And the child
grew, and waxed strong in spirit, and was in the deserts till the day of his showing unto Israel." He has
led Israel's host to the end of this great journey, and
now we believe that he is about to surrender his
captaincy. The tabernacle was then pitched at Gilgal, in the valley of Ajalon. We now have visible on
the field Joshua, Israel, and the enemy; above, the
sun and the moon—the former representing Jesus
Christ and the latter the tabernacle. Psalm lxxxix.
36, 37: "His seed shall endure forever, and his throne
as the sun before me. It shall be established forever as the moon, and as a faithful witness in heav-
en." His (David's) seed shall endure forever; but
"his throne as the sun before me." This can not refer to his temporal throne, for that perished many
centuries ago. It can not refer to the orb of day, for
his throne was to last as long "as the sun before me,"
and the sun still lasts. His throne is to last as long
as the Sun of Righteousness, who stands before the
Father. "It [David's throne] shall be established
forever as the moon, and as a faithful witness in

heaven." The relation of sun and moon bears a relation very similar to that maintained by Jesus Christ and the Church. Jesus Christ and the tabernacle led the sojourn to the planting of the one and the manifestation of the other. The sun and the moon witnessed these two events in a sullen stillness that lasted for the space of nearly a whole day. At the command of Joshua the luminaries stop overhead, while behind the screen the Captain of the hosts stops, and the tabernacle stays. Here it was set up and remained many years under David and Solomon. (1 Chron. xvi. 39; 2 Chron. i. 3.) The moon, representing the tabernacle, was not ordered to stand still, but to stop. Through the tabernacle God manifested himself to the people; the tabernacle reflected his light, just as the moon does the light of the sun. Here is found the highest motive for this miracle. This is what made this day more wonderful; it was not the act of stopping the sun and moon. Never before had "the Lord harkened unto the voice of a man." He had never before obeyed the voice of a man. Wherein had he obeyed the voice of a man? Just when Joshua spoke to the Lord and said: "Sun, stand thou still upon Gibeon; and thou, Moon, in the valley of Ajalon." We know that God had conversed with Adam, Enoch, Abraham, Isaac, Jacob, Moses, Aaron, and many others, but this is something higher than merely listening to man; it is harkening to the voice of a man, which he did on the field of Gibeon. It was really a double miracle: man, the instrument, executing the enjoinder, the sun and moon the visible parties enjoined; while the captain of Israel's hosts and the tabernacle, the invisible ones, pay a like obedience—making it both a physical and a spiritual miracle. The line that separates the two worlds, physical and spiritual, is but a curtain whose meshes are too close for our gross senses. The time is coming, says our hope, when we shall have our great reproach rolled from us, when we cease to eat manna in the wilderness, when the last struggle is being made, the last spiritual battle is being fought, and our hands reach out for the promise; then our visual sense will be quickened, the meshes of this curtain part; then we will realize with a perfect vision Joshua's miracle at Gibeon. At our bidding our spiritual sun will stand still till we make ourselves heirs, seizing on to the promise made to all the faithful of every age and every clime who have fought in the sight of the Lord and have followed the Mighty One. The Church has pitched its tent in the valley—this the stayed moon; Jesus Christ, the poised Sun, stands over it. These will stand till every enemy is subdued. The five encaved kings are the five human senses; it is against their hosts that we war. "Come near, put your feet upon the necks of these kings. . . . Fear not, nor be dismayed, be strong and of good courage: for thus shall the Lord do to all your enemies against whom ye fight."

THE UNSOLVED QUESTION SOLVED.

What moves these worlds along their orbits? Till now we have had a plumb-line; now we have none. The world does not know the cause of these motions; but the wall stands massive and high, the plumb-line drops from our hand, and we gaze up, up, up, above this bewildering coil, only to see the wall rise

higher and higher, till we are filled with astonishment and lose ourselves in reflections concerning
Him who has wrought all these things and who is
perfect in knowledge, who made the earth by his
power, established the world by his wisdom, and
stretched out the heavens by his discretion. We
believe light to be the cause of motion as seen in the
sun, moon, and stars. Jeremiah xxxi. 35: "Thus
saith the Lord, which giveth the sun for a light by
day, and the ordinances of the moon and of the stars
for a light by night, which divideth the sea when the
waves thereof roar." The ordinances of the moon
and of the stars were given for light by night. These
very ordinances of light lift the waves of the sea,
becoming a great attractive force.

Joshua, by command, stopped the sun and moon,
and these stood still; but without a command, under
the potent influence of light, they move on. The
cause of these motions, the wisest of to-day do not
pretend to know. The prophet Habakkuk gives the
cause that moves worlds. Habakkuk iii. 11: "The
sun and moon stood still in their habitation: at the
light of thine arrows they went, and at the shining
of thy glittering spear." "The sun and moon stood
still in their habitation." "Habitation" is from
habeo, "to hold." Now to whatever these hold constitutes to them their habitation. These hold to their
orbits; here we find them every time to a certainty.
Eclipses, moon phases, the seasons, years, the fixed
objects above us that the earth has been seeing since
its creation, all attest the truth of this statement.
These hold to fixed bounds or courses more rigidly
than compass-directed ships on smooth, open seas.

"At the light of thine arrows they went, and at the shining of thy glittering spear." No command, no material instrument moved these; it is light, the light of arrows, the shining of a glittering spear. The cause is repeated. Arrows, spears, and points have their uses as electrical appliances. We know that those planets nearest the sun move more rapidly along their orbits than those more remote; we know also that the intensity of light decreases as the square of the distance increases. By comparing the amount of light and heat received by the different planets to their different orbital velocities we find them in such close conformity that we are persuaded still more that light is the all-moving cause. There is a want of uniformity in the tables as given by various authors; these apologize for this lack of uniformity on the ground that it is due to errors in observations. They differ even as to the earth's polar and equatorial diameters. These difficulties are apparent when we are told that a difference of thirty-six one-hundredths of a second in the sun's parallax makes a difference in our distance from that body of nearly four millions of miles. This small distance in the angle would about equal the breadth of a human hair seen at a distance of one hundred and twenty-five feet. We believe also that the sun's reputed parallax is but a compromise among several observations. The amount of light and heat received by each of the planets depends upon its distance from the sun. These distances affect their orbits, their velocities—that is, the orbits and velocities are not what we say, unless the distances from the sun are just what we say. Arrows are offensive weapons; activity is illustrated by them. The spear is an emblem of authority. These are symbols of force. From them light leaps out and leads these great globes on. If the physical and spiritual worlds have special corners where they come together, so that the one can interpret the other, this then must be a copartnership corner. Jesus says: "I am the light of the world." This Light raises the dead, clothes the dry bones with skin and flesh, changes the forms of government; and our civilization, our government, our superiority, our abundance in all things that make us the head and not the tail, are the trophies of this light. Motion and activity are two of its elements. Like the sun, his apparent motion is westward, while, in fact, we are but turning to Olivet and Calvary. He is a trinity of God the Father, God the Son, and God the Holy Ghost. From him spiritual life comes—spiritual bread, spiritual drink, spiritual growth.

The Extent of Solar Influence.

"Not only life, but all the grand phenomena of force with which we are familiar upon this planet, have their origin in the sun. His radiations govern the movements of terrestrial atoms, and in these the movements of masses take their rise." It is the great physical trinity — color, heat, and chemical rays. These are working all the wonders around us.

CHAPTER XIII.

Political Contrast—Rain-Making—A Prophecy Being Fulfilled —Vegetable Diet Against Meat and Wine—A Literal Devil— His First Estate.

POLITICAL CONTRAST.

To what nations have the promises of prosperity, of plenty, of happiness, been made? Ecclesiastes x. 17: "Blessed art thou, O land, when thy king is the son of nobles, and thy princes eat in due season, for strength, and not for drunkenness!" Psalm xxxiii. 12: "Blessed is the nation whose God is the Lord." Deuteronomy xxxiii. 19: "They shall call the people unto the mountain; there they shall offer sacrifices of righteousness: for they shall suck of the abundance of the seas, and of treasures hid in the sands." Deuteronomy iv. 5-7: "Behold, I have taught you statutes and judgments, even as the Lord my God commanded me, that ye should do so in the land whither ye go to possess it. Keep therefore and do them; for this is your wisdom and your understanding in the sight of the nations, which shall hear all these statutes, and say, Surely this great nation is a wise and understanding people. For what nation is there so great, who hath God so nigh unto them, as the Lord our God is in all things that we call upon him for?" Deuteronomy xxviii. 1, 3-5, 10, 13: "And it shall come to pass, if thou shalt harken diligently unto the voice of the Lord thy God, to observe and to do all his commandments which I command thee this

(345)

day, that the Lord thy God will set thee on high
above all nations of the earth. . . . Blessed shalt
thou be in the city, and blessed shalt thou be in the
field. Blessed shall be the fruit of thy body, and the
fruit of thy ground, and the fruit of thy cattle, the
increase of thy kine, and the flocks of thy sheep.
Blessed shall be thy basket and thy store. . . .
And all people of the earth shall see that thou art
called by the name of the Lord [Christian nations];
and they shall be afraid of thee. . . . And the
Lord shall make thee the head, and not the tail; and
thou shalt be above only, and thou shalt not be beneath." Who have been the recipients of these blessings? Geographers tell us that "Christian nations
are noted for their superiority in civilization, mental
culture, and refinement of manners." To what nations have been made promises of adversity and sla-
very? Deuteronomy xxviii. 15, 29, 33: "But it shall
come to pass, if thou wilt not harken unto the voice
of the Lord thy God, to observe to do all his commandments and his statutes which I command thee
this day; that all these curses shall come upon thee,
and overtake thee. . . . And thou shalt grope at
noonday, as the blind gropeth in darkness, and thou
shalt not prosper in thy ways: and thou shalt be only
oppressed and spoiled evermore, and no man shall
save thee. . . . The fruit of thy land, and all thy
labors, shall a nation which thou knowest not eat up;
and thou shalt be only oppressed and crushed al-
way." Who are the recipients of this curse? It can
not be Christian nations, for these are noted for their
superiority, and are the ones called by his name.
Then it must be unchristianized nations. Where we

find the most debasing forms of idolatry there we generally find the lowest stage of men. The one hundred and fifty millions of Chinese, who are subjects of British lords, eat and enjoy but little of the labor of their hands or the fruit of their fields or flocks. These purchase luxuries for a people they know nothing about. Liberty is the direct trophy of the gospel. It gives freedom from assumptious lords as well as from the bondage of sin, thus elevating our minds, filling us with a nobler nature, breathing into us a knowledge of the fact that our place is above only, and that none can despoil us. Ecclesiastes vii. 7: "Surely oppression maketh a wise man mad." Psalm cxliv. 15: "Happy is that people, whose God is the Lord." Let the history of every nation attest the truth of the Psalmist.

RAIN-MAKING.

In considering this part of our work we do this without the plumb-line; we have no line to swing. Still, the wall continues massive and high. We write this in the face of failure and under a storm of ridicule from the public journals and even the pulpit. There are Bible statements that lead us in this opinion. We believe that the time will come when man will be able to produce condensations when meteorological conditions are favorable to this end. We never said nor intimated that man would ever be able to make the causes of rain; only to produce condensations under favorable conditions. To illustrate: It is now midwinter; a cold, damp atmosphere surrounds my room. I kindle a fire in the stove, and the temperature in the room rises. See those large globules of condensed vapors on the glass in the window? The atmospheric conditions were favorable and the lighting of a match produced a deposition of dew, in the same general manner that rain is produced from the clouds. This deposition was produced by artificial means. We did this; we produced this not by command, but by applying the means in our power. The question of rain-making, as it was called, agitated the public mind a few years ago. The government aided by giving means to an experiment at rain-making. This experiment was marked by failure, according to report as furnished by the newspapers. The experiment was the result of observations made at the great battles of our late war. After many of these copious rains fell. It was said also that rains fell almost daily in the most arid deserts of the Western plateaus during the continuation of heavy blasting along a railroad in that section, and ceased when the blasting ceased. Could we consider these the cause of the above-mentioned condensation? The operators in the above work attributed these rains to the concussions produced by the heavy discharges. During the first day's experiments copious rains did follow, whether Gen. Dyrenforth laid claim to it or not. We will furnish you with the basis for our belief, and comment briefly.

Job xxxviii. is a chapter full of the learning of to-day. In it is couched the learning which is sought in the colleges and higher institutions of the world. The causes or factors that bring rain are found in verses 22-27 of this chapter. These verses give the direct purpose of the rain. After giving the causes and the purposes of the rain, the great Lecturer

springs the question before us: "Hath the rain a
father? or who hath begotten the drops of dew?"

"Hath the rain a father?" "Father" seems to be
used as a verb: to adopt, to take the child of another
as one's own, to profess to be the author. Rain is
the creature of the Author of all things, as is man,
the ox, or the horse. Heat, water, and air are the
agents that place the waters above us in the clouds.
Has man a father? As a Creator and Preserver he
has. Then follows the order to multiply and replen-
ish the earth. "Hath the rain a father," one to adopt
it, to propose to be the author, the begetter from the
first created mother of causes? It must have, else
it is an orphan in a world of chance. Had the condensations that followed Gen. Dyrenforth's effort
been the result of this effort, then he would have
been the reputed father of this rain. In the same
sense man is the father of steam, as being directly the
begetter of steam from the agents fire and water.
He is the begetter of electricity from the agents water, copper, and zinc. The very question is suggestive; it comes in the most familiar, most comprehen-
sive term: "Hath the rain a father?" Who will
father the rain?

"Or who hath begotten the drops of dew?" Here
the terms are expressive: "Who, out of conditions,
hath begotten not dew, but fathered the drops?
Who begot the globules on our window?"

"Out of whose womb came the ice?" "Womb," or
matrix, a mold, the cavity in which anything is
formed and which gives it shape. This process of
ice-making is some one's, because it is symbolized by
a thing which is the possession of animal and man

only. The fixture for ice-making is a vacuum-pan,
from which the vapor is removed as fast as gener-
ated. The scientific physiologist need but watch the
process of ice-making as seen in the tropics to acquaint himself with the growth of viviparous or
oviparous animals from the embryo till birth. Had
we been told one hundred years ago that our Southern cities would manufacture their own ice under
August suns, what crank would then have believed
the story, much less have been foolish enough to
propagate such a story?

"Knowest thou the ordinances of heaven? canst
thou set the dominion thereof in the earth?" See
our remark in another place on the term "heaven."
Does the ability of setting up these ordinances or
laws in the earth depend on knowing or understanding the laws? We know that Job or no other man,
not even Gen. Dyrenforth, could operate these ordinances unless he understood them. We do not say
that to understand gives the ability to operate them,
but in this instance it is suggestive of ability. Then
the first work is to understand well the workings of
the law. Gen. Dyrenforth only followed in part
the instructions. He tried to learn the ordinances
as the experiment progressed. He should have
known the laws before he began the work of setting
them up in the earth. An investigating mind can
not read the above questions without being impressed with the thought that in some way there is a
practical utility in them, or God would not have
asked them. Greater sermons have been preached
by the scientific world from texts far less expressive.
From the falling of an apple Newton preached cir-

cular orbits for the planets; while Galileo, from the
motions of a swinging lamp, evolved the law that
marked the descent of this apple. Following the
foregoing questions comes a question which assumes
not only the answer, but suggests a process for obtaining that end. As we have said before, this
is a peculiar characteristic of this entire chapter.
"Canst thou lift up thy voice to the clouds, that
abundance of waters may cover thee?" Why did he
not ask: "Can you produce a precipitation, Job?"
The idea is this: "If you can lift up your voice to the
clouds, then the waters will come down upon you,
the place from whence the voice was lifted." "Lift
up thy voice" admits of three interpretations: 1. To
simply command the clouds to let down rain. 2. To
elevate the voice in pitch or loudness. 3. To elevate
the voice to the clouds, and there give utterance; or,
more definitely, elevate the vocalizing body to the
clouds, and speak in a language understood by the
clouds, that the clouds may obey. It must go to these
in the language of the law, or they never would understand, and we think the latter the interpretation
designed; while the second was that which produced
condensations after the memorable battles of Mexico
and those of the rebellion and the precipitations on
our arid Western plains, but were ineffective in the
experiments made by the government. The cause,
however, is apparent: the voice of the government
was not lifted to the clouds, but to a sky of burning
brass. "Voice," says Mr. Webster, "the sense of
the verb is to throw out or drive out sound," and
voice is the thing driven out or sound simply.

Psalm xciii. 3: "The floods have lifted up their

voice." The idea here is that of both our second and third interpretations. The floods increase the sound of sea-motion above the ordinary movement. The floods really lift higher their crests, the vocalizing bodies. Voice is a representative force. "Let us call on God in the voice of the Chuch." Here it is the power of the Church. Shakespeare says: "I have no words; my voice is my sword." Our nation participated in the experiment. The thought originated from the terrible conflicts of contending armies. The voice of a nation rings out from the tramp of its soldiers, the rattle of its musketry, and the boom of its cannon. These represent the sum of all the forces of a nation. Ask the hills around Bull Run, Fort Donelson, Shiloh, Fredericksburg, Richmond, and Gettysburg what made them shake and tremble on those fearful days of the rebellion and they will tell you that it was the thunders of a nation's voice. Ask why and whence came the rain that followed close on these. "To the clouds." A cloud is a collection of visible vapor or watery particles suspended in the atmosphere at some altitude. "Lift up thy voice to the clouds," the law and the limit. Our rain-makers lifted the voice of the nation when and where there were no clouds. So we miss the desired result every time we deviate from the word and the law. Come to my conditions, apply the means suggested, and success will crown every effort. It can no more fail than can the sun fail to shine.

"Abundance of waters." This means enough for every purpose. Does it not imply a scarcity? If it takes at any time the foregoing process of lifting the voice to the clouds, that an abundance of waters may

fall on us, then of a truth there are times of scarcity.
Jeremiah xiv. 22: "Are there any among the vanities
of the Gentiles that can cause rain? or can the heavens give showers? Art not thou he, O Lord our
God? therefore we will wait upon thee: for thou hast
made all these things." We do not believe that the
vanities of any sect or nation could cause rain. If a
scientist, this precludes the idea of vanity. Without knowledge we see ourselves only, and that
through a powerful glass. As knowledge increases
our eyes turn more from self till self is nothing in
the world of wonders spread out everywhere, that
teach us God. We go to self from God, and go to
God from self. The ability of the heavens to give
showers is as feeble as are the vanities of the Gentiles to cause rain. "Art not thou he, O Lord our
God?" He is the Author of all the causes. Man, in
every instance, in all his life, uses these causes to
answer every purpose in his life. The limit to which
he may extend his ability to use these causes we do
not know; it is extending in every direction. "Therefore we will wait upon thee." Humility toward God
and a persistent determination to find him in the
ways of his wondrous works place us where he has
promised to keep back no good thing. He says that
these ordinances are his servants. If we attribute
all to law alone, we become law-worshipers, base
idolators; then we worship the servant to the neglect
of the Lord of the house.

A PROPHECY NOW BEING FULFILLED.

Mark xiv. 9: "Verily I say unto you, Wheresoever
this gospel shall be preached throughout the whole

23

world, this also that she hath done shall be spoken of
for a memorial of her." The incident of the woman
and the alabaster box of ointment brought from the
Saviour indirectly a prophecy that comes within the
scope of modern readers to determine whether or not
it is a prophecy, and also to determine whether or not
it has been fulfilled, or is now being fulfilled, with
fair prospects for its final fulfilment. This prophecy was uttered by the Saviour on the night before
his crucifixion. This gospel is to be preached
throughout the whole world. The thing enjoined is
to tell what this woman has done. From a human
standpoint, no prediction ever went forth with so
many apparent impossibilities against its fulfilment. The Leader was being hounded before the
last tribunal, and he knew it. Of the twelve apos-
tles, one is now bartering his betrayal; another is to
deny him in the final struggle. He, the Leader, a
moment after the above utterances, is on his face,
praying that the hour might pass. The breath of his
fame extended over a circle of only a few hundred
miles, and that scarcely above mockery. Had Cæsar
—fresh from a hundred pitched battles, stained with
the blood of a million murdered men—said, "My
power, my dominion, shall extend throughout the
whole world," even the thoughtful would have shud-
dered with secret fears of such a possibility. Had
Napoleon, on his return from Elba, when his magnificent army moved toward Waterloo, said, "My dominion shall extend throughout the whole world," his
followers, to say the least of it, would have thought
the thing possible and probable. Before these, Alexander had sent his name throughout the then known

world till they say "he wept that there were no more worlds for him to conquer." Those that said such things felt that this world was his dominion. The kingdoms of these men, like themselves, were without foundation, and so went down with them. Is this gospel being preached? Is it not extending? The western hemisphere certainly was not known for fifteen hundred years after. Now it has spread, has been preached from Cape Horn to Cape Kaler, from Bering Strait to that of Magellan, from the Atlantic to the Pacific. Along nearly all the parallels of this great country, on all the rivers, lakes, and oceans, go up songs of praise to the great Prophet. "Whereso-ever this gospel shall be preached," at every altar, "throughout the whole world, this also that she hath done shall be spoken of for a memorial of her." No human agency could have wrought the wonders wrought by the gospel. How seemingly impossible, then, that this little flock without a shepherd, a lead-er, should rear a kingdom that should fill the earth as the waters cover the sea! Kings pass from the stage, their kingdoms go with them. Not so with this kingdom; the King was taken, but his kingdom grew on. The things that overthrew earthly king-doms were pillars to this. Fires purified, persecu-tions were pentecosts. Tell the story of this woman!

VEGETABLE DIET AGAINST MEAT AND WINE.

Historical.—Daniel i. 5, 8, 11, 12, 14-16: "And the king appointed them a daily provision of the king's meat, and of the wine which he drank. . . . But Daniel purposed in his heart that he would not defile himself with the portion of the king's meat, nor with

the wine which he drank. . . . Then said Daniel
to Melzar, . . . Give us pulse to eat, and water
to drink. . . . So he consented to them in this
matter, and . . . took away the portion of their
meat, and the wine that they should drink; and gave
them pulse [beans and peas]." "At the end of ten
days their countenances appeared fairer and fatter
in flesh than all the children which did eat the portion of the king's meat."

A Literal Devil.

The devil is the prince of darkness. If we take
away the *d* from his name, we have *evil*, wicked.
Dropping now the *e*, we have *vil*, depraved by sin.
Dropping the *v*, we have *il*, depravity. Leaving off
the *i*, we have *l*, the place of punishment for the wicked after death, the capital of this empire, the home of
this prince, the destination of the evil, the tendency
of the vile, the reward of the depraved. All combined is the devil. The last is his abode. Between
him and the pit are his subjects. Restoring these
letters and transferring, we have *lived*, the indefinite
past tense. Perhaps he did at one time live in light,
lived for all the word has in possibility. What a difference inversion makes! Is it a change of name,
or is it a change of all the elements of self that turn
one around? As *devil* ends with *l*, starting here we
return toward *life*. Conversion is all of it. The
devil lost his first estate, became the father of death,
and his name reversed. so that in looking back it
might ever remind him of what he was. Let us not
forget that a good name is better than rubies, more
to be desired than fine gold.